SOLIDARITY AND DIFFERENCE

SUNY series in the Philosophy of the Social Sciences
Lenore Langsdorf, Editor

SOLIDARITY AND DIFFERENCE

The Politics of Enlightenment in the Aftermath of Modernity

GEORGE TREY

State University
of New York
Press

Published by
State University of New York Press, Albany

Production by Susan Geraghty
Marketing by Fran Keneston

Printed in the United States of America

For information, address State University of New York Press,
State University Plaza, Albany, N.Y., 12246

Library of Congress Cataloging-in-Publication Data

Trey, George, 1961–
Solidarity and difference : the politics of enlightenment in the aftermath of modernity / George Trey.
p. cm. — (SUNY series in the philosophy of the social sciences)
Includes bibliographical references and index.
ISBN 0-7914-4017-6 (hardcover : alk. paper). — ISBN 0-7914-4018-4 (pbk. : alk. paper)
1. Postmodernism—Social aspects. 2. Enlightenment—Influence.
3. Habermas, Jürgen—Views on modernity. 4. Poststructuralism.
I. Title. II. Series.
HM73.T47 1998
300′.1—dc21 98-9418
CIP

10 9 8 7 6 5 4 3 2 1

CONTENTS

ABBREVIATIONS

CLC:	"The Cultural Logic of Late Capitalism
CPH:	"Concerning the Public Use of History"
D:	"Differance"
DE:	*Dialectic of Enlightenment*
EME:	"The Entwinement of Myth and Enlightenment"
FRPS:	"Further Reflections on the Public Sphere"
HH:	"Habermas and the Historians"
JG:	*Just Gaming*
JS:	"Justice and Solidarity"
KSD:	"A Kind of Settling of Damages"
LC:	*Legitimation Crisis*
LI:	*Limited Inc.*
LPC:	"Legitimation Problems in Late Capitalism"
LPMS:	"Legitimation Problems in the Modern State"
PC:	"The Postmodern Condition"
PDM:	*The Philosophical Discourse of Modernity*
SDC:	"On Systematically Distorted Communication"
STP:	*The Structural Transformation of the Public Sphere*
TCA:	*The Theory of Communicative Action*
TCT:	"Traditional and Critical Theory"
TD:	*The Differend*
TI:	*Totality and Infinity*
TNO:	"The New Obscurity"
TP:	*Theory and Practice*
TTCC:	"Towards a Theory of Communicative Competence"
UP:	"What is Universal Pragmatics?"
WE:	"An Answer to the Question: What is Enlightenment?"
WW:	"Work and Weltanschauung"

ACKNOWLEDGMENTS

The work that follows represents the culmination of an extensive study of the social theory of Jürgen Habermas. In the courseof this study, and in prior studies that contributed to this study, I have been positively influenced by numerous instructors and colleagues. Of these, I would like to acknowledge three in particular: David Ingram, Bill Martin, and Martha Reineke. All three have been a source of emotional, psychological, intellectual, and sometimes even physical support for many years. Without them I quite literally would not have been able to complete this work.

On an even more personal level I thank the two most important people in my life: Elly and Rebekah. Rebekah has always been a joy and inspiration to me. When everything seemed bleak and pointless, I could always count on her cheerful smile and happy voice for sustenance. Likewise with Elly. Without her love and encouragement I would have given up on this long ago.

Finally, this work is dedicated to Jean Trey, whose creative intellect has moved me from day one, and Paul Trey, with whom I have had more stimulating conversations than anyone I know. Thank you both for your patience with me and support for my idiosyncratic interests.

INTRODUCTION

In a social, political, cultural, and theoretical atmosphere that is either succumbing to, or embracing wholeheartedly, fragmentation, superficiality, and disparity, Jürgen Habermas has consistently defended unity, depth, and comprehensiveness. In short, Habermas has been, in the most traditional sense, a philosopher par excellence at a time when philosophy itself has become a questionable enterprise. Another way of stating this would be to say that Habermas has bucked recent theoretical trends—the refusal to systematize, unify, or commit to positions—through an appeal to the highest developments of eighteenth-, nineteenth-, and twentieth-century thought and their tendency to construct theoretical totalities. Yet another way of putting this would be to say that Habermas has thoroughly embraced the Kantian critical project at a time when it has become popular to separate it into its constitutive parts and then pick and choose elements that serve the ends of less ambitious endeavors. In short, Habermas has risked being a theoretician—a critical theoretician—at a juncture in intellectual history when being a theoretician in the tradition of Hegel, Marx, and Weber has fallen into ill repute.

The antithesis to Habermas's grand theory project is most clearly represented by writers that can be loosely organized under the banner of postmodernism. This includes the theoretical offspring of Nietzsche, Freud, and of course Heidegger. But who precisely falls into the postmodern camp is not as simple as it may seem. Obvious members are self-proclaimed postmodernists such as Lyotard and Baudrillard; less obvious, and considerably more problematic, are thinkers such as Derrida, Foucault, and Levinas. While they clearly share the same lineage as the straightforward postmodernists, and likewise share their suspicions concerning unity, totality, and even depth, they also depart from the others in ways that I consider to have important ramifications, philosophically and politically.

My aim in setting up this somewhat contrived dichotomy is to delve into the modernism/postmodernism debate—a debate that has already raged on for quite some time—from a perspective that questions the initial terms of the debate. Such an approach obviously owes a strategic debt to postmodernism, regardless of how it is characterized. But it also, as I will attempt to demonstrate, owes an equal, if not greater, debt to the tradition of critical social theory—which is as modern as theory gets. My aim, then, is to provide a characterization of the theoretical and practical significance of what I will hereafter refer to as the aftermath of modernity. The purpose of developing this concept is to depart from what I consider to be an often fruitless, at times acrimonious, and at worst reactionary debate. I will attempt to show the futility of being theoretically paralyzed for fear of being "metaphysical" and practically stilted for fear of being "irrational." In a nutshell, I will pit Habermas and his "postmodern" enemies against one another, once again, in a effort to survey somewhat different territory than the current debate is able to accommodate. Rather than defending one side or the other I will attempt to look beyond the modernity versus postmodernity dichotomy.

This project, stated as such, goes beyond what can be achieved in the following work. In fact, I will attempt to shed light on only one key issue in what I envision to be a project that could go in a number of directions and could broach a number of questions. The issue that I will pursue is enlightenment: a topic that has long been Habermas's pet project. In doing so I reveal without hesitation an affinity for his work. I would go so far as to say that Habermas raises all the right questions and provides plausible answers to the bulk of them. Having stated this, however, I want to be clear from the outset that my support for Habermas is far from unqualified. In fact, he has tended to move in disappointing directions in his reproaches to thinkers he considers to be postmodern. These responses are not entirely unfounded; nonetheless, they are far from being fully supported either. At the root of his positions and reactions with respect to the questions of postmodernism is his stalwart defense of the Enlightenment. As such, his work will be center stage in this book. With Habermas I would like to defend a notion of enlightenment; against Habermas, however, I will attempt to show the importance of constructing this notion outside of the parameters of the "unfinished project of modernity." Hence, I will be approaching the question of enlightenment in a manner that doesn't dismiss the valuable insights that have developed in postmodern of theory. In brief, I will be exploring the prospects for enlightenment in the aftermath of modernity. In order to so I will examine Habermas's normative work on communicative action—including discourse ethics—and his critical analyses of poststructuralism.

In recent years poststructuralism has replaced positivism as the most formidable nemesis of critical social theory. A great deal of Habermas's work in the 1980s focuses on the philosophical backdrop and social-political repercussions of poststructuralist criticisms of Western rationality. This was initiated with an essay titled "Modernity vs. Postmodernity" (1981) in which Habermas makes the controversial claim that the poststructuralist representatives of antimodern thought are "young conservatives" (1981, 13). His most complete evaluation of poststructuralism is found in *The Philosophical Discourse of Modernity* (1987). Here Habermas concentrates on how modernity's counter-discourses (such as Romanticism and Marxism) evolved into post-discourses that rely heavily upon Nietzsche's analysis of modernity.

I will be discussing these issues in some detail in the chapters that follow. Before describing the manner in which I intend to proceed, however, it is useful to briefly review Habermas's characterization of the relationship between the terms *modernity* and *postmodernity*. The term *modern*, he notes, has been used at various times in the history of the West. It was first applied to the postpagan Christian period that emerged in the fifth century C.E. Other points at which the term was widely used include the twelfth and seventeenth centuries in France as well as during the Italian and German Renaissances. The common denominator between these periods is that each marks a break from an old era and signifies the expectations of a new epoch. Habermas's main concern is with the concept of modernity that is schematized in terms of the dissolution of structures that were characteristic of the medieval epoch. This, of course, involves a number of stages that span from as early as the fourteenth century on into the nineteenth century. For all practical purposes, however, modernity came into its own during the sixteenth and seventeenth centuries.

Initially the newness of the modern period meant a return to the "grand old days," referring to the golden age of antiquity. This is exemplified in the art and literature of the Italian Renaissance. Later, as a consequence of the French Enlightenment, modernity came to refer to a newness that was independent of the past. A spirit of progress and self-determination was prompted by advancements in science and liberalization in the religious, political, and economic spheres. This futuristic orientation of the enlightened conception of modernity is of particular importance to Habermas (1981, 3–4).

The term *postmodern* emerged in the late 1950s and was used to describe anti-establishment trends in art. These trends themselves are continuous with late modern phases such as surrealism and dadaism. The term has enjoyed much wider circulation in the '70s and '80s. Currently talk about postmodern architecture, art, film, and so on, is all the rage and speculation on postmodern science, philosophy, and politics is increasing. While the term itself has a meaning that is as fluid as the reality that it is used to characterize, the common theme is that there is nothing new under the sun. The "post" indicates that we are beyond the modern-enlightenment myth that something can be created out of nothing. In contrast, postmodern "things" (art, literature, philosophy, etc.) tend to patch together disparate objects, themes, and ideas, with the intent of breaking up the facade of unity, coherence, and progress that modernity has attempted to present.

Late in the eighteenth century, when modernity apparently was in full swing, its first wave of critics appeared. For the sake of convenience I will encapsulate this movement under the general rubric of romanticism and its offshoots. The concern of romantic thinkers was that rationalization, for all its scientific and economic merits, generates dehumanizing side effects; it excludes from the human experience such things as imagination, emotions, spirituality, and aesthetic sensibilities. Romantic modernists renounced the reverence for antiquity, replacing it with an idealized view of the Middle Ages. Their intention was to revitalize what they perceived to be a loss of the internal aspect of human experience. Habermas claims that this resulted in a modern vision that extracted itself from its own historical context. "In the course of the 19th century, there emerged out of this romantic spirit that radicalized consciousness of modernity which freed itself from all historical ties." The immediate ancestors of the romantics Habermas labels "aesthetic modernists"; they in turn anticipate contemporary postmodern thought (1981, 4).

The feature that defines aesthetic modernism (from Baudelaire to Dali) is its altered sense of historicity. The past was portrayed as something to leap out of, rather than build upon. "Avant-garde" became the theme that supplied the prescriptive force for an engaged approach to life that proceeds toward an undefined, indeterminate, but utterly new future. This extreme effort to break from the continuity and progress that marked status quo modernism was the reactive product of an increased awareness of the limitations established by traditional norms. According to Habermas, the attitude that accompanied this vision was that of a naughty child. Aesthetic modernism fed upon the act of breaking rules, resulting in its inability to establish anything with political substance. This is most evident in the "failed" avant-garde movements of the mid-twentieth century. The surrounding questions are concerned with whether the creative energy of modernity is spent. If so, is this a consequence of the infiltration of system into the lifeworld that results in the lifeworld's being "colonized" and exploited for the sake of system imperatives? This in turn raises a further question. As Habermas puts it: "Thinking more generally, does the existence of a post-avant-garde mean there is a transition to that broader phenomena called postmodernity?" (1981, 4–6).

The immediate consequence of the crisis produced by this historical juncture is "neoconservatism": a return to religious and traditional values that supposedly will resupply the meaning that has been swept away during the evolution of modernity. Habermas notes several ways in which this is problematic. Conservative critics of modernity have no way of accounting for social and economic advancements that have been made. This is because their analysis fails to grasp the extent to which negative cultural phenomena are tied to the mode of production. The cultural crises that they identify are a sign of a much deeper problem that falls from constitutional incongruities in the modern lifeworld. "I would describe this subordination of the lifeworld under system imperatives as a matter of disturbing the communicative infrastructure of everyday life." Habermas's point is that the central problem of the late phase of the modern epoch is a disruption of communicative rationality caused by the modern productive mode. It is not repressive norms that have stilted modern creativity; on the contrary, the breakdown in the structures of the lifeworld has inhibited the production and transmission of values and norms that are essential to maintaining the modern vision. As such, Habermas contends, the ideals of enlightened modernity need to be reappropriated and applied critically to the prevailing conditions that have brought about all the talk of postmodernity.

The feature of modernity that is central to Habermas's modernism falls from the differentiation of the rational substance of traditional religion and metaphysics into three distinct spheres: science, morality, and art. These three spheres correspond to the three types of validity claims that Habermas identifies as being raised in a formal discourse: truth, rightness, and truthfulness. Rational differentiation (which takes place within the modern lifeworld) gives rise to discourses that pertain to knowledge, justice, and taste. The ideal espoused by Enlightenment thinkers was that these discourses could be institutionalized in such a way that they would provide the foundation for a rational society. Unfortunately, this has not taken place. The three spheres have come under the control of experts who administer knowledge-based power independent of the general public. Rather than symmetrical public discourse, we have experts producing monologues that shape our thinking on the issues that they address. Contrary to the neoconservatives, however, Habermas refuses to see this phenomenon as an inherent repercussion of modernity. Rather, he claims, it is a function of communicative distortions that are associated with the capitalist economic mode. The normative content of modernity need not be renounced simply because it is distorted by a contingent productive mechanism. Hence, the solution to the crises of late modernity is to be found in the structures that constitute the modern lifeworld, not some indeterminate postmodern future (1981, 8–9).

Habermas develops his case by filling out the critique of aesthetic modernism. Rather than pursuing the Enlightenment goal of integrating art into public life, art movements, due to the outlandishness of their product, have become more and more detached. As such, art is negated as a distinct component of cultural life, rendering it impotent. When the boundaries separating the discursive spheres that constitute the modern lifeworld are obliterated, when moral and scientific discourses are renounced in favor of the expressive discourse of art, the potential for collective transformation of society is eliminated. In response, Habermas offers this proposal:

> I think that instead of giving up modernity and its project as a lost cause, we should learn from the mistakes of those extravagant programs which have tried to negate modernity. Perhaps the types of reception of art may offer an example which at least indicates the direction of a way out. (1981, 11)

Enactment of this proposal requires that language games be established that center on art. Art can then be reintegrated into the lifeworld, making it once again publicly accessible. Discourses that are concerned with expressive validity claims will set a precedent for reintegrating discourses concerning knowledge and justice. As such, art can pave the way toward a reactivation of the normative content that is stored in the modern lifeworld.

While an interesting proposal on a strictly theoretical level, Habermas recognizes that it falters practically: "If I am not mistaken, the chances for this today are not very good. More or less in the entire Western world, a climate has developed that furthers capitalist modernization processes as well as trends critical of cultural modernism. The disillusionment with the very failures of those programs that called for the negation of art and philosophy has come to serve as a pretense for conservative positions" (1981, 13). Habermas's pessimism on this count is underscored by his own analysis of the conditions that prevail in advanced modern societies. In a sense, then, his philosophical and political commitments to modernity begin from a position of frustration if not futility. The sorts of normative discourses that are necessary to break the stranglehold of capitalism are fundamentally precluded by that very set of limitations.

The position that I will attempt to develop is that two intertwined levels of normativity have developed during the modern epoch: the level that Habermas refers to, which ensures that validity claims are addressed rationally and fairly; and the level that enables activities to be conducted by individuals and collectives that are strategically positioned within the power/knowledge configurations that constitute advanced capitalist societies—preserving the communicative asymmetries that maintain their advantages. The fact that this bilevel set of norms is formally contained in the structures of the lifeworld serves as a smoke screen that cloaks a communicative structure that is not so much distorted as it is fine-tuned to protect the interests of those who have learned and mastered the norms that ground modern action related to political power and economic hegemony. So long as the illusion that the way to generate change is to engage in discursive practices that follow the letter of modern normativity is maintained, those individuals and groups that aspire to bring about change in accordance with these rules will be effectively subdued. They will be rendered impotent by system imperatives that have, for all intents and purposes, cornered the lifeworld that provides their foundation. One needs simply to look at activist groups that are in existence today to confirm this. While participants enjoy rich discourse and establish solidarity among themselves, they rarely make an impact simply through dialogue. By relying on the questionable normative content of modernity to ground his theory, Habermas by his own admission renders a complementary set of political practices implausible.

This criticism is one that is fostered by Habermas's own analysis of advanced capitalism. He is acutely aware of the way that the communicative paradigm of capitalism has seeped into all spheres of late modern life. He does not, however, proceed with an assessment of the discourses that enable this to occur. On the contrary, he persistently returns to the type of analysis that was first introduced in his earliest work. An ideal model of healthy social and political communication is used as a standard against which existing communicative patterns are measured. This facilitates the detection of distorted communication, which is an initial step in a process tailored toward bringing it under the regulation of agreed-upon standards of legitimacy. If, however, the discourse is already regulated by a set of norms that are inseparable from modern norms, then an alternative approach to discursive practices that is less indebted to the "talking cure" needs to be developed.

The points that I have sketched in this introduction will be elaborated in the book that follows. My objective is to take one of Habermas's central claims—that a politics of emancipation is by necessity a politics of enlightenment—and explore the conditions of its development such that the dubious status of modern normativity is rigorously questioned. My aim is to think through the problems of such a politics in lieu of a waning modernity. In doing so I will provide a thorough critical analysis of Habermas's conception of the relationship between the ideals of the Enlightenment and the development of modern societies. I will argue that Habermas unnecessarily links the concept of enlightenment to modern social, political, and economic developments. This is an important issue if, as postmodernists have contended, some of the basic structures of modernity have fallen into dissolution. While I am not prepared to embrace postmodernism, a number of issues raised by critics such as Jean-François Lyotard and Fredric Jameson need to be taken into consideration. In my analysis of these figures—with respect to the question of enlightenment as well as Habermas's modernism—I will argue for a middle position that will be characterized as the "aftermath of modernity." This characterization will enable a critique of Habermas's enlightenment positions with respect to several key political, cultural, and theoretical debates. These are loosely organized under the banner of neoconservatism. In response to his modernist approach, I will consider the preliminary features of a politics of enlightenment that is compatible with the aftermath of modernity. In doing so I will appeal to several recent French philosophers (primarily Foucault, Derrida, and Levinas) who, I believe, avoid the modern/postmodern dichotomy. My aim will be to preserve a conception of normativity and a strong sense of emancipation, along with Habermas's commitment to the Kantian ethical project. I will contend that in order to keep these concepts both theoretically and politically viable, it is necessary to move beyond the limits of Habermas's conception of modernity.

In the first chapter I will situate my project in terms of a dialectic of enlightenment that has been developing for over 200 years. The point of departure for this discussion is Kant's famous essay "What Is Enlightenment?" I argue that this, as well as several other of Kant's "occasional" writings, provides a firm philosophical basis for further discussion of the question of enlightenment. This question will be followed historically through the nineteenth century and proceed to the seminal work by Max Horkheimer and Theodor Adorno, *Dialectic of Enlightenment*. In the present work I identify two strains of enlightenment thought: one that is more compatible with Habermas's vision and another that points in the direction of a form of enlightenment that moves beyond the parameters of modernity. I will proceed to show how this alternative to the traditional, Habermasian, conception of enlightenment is both plausible and, to a certain extent, compatible with Habermas's own analysis of advanced modern societies. This chapter concludes with an analysis of the political possibilities that emerge in the wake of modernity.

Chapter 2 deals extensively with issues surrounding the modernism/postmodernism debate. I begin by detailing Habermas's views on the development of modern societies. Particular attention is paid here to the way that Habermas characterizes the normative content of such societies. As a foil to this, I discuss the work of Lyotard and Jameson. In the course of doing so I distinguish between what will be referred to as descriptive postmodernism and "normative" postmodernism. This enables a fuller characterization of the political possibilities that lie outside of the modern/postmodern dichotomy. I conclude the chapter by arguing that both the modernist and postmodernist views miss something crucial about the current historical-political climate and why it is more relevant to refer to this atmosphere as the aftermath of modernity.

In chapter 3 I take up Habermas's version of the politics of enlightenment: his theory of communicative action. Here I argue that the normative aspirations of this theory, in their most abstract form, can indeed be separated from the capitalist mode of production. When the theory becomes more concrete, however, particularly with respect to law, morality, and emancipation, this separation falters. My contention is that philosophical distinctions between what could be called, in conventional Marxian terms, base and superstructure, run the political risk of integrating into a normative theory the very distortions that the theory is designed to mitigate against. I conclude with a discussion of the prospects for going beyond foundationalism in the direction of a historically fortified materialism.

Chapter 4 addresses specific examples of the politics of enlightenment that Habermas forwards, arguing that when examined in the context of real political action, it tends toward fortifying a quasi-liberal status quo. This is exemplified in several debates that Habermas has participated in concerning the issue of neoconservatism. Beyond this I attempt to gauge the way that a Habermasian politics of enlightenment would pertain to watershed political events of contemporary relevance.

In the final chapter I develop my own position on the politics of enlightenment. I argue that the key to such a politics is to be found in Habermas's theory of the lifeworld. My claim is that this theory is incompatible with his version of communicative action. I suggest an alternative to this that opens further political possibilities. In conclusion I argue for a radically egalitarian form of communicative action that is based on Habermas's discourse ethics and recent French philosophy.

Before proceeding with this task I would like to address an inevitable objection to the project that I here propose. The purist will say that this is not an authentic work in Habermas scholarship. Much of Habermas's recent work is not even addressed. Many of the positions that I attribute to him are rooted in a period that he has in some ways moved beyond. Finally, the interpretations that I offer of Habermas's work are not always in line with the standing orthodoxy. To all of these objections, I would enthusiastically plead guilty as charged. I am not a Habermas scholar. I certainly wouldn't claim to be one of the most astute readers of his work (although I did have the good fortune of working closely with David Ingram, who is one of the most astute readers of Habermas). And on a certain level this isn't really even a book about Habermas. My interest here is primarily in a set of ideas, theories, debates, and political problematics that arose within the framework of the neoconservative movement that swept the Western world in the 1980s. Habermas, in my estimation, played a crucial role in trying to come to grips with these watershed events. It is his courage and conviction that I wish to bring into play in this work, not the letter of the theoretical law of Habermas scholarship (for which I have a great deal of respect). Habermas's work during this era is comparable to the postwar work of his first-generation predecessors. Therefore, I proclaim (at the risk of sounding overly ambitious and possibly pompous) this to be a work in critical social theory as I believe it is best done: utilizing the theoretical resources that are at our disposal for the sake of gaining insight into the most urgent social and political problems of our time. If this book sheds any light at all on such matters, I will be satisfied.

CHAPTER 1

Dialectic of Difference: Enlightenment and Its Other

Enlightenment, whether considered as an historical process or a philosophical concept, has sparked a great deal of debate in contemporary social theory. Numerous events have occurred in the twentieth century—the rise of Nazism, the war that didn't end all wars, the development and deployment of nuclear weapons, the flagrant exploitation of "Third World" nations, and the rise and fall of "communism" just to name a few—that have prompted questions as to whether the objectives stated by Kant in 1784 have been, or are being realized:

> Enlightenment is man's emergence from his self-imposed immaturity. Immaturity is the inability to use one's understanding without guidance from another. This immaturity is self-imposed when its cause lies not in lack of understanding, but in lack of resolve and courage to use it without guidance from another. Sapere Aude! "Have courage to use your own understanding!"—that is the motto of enlightenment.

The all-important question for social theorists is whether the atrocities of the current century are a sign of immaturity or a function of the very maturation process that Kant so enthusiastically lauds. If the former is true, and further enlightenment is the solution, then enlightenment must be a basic tenet of any social theory. If the latter is the case, then social theory must cut against the grain that has been constituted by "enlightened" thought.

The poles that I have characterized, although construed a bit too simplistically, represent, in a sense, the theoretical presuppositions of two prominent schools of social thought: critical theory and poststructuralism. Critical theorists feel that the project of enlightenment must be continued by reconceptualizing it in a manner that is compatible with existing social and political conditions. Poststructuralists, in contrast, are less willing to accept the traditional concept of enlightenment in any form. Oddly enough, both schools are committed, in one way or another, to working through this problem by rethinking the Kantian critical project.

The publication in 1982 of the notes that were to be the third and final volume of Hannah Arendt's *The Life of the Mind*[1] issued in a post-structuralist wave of scholarship on Kant's "political philosophy." This work focuses not so much on his more explicitly political writings, but rather on the third Critique. The neo-neo-Kantianism to which Arendt's Lectures gave rise developed what could be referred to as the politics of judgment.[2] In these fragments, Arendt attempts to dismiss Kant's "less than serious" dabblings in philosophical journalism in order to ferret out the political philosophy that he never quite wrote. She bases her analysis primarily on the notion of judgment developed in the third volume of the critical trilogy. This focus locates Kant's political philosophy in a rather paradoxical way. It would be hard to imagine a thinker more distinctively modern than Kant; yet the politics of judgment that Arendt gives impetus to in her lectures has taken on a surprisingly postmodern character.[3] The expression of this is most notably found in the writings of Jean-François Lyotard.

The main alternative to the postmodern Kant that the neo-neo-Kantians have manufactured is the more conventional Kantianism developed by thinkers such as John Rawls and Jürgen Habermas. Their attempts to write Kant's "fourth Critique" concentrate on the second increment of the critical trilogy. In doing so they remain firmly within the modernist tradition that Kant, in a sense, initiated. While my sympathies lie with the ethical content of this more likely approach to a Kantian political philosophy, there is a tendency, in my estimation, to ignore important structural changes that challenge some of modernism's most cherished principles. This is most clearly evident in Habermas's work. In his efforts to revive the ethical-political content of the modernist tradition, he tends to dismiss the "realities" of the postmodern condition. While I am not willing to fully embrace either the descriptive or normative dimensions of postmodernism, I do think that it is necessary—both philosophically and politically—to query with seriousness its threat to the tradition of enlightenment thought. In doing so, I will take up several of Kant's writings that Arendt, citing Schopenhauer favorably, claims do not seem to be "the work of this great man, but the product of an ordinary common man" (Arendt 1982, 8). My aim is to trace a line from Kant to Habermas that explores the territory between nostalgic modernism and cynical postmodernism.

The pivotal work in my analysis will be Max Horkheimer and Theodor Adorno's *Dialectic of Enlightenment*. This remarkable book provides, in a number of ways, a context for the debate between the modernists and postmodernists on the question of enlightenment. I will explore this further by taking into consideration Michel Foucault's reflections on the question of enlightenment. My argument will be that Foucault is not opposed to enlightenment per se, but rather to a specifically modern, humanist conception of enlightenment that lends itself to a particular type of immaturity. This situates Foucault as one of those key figures whose work lies between the modern/postmodern dichotomy. From there I will proceed to argue that Habermas's most recent assessment of late modern society comes to conclusions that are not incommensurate with Foucault's views. My aim in doing so is to provide a framework for discussions in subsequent chapters that will show that while late modern (advanced-capitalist or postindustrial) societies are in concrete terms not postmodern, a theory of enlightenment that is sensitive to the conditions of late modernity must take into consideration countermodern critiques. In doing so I will attempt to thematize the basic issues that are relevant to a politics of enlightenment appropriate to the aftermath of modernity.

THE POLITICS OF ENLIGHTENMENT: PHASE 1

In this section I will discuss three of Kant's essays that raise important issues concerning the conditions for a politics of enlightenment.[4] These writings inform the conception that I will develop later. Kant attacked the question of enlightenment most directly in his famous essay "An Answer to the Question: What Is Enlightenment?."[5] In this short, but pithy, treatise, he develops a compelling case for the significant role that autonomy must play in a theory of enlightenment. Stating Kant's thesis once again:

> Enlightenment is man's emergence from his self-imposed immaturity. Immaturity is the inability to use one's understanding without guidance from another. This immaturity is self-imposed when its cause lies not in lack of understanding, but in lack of resolve and courage to use it without guidance. (41)

While on the surface this might appear to be a radically individualistic view of autonomy, a closer look shows that Kant has a subtle understanding of the conditions that must obtain in order for autonomy to be a viable possibility. He thematizes this in terms of a strong principle of freedom—a freedom that takes shape in the context of changes occurring in both the political structures and the moral fabric of an emerging modernity. "But that the public should enlighten itself is more likely; indeed, if it is only allowed freedom, enlightenment is almost inevitable."

We see in Kant's thinking the development of a dialectical conception of enlightenment. On the one hand, autonomy or self-determination requires a substantive, concrete form of freedom. One can surmise that for Kant this involves secular authority, market economies, republican forms of government, and a separation between state and civil society. On the other hand, in order to see clearly what is required to bring about a substantive form of freedom, subjects must already be autonomous. From an ahistorical point of view it would appear as though Kant's initial theory of enlightenment turns into a dilemma. But from the perspective of developing forms of life, the dilemma takes shape as a field of genuine social and political possibilities. These possibilities, which are dependent upon necessary a priori conditions, find their conditions of sufficiency within a newly emerging realm of political discourse.

> However, insofar as this part of the machine also regards himself as a member of the community as a whole, or even of the world community, and as a consequence addresses the public in the role of a scholar, in the proper sense of that term, he can most certainly argue, without thereby harming the affairs for which as a passive member he is partly responsible. (42)

As such, the dialectic of enlightenment is located within the public sphere of bourgeois society.[6]

Kant further historicizes his position by pointing out how one of the sure signs of enlightenment is the realization that enlightenment is not a state to achieve, but rather a process to participate in. This highlights the importance that he attributes to public debate as a vehicle for generating enlightenment. A vibrant public sphere seems, for Kant, to be the most important structural constituent of the dialectic of enlightenment: at the social and political level it provides for a critical transformation of impediments to substantive freedom; at the individual level it provides a forum in which personal integrity and mutual respect can be fostered. Together these two aspects of the public sphere enable a strong sense of solidarity as well as a contextualized model of autonomy.

The theory of enlightenment developed thus far is principally conceptual. While I have focused upon Kant's appreciation of the historical embeddedness of the possibility for enlightenment, as a theory of enlightenment these contingencies are underdeveloped. In order to see more clearly the philosophy of history that is in the backdrop of this conceptual schema, it is useful to turn to Kant's sketch in "Idea for a Universal History with a Cosmopolitan Intent."[7] Here he develops a series of theses that serve to illustrate the telos of enlightenment. Kant introduces this essay by bringing into play the noumenal/phenomenal distinction that is so important to his epistemology and moral philosophy. In this context he frames it in terms of the course of history in relation to the autonomous subject. Humans don't plot out a desirable course for history and then construct a plan of action that will lead to the determined objective. Rather, the natural process of history, in conjunction with the determinate aims of discrete communities of actors, moves in the direction of fulfilling enlightenment ideals.

The spark for this process is conflict and antagonism, followed by progressive resolution; it is fueled by the transcendent rationality to which Kant continuously appeals. Institutionally this process is objectified in political and social structures that are repeatedly transformed as they outlive their usefulness. Morally it builds toward a concept of right that facilitates the flourishing of human freedom. The ultimate logic of this, Kant suggests, leads us to a concept of internationalism based on shared values and preserved by a system of universal law. In other words, history moves toward a cosmopolitan state premised on general conditions of toleration and cooperation. Hence, Kant provides a philosophy of history that serves as the normative-empirical foundation for a strongly emancipatory theory of enlightenment.

The utopian aspirations of this theory are reflected on more freely in "To Perpetual Peace: A Philosophical Sketch."[8] In this essay Kant develops a set of principles that focus on the maintenance of peace between sovereign nations. Based on the preceding discussion, as well as comments to that effect in Kant's essay, it can be inferred that he sees the ultimate condition of enlightenment to be harmonious coexistence on a global scale. Before discussing several of the key tenets of perpetual peace, it is important to note that the more conservative side of Kant is also on display in this essay. He is suspicious of unlimited democratization; assumes a very Hobbesian theory of human nature—one that doesn't do service to his own rich conception of the dialectical relationship between the noumenal and phenomenal constituitives of human being; and he assumes, too, that coercion is necessary if politics and morality are to be squared.[9] In spite of this, Kant summarizes several of the most important features of his theory of enlightenment in a provocative manner. The ones that will concern me here deal with the relationship between universal morality and contingent political institutions.

Kant sets up the discussion of perpetual peace by opposing his views to the "pragmatics" of political functionaries and their disdain for the visionary aspirations of theorists. This situates the ideal of peaceful coexistence in terms of the dialectic of enlightenment by pitting forces of conservancy against the radical possibilities that contest the established common sense. The former reduces humane existence to the determinations of the phenomenal realm; the latter recognizes the need for noumenal transcendence, made concrete in the political sphere, in order for conditions of enlightenment to be secured.

> The state of peace must therefore be established, for the suspension of hostilities does not provide the security of peace, and unless this security is pledged by one neighbor to another (which can happen only in a state of lawfulness), the latter, from whom such security has been requested, can treat the former as an enemy. (111)

Kant's point is that the impulses of self-preservation will not suffice to sustain conditions of peace. Perpetual peace requires the rule of law. This appeal to the transcendental-universal aspect of his moral theory illustrates the way in which the ethical abstraction embodied in the categorical imperative can be brought to bear in an institutional context. While the specific status of the relationship between noumenal ideals and phenomenal practices remains underdeveloped, it is clear that he sees this *possibility* as necessary for formulating a politics of enlightenment.

Kant attempts to specify more precisely the institutional form that this would need to take. His two key points pertain to the establishment of republican governments at the national level and some type of international confederation of nations. The first of these doesn't demonstrate a great deal of political imagination; the second, however, points to important limitations of the nation-state at the outset of its development. In order to achieve peace at all, there must be a network of relations established between all political entities. This addition marks an important development over the Hobbesianism of his view of the social contract. Relations between nations would have to be grounded in the concrete political expression of the categorical imperative.

In summary I would like to stress the following points: First, for Kant it seems possible for one to uphold moral principles outside of the context of an enlightened society. In fact, the possibility for moral self-determination must precede the setting up of just institutions. What is crucial for Kant's dialectic of enlightenment is that the possibility for moral self-determination begins to converge with the development of modern political institutions. Second, a concrete form of autonomy is needed in order for this convergence to take place. In other words, the transcendental moral subject must find her/his place in the phenomenal world. Kant situates the possibility for this in terms of a philosophy of history that has as its end the achievement of enlightened societal structures and relations. Finally, this end can only be fulfilled within intersubjective networks that are sustained in order to generate solidarity. Kant's appeal to the public sphere and the importance of internationalism specifies this need. While I recognize that my interpretation of Kant is contestable,[10] I want to emphasize that if the radical side of Kant is ferreted out, his views on enlightenment offer a wealth of resources.

THE POLITICS OF ENLIGHTENMENT: PHASE 2

My argument thus far has been that Kant, in a sense, develops a notion of a dialectic of enlightenment that is relevant to my present concerns.

His analysis, however, is weak on a number of scores. The most flagrant of these is his naivete concerning political economy. For Kant, the economy played no role in the normative structure of society. His focus is almost exclusively on civil society and the state. Critical theorists after Kant, however, became increasingly aware of the contradictions between an enlightened society and the capitalist mode of production. Hegel, for example, saw that the logic of capitalism entails a state of perpetual unrest in that expansionism and fierce competition leads to warfare. And of course Marx's contribution to this scarcely needs to be mentioned. Where both Hegel and Marx uncritically followed Kant concerned his teleological view of history. As Kenneth Baynes puts it,

> Kant's predictions about the course of historical and political events have not fared any better than Marx's. Nature has produced neither just political orders nor a condition of international perpetual peace. If Kant's teleological conception of history is unjustified, what consequences does this have for his assumptions about the unity of practical philosophy?[11]

It is this question that prompts the next phase of the politics of enlightenment.

When Max Horkheimer and Theodor Adorno wrote *Dialectic of Enlightenment* (DE),[12] they were overwhelmed with the phenomenal events that seemed to undermine the viability of a politics based on rationally grounded transcendental morality: the aforementioned developments that have marred the record of twentieth century "enlightened" societies. The way that one interprets these events will largely determine how one is disposed toward the question of enlightenment. If *the* Enlightenment leads directly to these atrocities, then critique must mitigate against Enlightenment norms; if, on the contrary, these events are radical deviations from the norms of the Enlightenment, then critique should attempt to defend the validity of these norms and consider ways in which they can be brought to bear on existing social and political conditions. This is the set of problems that Horkheimer and Adorno attempt to analyze. I will now address their interpretation of the dialectic of enlightenment.

While critics of the Enlightenment can be found at nearly every juncture of its development, it is Horkheimer and Adorno's critique that is most pertinent to the concerns of this book. They state the following thesis: "myth is already enlightenment; and enlightenment reverts to mythology" (DE, xvi). It is this proposition that prompted them to radically reformulate the project of critical theory.[13] An important catalyst for this reformulation was their observation that the process of social organization, driven by the development and intensification of rationality, so effectively subdues nature that humanity, being a natural entity, falls victim to its own progress. This is exemplified by the impulses of the Enlightenment:

> For the Enlightenment, whatever does not conform to the rule of computation and utility is suspect. So long as it can develop undisturbed by any outward repression, there is no holding it. In the process, it treats its own ideas of human rights exactly as it does the older universals. Every spiritual resistance it encounters serves merely to increase its strength. (DE, 6)

Enlightenment turns against the original intention of rationally emancipating individuals from mythological worldviews. By failing to reflect critically upon its own historical development, the Enlightenment becomes encased in a mythological fortress that protects it from the harsh truth of its own reality: that it creates a technological despotism that deprives individuals of their personal identity, linkage to nature, and spirituality.

In defense of these claims Horkheimer and Adorno provide a comprehensive critique of the entire tradition of Western rationality.[14] From the outset, enlightenment, under any name, has simply articulated the presiding myth via the language of rationality.[15] As such, there are notable similarities between mythological and enlightened thought. Both, to a certain extent, attempt to provide a unified picture of reality; they share the objective of mastering nature; and each structures itself on the basis of power hierarchies. Mythology and enlightenment are both motivated by a deep fear of the unknown, driving each to the conclusion that mysterious elements of reality must be subdued through explanation. It was a specific type of explanation—scientific—that gave rise to the historical Enlightenment. Horkheimer and Adorno indicate a number of consequences that fall from this. The most important of these pertain to modes of communication and social organization (DE, 8–18).

Modes of communication are dependent upon forms of discursive language. In mythological discourse the language is symbolic: the signifier and signified are united in the symbol. Or, to put this in another way, processes of reference are perceived to create a unified whole. This unity translates into social unity, for the meaning and truth objectified in language plays an important role in corporate ritual practices that are repeatedly used to create a sense of communal cohesion. As distinctions between literal and figural discourse came to be drawn, the former, without recognition of fictional residue, was deemed the language of truth. This began in ancient Greek philosophy and reached its pinnacle in enlightened positivism. The theme that is common to all phases of this history is a compulsion to assert humanity's superiority over nature.

Consequently, discursive development reflects a desire to describe, understand, and ultimately dominate nature. Hence, the signifier ceases to provide social coherence by representing a shared truth and meaning. Rather than symbolizing the horizontally organized communality of humanity and environment, it becomes a manipulative implement that serves the compulsion to vertically administrate social and natural reality (DE, 17–18).[16]

As I mentioned, Horkheimer and Adorno contend that the discourses of rationalistic philosophy, and later of enlightened science, retain a number of characteristics typically associated with their mythical antecedents. The most significant remnants are the power associated with linguistic mastery, the use of technical vocabulary to systematize and totalize, and the development of linguistic apparatuses that facilitate the hierarchical ordering of subject matter. Whereas in prerational societies the priest, as the possessor of symbolic meaning, was the most powerful member, now the scientist, whose discourse is laced with facts and figures, reigns. While operating under the guise of neutrality, the ideology of scientific rationality permeates all spheres of social existence. This is achieved, the authors claim, through the proliferation and dissemination of scientific language.

> Language itself gave what was asserted, the conditions of domination, the universality that they had assumed as the means of intercourse of a bourgeois society. The metaphysical emphasis, and sanction by means of ideas and norms, were no more than hypostatization of the rigidity and exclusiveness which concepts were generally compelled to assume wherever language united the community of rulers with the giving of orders. As mere means of reinforcing the social power of language, ideas became all the more superfluous as this power grew, and the language of science prepared the way for their ultimate desuetude. (DE, 22)

To summarize, Horkheimer and Adorno claim the following: mythical discourse precedes and influences metaphysical discourse, which precedes and influences scientific discourse. While passionately seeking to purge itself of all mythical and metaphysical characteristics, enlightened science fails to reflect on its own discursive evolution. As such, the remnants that I mentioned above translate into a new social mythology involving an unqualified faith in reason, an uncritical acceptance of market relations, and an overenthusiastic reception of full-scale capitalism (DE, 20–23).[17]

Horkheimer and Adorno go on to claim that the mythological foundation of enlightened modern society is a dogmatic aversion for theory. Thinkers in the Enlightenment tradition are, in a sense, antithinkers. They no longer feel compelled to theorize about the good or the nature of reality. Now it is simply the matter of learning the laws of nature and mathematics and applying them to the matters at hand. This procedure, according to Horkheimer and Adorno, is conducted under the jurisdiction of a totalizing presupposition: that all of the natural order can be systematically understood and exploited for the "good" of humanity. As a result of rigid adherence to this presupposition, negative consequences go undetected. "What appears to be the triumph of subjective rationality, the subjection of all reality to logical formalism, is paid for by the obedient subjection of reason to what is directly given" (DE, 26).

While the repercussions of this mind-set for philosophy and science are significant, according to Horkheimer and Adorno, the influences on the way that everyday life is conducted are devastating. The same rigorous schemes of classification and ordering used to characterize natural phenomena are implemented in manufacturing facilities and social institutions. Individuals become cogs in the capitalist machinery. Conventions of expediency are enforced with such proficiency that behavioral norms are rarely questioned. This is accomplished by carefully monitoring and maintaining individual components of the collective unit, ensuring its smooth operation. The basic truth undergirding the modern facade of individuality and freedom is that power rules. This, according to Horkheimer and Adorno, is the dark mythical undercurrent of enlightenment (DE, 28–29).

The preceding analysis raises serious questions about the idea of a politics of enlightenment. Kant's dream of modern progress seems to have turned into a postmodern nightmare. Yet I would contend that the authors of *Dialectic of Enlightenment* don't depart from Kant's most basic ideals. They challenge the teleological view of progress by positing an alternative interpretation to the idealist metanarrative.[18] Likewise they root themselves in, and expand upon, the classical critique of political economy.[19] Finally, they argue convincingly that *the* most important feature of Kant's optimism concerning the prospect of an enlightened society—that being the potential for human autonomy—is virtually impossible within the parameters of his analysis. This, however, does not amount to the dismissal of Kant's ideals. In fact, they repeatedly appeal to principles such as self-determination, the need for public discourse, and the basis for this that can only be provided for within the context of a vital community. While Horkheimer and Adorno are hesitant to frame this positively in terms of a politics of enlightenment, their negative appeal to these values clearly situates them within Kant's set of questions.

All the same, the main essay of *Dialectic of Enlightenment* leaves the reader somewhat confused as to whether Western rationality and enlightenment are inherently bad or simply misdirected. An Adornoesque pessimism certainly prevails, giving the impression that reason and enlightenment are fraught with deep conceptual problems that translate into authoritarianism and domination. Nevertheless, the critique pursued is of existing *forms* of rationality and a specifically modern *form* of enlightenment. While the seeds of these forms are traced, in almost Heideggerian fashion, back to the golden days of ancient Greece, the concrete examples are all linked to a distinctly modern conception of science, as well as the modern mode of production. Unlike Heidegger, however, the authors don't clearly dismiss rationality and enlightenment in general. There is at the very least a restless ambiguity in the text.[20] This is intensified in light of the different attitudes expressed in the two excursuses that follow. Given that the excursuses were independently authored, it can be inferred that the tension is explicable in terms of differences between the individual views of Horkheimer and Adorno. I will proceed under the assumption that this is the case.[21]

THE POLITICS OF ENLIGHTENMENT: PHASE 3

As I mentioned above, during the course of this analysis a model for critical-theoretical studies of society is formulated. This model can be developed in two directions that are relevant to the question of a politics of enlightenment. These two directions are delimited by the excursuses that follow the main essay in *Dialectic of Enlightenment*. The first, authored by Adorno, views enlightened thought to be inherently *suspect*. The second, authored by Horkheimer, indicates that it is not enlightenment as such, but rather its perversion, that is the source of modernity's rationality-related problems. In this section I will argue that Foucault develops Adorno's thesis while Habermas elaborates Horkheimer's.[22]

In the first excursus the author (Adorno) initiates his interrogation of Western rationality with the stunning claim that Homer's Odysseus is the prototypical bourgeois individual. He proceeds by offering an interpretation of *The Odyssey* which contends that Odysseus's experiences initiated a continuous history of instrumental rationality that reaches full fruition in the Enlightenment.[23] This unaltered model for rational cognition is established by the cunning acts of the epic voyager. Odysseus faces a number of mythical-natural obstacles during his trek. The strategy that he develops for overcoming these impediments employs a submissive yet manipulative form of rationality. Nature is not confronted in a face-to-face struggle; it is outmaneuvered and subdued from behind (DE, 58–60).

Adorno characterizes Odysseus's encounter with the Sirens as the paradigm for all succeeding implementations of instrumental rationality:

> It is impossible to hear the Sirens and not succumb to them; therefore he does not try to defy their power. Defiance and infatuation are one and the same thing, and whoever defies them is thereby lost to the myth against which he sets himself. Cunning, however, is defiance in rational form. (DE, 58–59)

Odysseus gains the upper hand, but not without consequence. In order to overcome the order of nature, he submits to self-imposed bondage (by strapping himself to the mast of the ship). For Adorno, this represents the inevitable paradox of instrumental reason. In order to win, one has to lose. It also provides a model for the type of human behavior that flourishes under the capitalistic economic structures of enlightened modern society. In order to get ahead, one has to submit to self-sacrifice and must be willing to sacrifice anyone that stands in the way. Adorno concludes that Western rationality is inherently plagued with this "negative dialectic." The historical Enlightenment simply intensifies the irrationality that has always infected reason, producing the above-mentioned social consequences (DE, 55–60).[24]

Habermas makes the point that this critique of enlightened thought is so comprehensive that it ultimately denies its own critical foundation. From the very beginning, Adorno claims, Western reason is tainted with the sinister paradox faced by Odysseus. Likewise, the possibility that rationality has any positive critical content is dismissed. Yet, to use Habermas's phrase, he retains a "residual faith in a de-ranged reason" (1987b, 186). As such, his analysis, like the tradition he criticizes, is rooted in a paradox: it uses the tools of Western rationality while denying that they can have any positive application. While I don't entirely endorse Habermas's assessment of Adorno, the general dilemma that he identifies needs to be contended with. If social theory is to take seriously Adorno's critique while still maintaining—at least theoretically—its relationship to the ideal of collective emancipation, this problem needs to be addressed. I think that Foucault offers insight into how this might be accomplished.[25] While not a direct understudy of Adorno's, Foucault's entire corpus of work represents a concern with the questions raised in the first excursus of *Dialectic of Enlightenment*.[26] As such, he can legitimately be characterized as picking up where Adorno left off.[27]

In "What Is Enlightenment?" (hereafter WE) (1984), Foucault takes up the question addressed by Kant in the latter part of the eighteenth century and, in a sense, by Horkheimer and Adorno in *Dialectic of Enlightenment*. He suggests that the question as to the inherent goodness or baseness of the Enlightenment is irrelevant. By focusing on the conceptual point that tormented Adorno, and the question as to whether enlightenment contains an "essential kernel of rationality," theory will be "blackmailed" by the Enlightenment (subdued by the dialectic of liberation and domination). The essential theoretical project is to identify the boundaries that are established by the Enlightenment attitude and to determine the points at which these limits are susceptible to pressure. "The point, in brief, is to transform the critique constituted in the form of necessary limitation into a practical critique that takes the form of a possible transgression" (WE, 42–45).

It is naive, in Foucault's judgment, to think that a totalistic analysis of the repercussions of rationality on social existence (such as that conducted by Adorno) is even possible. Social theory should focus on grasping points at which change is urgently needed and attempt to determine tactics that are capable of achieving the desired alteration. Such a strategy would dispense with Adorno's sweeping generalizations while retaining the analytic acuity that enabled him to identify specific instances that confirm his hypothesis. Foucault describes this project as being genealogical in design and archaeological in method. "It is not seeking to make possible a metaphysics that has finally become a science; it is seeking to give new impetus, as far and wide as possible, to the undefined work of freedom" (WE, 46). As such, the problematic element of Adorno's critique (its totalistic dimension) can be eliminated without sacrificing the critical wealth of his analysis (WE, 45–47).[28]

In the second excursus of *Dialectic of Enlightenment*, Horkheimer suggests that the undistorted "kernel of rationality" that Adorno seems to think is nonexistent and that Foucault is unconcerned with might be worth pursuing. While concentrating on the negative dimensions of Western reason, as manifest in enlightenment morality, Horkheimer implies that this isn't the necessary end of reason.

Horkheimer clearly rejects instrumental reason. Rationality of this sort, he claims, is in line with the Kantian conception of enlightenment and reason.[29] The task of reason here is to systematize and put things in their proper order. This will ensure that humanity reaches maturity and preserves itself as a species. Horkheimer agrees with Adorno that this organizational fetish is the most dangerous product of the Enlightenment, but suggests that critique should be directed specifically at rationality and enlightenment as conceived within capitalistic socioeconomic structures. It is the combination of a specific type of reason and a specific mode of production that causes the devastating consequences associated with the historical Enlightenment. It doesn't necessarily follow from this that reason is inherently distorted. It is paradoxical, rather than predictable, that the Enlightenment should result in its own antithesis. This, for Horkheimer, occurred due to a fatal practical flaw: Enlightenment thought failed to fully incorporate the need for internal criticism. One can infer from this that Horkheimer would accept an adequate concept of enlightenment. By indicating that reason has assumed a perverse *form*, he leaves open the possibility that a more reflective rationality might be the answer to the problem created by its irrational opposite (DE, 85–93).

This is precisely the position held by Habermas. His well-known approach is to develop a normative theory of action that is based on distortion free rational discourse. He situates this project vis-à-vis the dialectic of enlightenment in "The Entwinement of Myth and Enlightenment."[30] Habermas attacks Horkheimer and Adorno for overgeneralizing and oversimplifying the dialectic of rationality. By excluding from their analysis all but the most positivistic of sciences, neglecting the important role of reason in formulating standards of morality and justice during the modern epoch, and declaring that all contemporary art is simple entertainment, the fruitful contributions that the Enlightenment has made are ignored. In response, Habermas contends that the development of science has been driven by a rich internal dynamic, that enlightened conceptions of justice and morality tend toward universality, and that the visions of avant-garde art have emancipatory possibilities. Habermas does not praise these qualities at the expense of the important critical insights provided by Horkheimer and Adorno. Rather, he takes their insights to be indicative of the need to rigorously apply critique to Enlightenment thought and social practices. In doing so, the normative content of modernity that remains undefiled by purposive rationality can be extracted and developed, continuing the dialectic of enlightenment.

Habermas concludes by claiming that theory must accept the fact that myth and enlightenment are to a certain extent entangled. This does not mean, however, that social criticism should turn against rationality. Rather, it should accept, for pragmatic purposes, the presuppositions of rational discourse, allowing the efficacy of the better argument to shape social-political reality. "Only a discourse which admits this everlasting impurity can perhaps escape from myth, thus freeing itself, as it were, from the entwinement of myth and Enlightenment" (Habermas, 1982).

At the programmatic level, Habermas and Foucault come down on the same foot. Both consider the aim of a politics of enlightenment to be that of generating critical insights that move in the direction of discourses of emancipation. At other levels, however, they are quite different. While Foucault sees little merit in what has taken place as a result of the historical Enlightenment, Habermas praises its contributions to truth, freedom, and justice (the normative foundations of modernity). They differ significantly at the level of strategy as well; Foucault suggests the need for transgression, while Habermas seeks progression in the form of establishing a continuum with pure Enlightenment ideals. While both see the need for a notion of enlightenment, Habermas's is unequivocally modern whereas Foucault moves in a postmodern direction. It is this direction that I will attempt to come to grip with in the pages that follow. Habermas's claim that there are unambiguously positive products of the modern Enlightenment strikes me as being mistaken. The concepts of truth, freedom, and justice to which he appeals are far more bound up in the capitalist economy of modernity than he cares to recognize. These are claims that I will develop in subsequent chapters. I will attempt to show that Habermas's own analysis of advanced capitalism in many ways confirms my position. It provides, in a sense, the prelude to a theory of the politics of enlightenment that moves beyond the normative structures of an unenlightened modernity.

While the normative appeal of Habermas's communicative resolution to the impasse presented by the dialectic of enlightenment is strong, the force of Horkheimer and Adorno's analysis causes one to question its viability. Furthermore, Habermas's most comprehensive assessment of the late-modern condition is even bleaker. He describes a scenario in which systems driven by money and power have come to permeate all spheres of human life. The following passage sums up his analysis:

> The legal-administrative means of translating social-welfare programs into action are not some passive, as it were, propertyless medium. They are connected, rather, with a praxis that involves isolation of facts, normalization, and surveillance, the reifying and subjectivating violence of which Foucault has traced right down into the most delicate capillary tributaries of everyday communication. The deformations of a lifeworld that is regulated, fragmented, monitored, and looked after is surely more subtle than the palpable forces of material exploitation and impoverishment; but internalized social conflicts that have shifted from the corporeal to the psychic are not therefore less destructive.[31]

In other words, a domineering modern system has chopped the modern lifeworld into bits and pieces, severely limiting the possibility for a politics of enlightenment. In spite of this, Habermas continues to insist, albeit in more localized form, that the appropriate strategy in light of this predicament is to form collectives of solidified consciousness that can establish patterns of communicative action within specifically politicized spheres. The aim is to "sensitize the self-steering mechanisms of the state and the economy to the goal-oriented outcomes of radical democratic will formation" (PDM, 368). If Habermas's own characterization of advanced capitalist society is taken seriously, however, then it would seem that the system is already beyond the point that it can be sensitized through reform movements.

In this final phase of the politics of enlightenment we seem to have come full circle. On the one hand we have the noumenal factors that make it possible to theorize about ideal discourse; on the other we have the rational utility maximizers of advanced modern society who would make Kant's race of devils quake in their boots. While Habermas's attempt to mediate this discrepancy involves "building up restraining barriers for the exchange between system and lifeworld and of building in sensors for the exchange between lifeworld and system" (PDM, 364), I would argue that the more appropriate strategy is to break down or dismantle the structural barriers that prohibit the development of "radical democratic" political processes. In other words, if we are to thematize a politics of enlightenment that is appropriate to the aftermath of modernity, we can't simply rehash that which has brought us to the present impasse.

WHAT IS ENLIGHTENMENT?

The analysis that I have developed up to this point is provisional at best. My main objective has been to illustrate the claim that there is more than one way to develop a politics of enlightenment. The approaches suggested by both Habermas and Foucault have their respective merits and problems. I focus on these approaches for two main reasons: First, because Habermas's work is identified almost completely with the project of rehabilitating the idea of enlightenment after Horkheimer and Adorno's critique; this is true to such a degree that the remainder of this book will focus on Habermas. Second, because Foucault alludes to an approach to the question of enlightenment that moves away from the modernist conception that Habermas embraces. As such, he suggests the possibility of developing a theory of enlightenment that is compatible with conditions that I will refer to as the aftermath of modernity. Nevertheless, Foucault merely makes allusions whereas Habermas has a comprehensive theory. In the pages and chapters that follow I will aim at substantiating these allusions by way of a critique of Habermas that takes up the question of enlightenment in a serious fashion. This will require that I draw on a number of sources that may at first glance appear to run contrary to the objective of theorizing a politics of enlightenment.

In order to begin thinking about such a politics I would like to turn to Derrida's essay "The Ends of Man."[32] I will argue that the title for this paper could just have easily have been, "What Is Enlightenment?" In doing so I will attempt to show how Derrida's concluding remarks in this essay bear upon the fundamental Enlightenment values that Habermas so relentlessly defends, and to raise questions as to whether these are really the values that are seminal to enlightenment.

I will begin, as does Derrida, with the question of internationalism.

The context in which this paper was presented, an international philosophical colloquium, prompts Derrida to consider the relationship between the political and the philosophical. His claim: "Every philosophical colloquium necessarily has a political significance." Further, he asserts that the international dimensions of this particular colloquium complicates its political significance. Finally, the specific events that were taking place at the time of this writing, "the weeks of the opening of the Vietnam peace talks and of the assassination of Martin Luther King," along with the fact that "the universities of Paris were invaded by the forces of order . . . and then reoccupied by the students in the upheaval," further problematizes the question. What, then, does this have to do with internationalism, and, more importantly, what does internationalism have to do with enlightenment? The first aspect of this question, as Derrida indicates, presupposes the formation of national identities and assumptions about the conditions under which those identities can converge. These assumptions seem to be of an enlightenment bent: Derrida chooses to concentrate on certain democratic presuppositions that depend upon the nexus between a formal category and a practical orientation. This nexus is both the condition that gives rise to the possibility of internationalism—"the colloquium can take place only in a medium, or rather in the representation that all the participants must make of a certain transparent ether, which here would be none other than what is called the universality of philosophical discourse"—and the condition that brings about reaction when things begin to get dangerous—"a declaration of opposition to some official policy is authorized, and authorized by the authorities, also means, precisely to that extent, that the declaration does not upset the given order, is not bothersome."[33] Hence, internationalism is fundamentally communicative, but likewise is confounded both internally and externally by the *limits* of communication.

With respect to the second aspect of the question, the relationship between internationalism and enlightenment, Kant's role becomes more explicit. In order to have enlightenment, we need to achieve perpetual peace, which necessitates the establishment of a world community. Kant is concerned with the role of law in the formation of such a community, but in the backdrop of his conception of law formation is an implicit appeal to the complex principle of democracy. Sorting through some of the loose threads here we can see the following set of conditions converging. Internationalism, as a political or even philosophical objective, presupposes some notion of enlightenment. At the same time it assumes some notion of nationality, which serves as the particular in relation to the international universal. This is mediated by a principle of democracy—constituted at the nexus of form and content, theory and practice—that is driven by a set of principles that emerged within the context of the historical Enlightenment. The field of enquiry circumscribed by this set of intersections establishes a context within which the question of enlightenment can be raised—by Derrida no less than Habermas.

Returning to those enlightenment values to which Habermas constantly appeals—truth, freedom, and justice—I think it is safe to say two things: (1) Derrida the philosopher doesn't oppose such values, but (2) Derrida as the sort of postmodernist that Habermas characterizes[34] him as being, does raise problematic questions about the "value" of these values. These questions revolve around how we "read us"—the way in which we interpret the limits and possibilities of collective social and political action. While I think that it would be wrong to say that Habermas doesn't carefully consider the possibility for social and political action, I also think he does so in a manner that confines these possibilities to a fixed understanding of what the term *enlightenment* can mean. The obvious reason for this is that the conception of enlightenment that rests at the base of his theory of communicative action requires a fairly straightforward understanding of the range of possibilities for human aggregation. Following three points that Derrida makes at the end of "The Ends of Man," I would like to explore a somewhat different reading of collective action than can be accommodated within Habermas's procedural approach.

While Habermas is quite obviously interested in the conditions that must obtain in order for validity claims to be raised and redeemed, the analysis of these conditions forces him into the nebulous structures of the modern lifeworld. He accounts for these as linguistic structures and proceeds to consider the manner in which they lead to the production of meaningful utterances that can be put into play within specific forums of discourse. The relationship, in his analysis, between the lifeworld as the basis for discourse, and particular arenas of discourse, fails to consider any but a fairly conventional notion of enlightenment. This is the point at which Habermas resists reading collective action carefully enough. The appropriation of the linguistic basis of discourse within particular discursive formats is relatively unproblematic for Habermas. In a Derridean formulation, however, this is where semantic stability can be quite radically altered. As Derrida puts it, "it is a question of determining the possibility of meaning of the basis of a 'formal' organization which in itself has no meaning, which does not mean that it is either the non-sense or the anguishing absurdity which haunt metaphysical humanism." My sense is that Habermas's concern with postmodernism is precisely this non-sense that Derrida is quite determined to distance himself from. At the same time he is careful not to retain a safe but implausible anthropology. While I won't attempt to spell out the full implications of Derrida's views on semantic indeterminacy at this point, I do want to emphasize that they seem to pose important questions concerning the relationship between the semantic mode of production that operates in Habermas's conception of the lifeworld and the value production that operates under conditions regulated by ideal speech. This, as I will discuss in the final chapter, raises challenges that must be addressed within the framework of the theory of communicative action.

By introducing Derrida at this point I have simply intended to show that a serious enquiry into the prospects for enlightenment needs to take into consideration various possible approaches to the basic question of enlightenment. I will be pursuing these possibilities in the following chapters. Habermas may be right that the risk of exploring what lies beyond Enlightenment humanism is too great to consider. He likewise may be right that most of the theorists that "gesture" away from the Kantian project of a politics of enlightenment are risking the loss of enlightenment possibilities. At the same time, however, issues pertaining to culture, gender, and even class continue to play a marginal role in his analysis. For him the basic form of enlightenment has already been determined by the normative developments of modernity. Derrida's counter-Enlightenment respect for alterity seems to be one way of keeping open the teleological question. In doing so it also preserves the question of enlightenment.

My objective in this chapter has been to show that the question of enlightenment cannot be neatly compartmentalized as a subdivision of the debate between modernists and postmodernists. There is no compelling case to be made that a postmodern conception of enlightenment is impossible or even unlikely. I have argued that the common thread that runs through both approaches to the question of enlightenment can be traced back to Kant's writings on the subject in the waning years of the eighteenth century: a time when both the possibility for, and impossibility of, enlightenment was being expressed through new-found freedoms as well as new forms of domination. This tension, which Kant was vaguely aware of, generated the dialectic of enlightenment that was taken up critically by Max Horkheimer and Theodor Adorno in the middle of the twentieth century. It is their essays that reintroduce the significance of grappling with the important questions that surround interpretations of the Enlightenment. I have argued, by appealing to the work of Habermas, Foucault, and Derrida, that a number of resources must be brought to bear on the question of enlightenment if a fruitful theoretical model is to be developed.

It is the development of this model that I will pursue in the chapters that remain. The issues introduced in this chapter—such as the modern/postmodern debate, the state of advanced capitalist societies, and the status of enlightenment norms—will be taken up in further detail. My intent in doing so is to thoroughly rethink the question of enlightenment in such a way that a concept of enlightenment that is relevant to the aftermath of modernity can be articulated.

CHAPTER 2

Modernity, Late Modernity, Postmodernity: The Theory and Practice of Enlightenment

The central question in chapter 1 concerned the conceptual status of "enlightenment." I argued there that a politics of enlightenment could be formulated without any necessary or absolute linkage to the historical Enlightenment, particularly the normative terms of the Enlightenment. The point in doing so was to show that enlightenment was not by necessity a product of modernity. This, of course, leads to complex issues concerning if and how modernity can be distinguished from postmodernity. In this chapter I will take up those issues directly. I will develop this along the following lines:

1. I will provide an analysis of Habermas's account of the development of modern societies up until the present.
2. I will then bring into play the views of several noted postmodernists that will serve as a critical foil to Habermas's defense of modernism.
3. Finally, I will draw a distinction between descriptive and normative postmodernism that facilitates the development of the idea of the aftermath of modernity.

HABERMAS ON THE DEVELOPMENT OF MODERN SOCIETIES

In *Critique, Norm, and Utopia*, Seyla Benhabib contends that critical social theory must have two related components. The first, which she labels "explanatory-diagnostic," utilizes empirical data, compiled through scientific research, to identify structural weaknesses in the existing social-political system; the second, deemed the "anticipatory-utopian" component, projects from this analysis a theory of transformation that aims at a more humane form of existence. Insofar as critical theory "addresses the needs and demands expressed by social actors," the second component must include a theory of action. With the advent of *Dialectic of Enlightenment*, critical theory all but lost this important feature—resigning it to quietism.[1]

Considering the historical circumstances faced by Horkheimer and Adorno, it is little wonder that critical theory reached a postwar stalemate. The "realities of the cold war, the moral and political horrors of Stalinism, and the conservative-restorationist tendencies of some Western democracies in the aftermath of WW II did not leave much room for hope."[2] Disillusioned by what they considered to be a pervasive instrumentalism that infects all forms of rationality, Horkheimer and Adorno lost faith in the scientific tools needed to develop the explanatory-diagnostic phase of theory.[3] As such, their account of the concrete present (explanatory-diagnostic) did not give rise to a remedial theory of social-political change (anticipatory-utopian).[4]

Benhabib credits Habermas with reviving the two-dimensional approach to critical theory. "In this respect, it is one of the great merits of Habermas' critical social theory to have restored that moment of genuine collaboration between philosophy and the social sciences, and to have developed an empirically fruitful explanatory-diagnostic theory of late-capitalist societies."[5] By not ultimately passing judgment against reason, Habermas is able to utilize scientific analyses that cast the present in critical light without conceding a futuristic vision. In this section I will focus on Habermas's account of advanced capitalist society. The questions that I will pursue are these: Does Habermas's account of modern norms square with his analysis of the development of modern societies? And does his final analysis of modern societies leave room for a politics of enlightenment? I will begin by examining Habermas's concern in the 1970s with the question of political legitimation and will proceed to his more recent work where he develops a bilevel theory of society.

While Habermas considers his project to be rooted in the Marxist tradition, he recognizes the need to revise considerably the original critique of political economy. Marx's analysis of nineteenth-century capitalism led to the conclusion that the economy would collapse under the pressure of its own contradictions, paving the way for an emancipated socialist future.[6] To him it was inconceivable that political interventions would be used to offset self-contradictory patterns in the liberal market economy.[7] This, however, is precisely what has happened. As a result, Marx's prediction that socialism and communism would replace capitalism has not materialized.[8]

It is generally agreed that Marx correctly assessed the crisis potential of liberal capitalism; free market economies are undermined by their own dynamics.[9] The twentieth-century scenario, however, is considerably more complex then the one faced by Marx, placing additional burdens on the social analyst. David Ingram sums this up as follows:

> For Marx, it was sufficient to show that so-called free exchange of equivalents in the market involved coercion, exploitation, and the promotion of class interests. But now that the state plays a leading role in manipulating the market, ideology critique can no longer take the form of a critique of the economy. Instead, it must focus on the legitimacy of political decisions that have been made through formal democratic channels. Justification for such a critique resides in the conviction that Western-style democracies fall short of the standards of rational dialogue—equal access to publicity, freedom from systematically distorted communication, and so on—that they ostensibly embody. (1987, 173)

Habermas, in his reformulation of Marxist analysis, focuses on the increasingly important role of the superstructure. Twentieth-century capitalist economies are permeated with bureaucratic-administrative politics. As such, "a purely economic analysis is not the basis for accurate prognoses."[10] This, of course, breaks sharply with classical Marxism (the base/superstructure model): a necessary move given present conditions. What Habermas retains of classical Marxism is the conviction that theory and practice should not be sharply separated. "I'm convinced that the left in general, and the Marxist Left in particular, can claim one advantage over all other political forces. This is the belief in the possibility of introducing theoretical analyses with a middle- or long-range perspective into day-to-day politics" (Dews 1986, 79). In the section that follows I will examine Habermas's assessment of liberal and advanced capitalism (explanatory-diagnostic), using *Legitimation Crisis* (LC) as the main text. This provides an informative account of the conditions and tendencies prevalent in mature capitalist economies as well as the backdrop for his theory of social-political change (anticipatory-utopian). Habermas argues that advanced capitalism, like capitalism in earlier forms, exhibits tendencies that will lead to crisis. He contends that the solution is a form of democracy premised on undistorted political discourse. My critical remarks will focus on the theory/practice issue.

Habermas accounts for liberal capitalism in terms of three criteria: the determining principle of organization, the possibility for social evolution, and the types of crises that develop.[11] The determining principle of social organization is located in the relationship between wage-labor and capital. This in turn is maintained through a system of prohibitive civil law. Economic activity is determined solely by the market; direction and maintenance are left to the "invisible hand." The invisible hand also serves as the primary social steering mechanism, resulting in a decentralized, depoliticized social structure.[12] Government is restricted to enforcing civil law, establishing minor economic regulations, satisfying needs that cannot be met by the private sector, and structuring an environment that is conducive to accumulating wealth. The potential for social evolution is intensified in liberal capitalism as the development of industry greatly increases productive capacity. Further, the relationship between the state and economy is refined and minimized. A "production morality" also emerges (Weber's Protestant work ethic) that emphasizes accumulation of wealth while sidestepping the "traditional" mediations that limit the free movement of capital (LC, 20–22).

Crisis tendencies in liberal capitalism are all linked in some way to the opposition between wage-labor and capital. Class domination is exposed when standards of living for laborers become intolerable. At this point social-structural deficiencies are manifest, resulting in a crisis that moves quickly from the economy to all components of the social system. Due to the rapidity with which crises reach system threatening proportions, liberal capitalism evolves into advanced capitalism. A considerably larger role is now played by the administrative-political system, making previously explicit class domination less evident.[13] As such, legitimation deficits initially go undetected as the economic trauma that clarifies them is clouded by interventionary programs (LC, 23).

Advanced capitalism is based on three internal systems: the economic system, the administrative system, and the legitimation system. The economic system is foundational and is composed of three subsystems:

1. The competitive market system, which is characterized by labor-intensive production, low salary levels, and a lack of rationalization.
2. The monopoly market system, where production is capital-intensive, labor is well paid, and there is a high level of rationalization.
3. The system that serves the needs of the government (military, infrastructure maintenance, etc.), which is both labor- and capital-intensive, supports a well-organized labor force and is not highly rationalized. (LC, 34)

The input for the economic system is labor and capital; the output is consumer products. It is at the output level that crisis tendencies appear due to breakdowns in distribution regulation. This results in a crisis in government finance, permanent inflation, public poverty, and a disparate concentration of wealth. Insofar as the government plays a critical role in the administration of the economy, economic crises place pressure on the political administrative system (LC, 45–46).

The primary function of the political-administrative system is to replace the liberal market with a global regulatory strategy that seeks to sustain economic growth, establish a stable currency, minimize unemployment, and maintain a balance of trade.[14] Doing so requires a number of interventions: the state coordinates international economic activities by forming blocs, facilitating imperialistic ventures, and monitoring trade when unfavorable imbalances develop; the domestic economy is bolstered by government contracts for nonconsumable products (military spending and certain types of technological projects), stimulating the economy by creating jobs (at a number of levels), and using raw materials; sectors of the population that are economically marginalized by the market receive compensation through social-welfare programs; both the material and immaterial infrastructures are maintained and improved; various levels of public education are made available so that productivity can increase across the board; and the costs of capitalism's negative side effects, such as unemployment and environmental pollutants, are covered (LC, 35–36; LPC, 647).

The input for this system is public loyalty; the output is a range of administrative decisions that are executed through sovereign authority. Administrative failure leads to a rationality crisis, which generates a legitimation crisis as the "masses" retract their loyalty. "The legitimation crisis is directly an identity crisis. It does not proceed by way of endangering system integration, but results from the fact that the fulfillment of governmental planning tasks places in question the structure of the depoliticized public realm and, thereby, the formally democratic securing of the private autonomous disposition of the means of production." At this level, crisis threatens the entire system (LC, 46–47).

These crisis phenomena are reflected in the sociocultural system, which has as its input the output from the previous two systems. Disturbances produced by output crises in these systems lead to withdrawal of public support for the system as a whole, which threatens its legitimacy. Insofar as the output of the legitimation system is social integration, crisis here leads to a motivation crisis: unwillingness on the part of the public to perform economically necessary tasks.

> Only a rigid sociocultural system, incapable of being randomly functionalized for the needs of the administrative system, could explain how legitimation difficulties result in a legitimation crisis. This development must therefore be based on a motivation crisis—i.e. a discrepancy between the need for motives that the state and the occupational system announce and the supply of motivation offered by the sociocultural system. (LPC, 660)

Habermas claims that this crisis sequence is a "consequence of the fundamental contradictions of the capitalist system." The economic system fails to meet the consumptive demands of the population and the political system is unable to compensate through rational administrative decision-making. This renders the system of legitimation (which is central to the preservation of the system in general) ineffective, creating a motivation crisis that cripples the sociocultural system. Therefore, the crisis center is at the level of legitimation (LC, 48–49).

Given the centrality of legitimation crisis in Habermas's analysis of advanced capitalism, as well as his normative theory, further consideration is warranted. In "Legitimation Problems in the Modern State" (LPMS), Habermas documents the importance of political legitimation in the development of the bourgeois epoch. A political institution's ability to establish societal norms depends upon its claim to legitimacy. For the modern state this is particularly important as democratization and the emergence of a public realm that is accessible to the masses places increasing demands on the means by which legitimacy is established and maintained. Whereas previously legitimacy claims were substantiated by an appeal to the authority of a higher order (God or Church), now they must be redeemed as validity claims in a process of political discourse (LPMS, 178–83).

With the replacement of traditional means of legitimation by a rational-discursive mode, formal conditions of justification needed to be established. Two competing models emerged: state of nature theories and transcendental theories. The former argues that will formation is shaped by an original social agreement, while the latter claims that it follows from a set of universal presuppositions. While in many respects these two theories are at odds, they share the view (which is all-important for Habermas) that legitimation must be the product of consensus rather than an appeal to de facto authority. "In both traditions, it is the formal conditions of possible consensus formation, rather than ultimate grounds, which possess legitimating force." The objective is to establish a political order that would be agreeable to everyone on the basis of arguments forwarded in an arena of free discourse. This requires a communicative structure within which valid and invalid claims can be distinguished. "Only the rules and communicative presuppositions that make it possible to distinguish an accord or agreement among free and equals from a contingent or forced consensus have legitimating force today." Malfunctions in this communicative structure confound the norm-producing capacity of the modern state (LPMS, 184–88).

While the original ideal of the modern state was political minimalism, as the industrial revolution blossomed and the popular masses began to feel the contradictions of large-scale capitalism, it became clear that the state would have to take a more active role (as I discussed previously). This leads to a paradox that makes the late modern state precariously susceptible to legitimation crises.

> On the one hand, the definition of deficiencies and the criteria of success of dealing with them arise in the domain of political goal-settings that have to be legitimated; for the state has to deploy legitimate power if it takes on the catalog of tasks mentioned above. On the other hand, in this matter the state cannot deploy legitimate power in the usual way, to push through binding decisions, but only to manipulate the decisions of others, whose private autonomy may not be violated. Indirect control is the answer to the dilemma, and the limits to the effectiveness of indirect control signal the persistence of this dilemma. (LPMS, 195–96)

Insofar as the legitimacy of the state rests primarily on its ability to maintain the economy, it will remain intact only if one or the other of two sufficient conditions is met: (1) that it continues to successfully suppress economic dysfunctions; or (2) that the modern standard of acceptable legitimation is lowered. Meeting the first condition is confounded by the dynamic of the economy; meeting the second condition is regressive and contrary to explicit modern ideals. Hence, a legitimation crisis is virtually inevitable (LPMS, 195–200).

A legitimation crisis would make explicit the scope of administrative functions, exhibiting the lack of traditional legitimacy and issuing in an unprecedented mandate for discursive processes of legitimation. "Thus, the forcible shift of things that have been culturally taken for granted further politicizes areas of life that previously could be assigned to the private domain." This, for Habermas, sets the stage for either a repoliticized public realm of discourse or a regression to some form of totalitarianism (LPC, 655–60).[15]

Legitimation crises occur mainly because the general population has been excluded from "meaningful" participation in the political sphere. So long as the powers that be can disguise the lack of genuine democracy by administering to the consumptive wants and needs of the people, deep systemic problems remain latent (specifically the problem of class conflict—LPC, 659). They will surface, however (Habermas argues), when the internal contradictions of the welfare state economy become manifest. As such, a remedy that establishes meaningful political participation must be developed or modern society will become vulnerable to totalitarian domination.

> If this is correct, a legitimation crisis can be avoided in the long run if the latent class structures of advanced capitalist societies is transformed or if the pressure for legitimation to which the administrative system is subject can be removed. The latter, in turn, could be achieved by transposing the integration of inner nature in toto to another mode of socialization, that is, by uncoupling it from norms that need justification. (LC, 94)

Insofar as the former is obviously preferable, the anticipatory-utopian dimension of theory must point toward a system in which dialogical participation provides legitimation. That this is possible, according to Habermas, is formally demonstrated through an analysis of the universal-pragmatic content of speech acts. The following provides an account of Habermas's attempt to develop the results of his reconstruction of communicative action into an anticipatory-utopian theory.

This theory rests on the view that practical questions (questions of norms and action) can be responded to with claims that have universal validity: "that the values and norms in accordance with which motives are formed have an immanent relation to truth" (LC, 95). As such, moral development can be "logically reconstructed," facilitating the explanation of motivational development. This is significant in that at the highest developmental stages of moral consciousness, a universal morality emerges that is rooted in a "fundamental norm of rational speech" (LC, 95). Hence, a connection is drawn between rationally conducted discourse and the establishment of universal norms. This indicates that there can be a link between legitimation and truth—something that "must be presumed to exist if one regards as possible a motivation crisis resulting from a systematic scarcity of the resource of meaning" (LC, 97).

Legitimation claims without truth content suffice for psychological purposes only; when crises arise they lose their effectiveness. This creates something of a dilemma, as the claim that practical statements can have truth content is at best dubious. In defense of his position Habermas appeals to the consensus theory of truth. In discourse, the validity of a norm is argumentatively tested by the constituency that it will affect. This produces rational agreement that can be subjected to further discursive scrutiny if deemed appropriate. Discursively established norms are true insofar as general agreement is the criterion for truth (LC, 104–6). In a later formulation Habermas provides these criteria for normatively redeeming validity claims: (1) the statement must be true; (2) it must be appropriate to the relevant normative context; and (3) the speaker's intention must be properly expressed and received. "Thus the speaker claims truth for statements or existential propositions, rightness for legitimately regulated actions and their normative context, and truthfulness or sincerity for the manifestation of subjective experience" (1985, 163–64). Truth content is embedded in the propositional component of any speech act uttered in discourse; and truth is the foundation for universality. As such, all utterances that meet these three requirements, discursively tested under appropriate conditions, can be deemed universally valid.

With this in mind, Habermas lays out a platform for discourse on practical questions (this is a practical interpretation of the ideal speech situation). Discourse, as he defines it in this context, is a communicative form that takes place outside the realm of "experience and action" (LC, 107). The general rules are: that the topics under discussion be limited to validity claims; that types of arguments remain unrestricted with the exception that they stick to the validity claim in question; that the only force employed be argumentative; and that there be no self-interested motives. Dialogue under these conditions results in the establishment of norms that reflect the general interest of participants (LC, 107–8). Habermas considers this to be an idealized model for public debate concerning questions pertinent to the life of a community. Its viability rests on the purportedly established fact that the intersubjective structures of language usage allow for agreement on questions of practice that can be translated into universal norms. As such, there is no need for a higher order of validation than consensus.

In support of this Habermas argues that the hypothetical ideal speech situation (the above-described platform) is the presupposition underlying any communicative practice. It is the prerequisite for acceptance of the fundamental norms of rational speech. The ideal speech situation, coupled with the language of discourse (natural language), provides the theoretical ground for politically determined universal norms. "This, if you will, transcendental character of ordinary language . . . can be reconstructed in the framework of a universal pragmatics" (LC, 110).

In summary, Habermas's explanatory-diagnostic analysis of late modern capitalism reveals that the dominant mode of action is strategic. This operates via a distorted communicative medium that relies on perlocutionary force to accomplish purposively defined objectives (those of the political regime or the monopoly capitalist complex). While considerably more systematic than Horkheimer and Adorno's analysis in *Dialectic of Enlightenment*, the conclusions do not conflict. Habermas, however, is not resigned to quietism, as would seem to be the case under one reading of his mentors. In his reconstruction of language usage, he points out that the distorted communication patterns that operate under the advanced-capitalist rationality paradigm exclude the intersubjective aspect of the double dimensional semantic structure that is characteristic of ordinary language. By reactivating the intersubjective element, via a systemic shift toward substantive political discourse, the way toward a society that operates on the basis of communicative rather than strategic action is paved. The main point of Habermas's anticipatory-utopian theory is that increasing democratization through a revitalization of the presently distorted realm of public communication is the only palpable solution to the crises of the welfare state.[16]

At this point I would like to raise several issues that will be developed more thoroughly in subsequent chapters. These comments will thematize the reservations that I have about the relationship between theory and practice in Habermas's work (this will be addressed more directly in chapter 4). As I noted in chapter 1, Habermas is sympathetic to, while still critical of, the aspirations of the Enlightenment. At the core of enlightened thought is the notion that all human enterprises must proceed from demonstrable foundations. Habermas contends that relinquishing this in the political sphere leads either to quietism (which he claims is the case with Horkheimer and Adorno) or, worse yet, political nihilism (which he associates with poststructuralism). Habermas considers a reformulated Enlightenment project, with built-in reflexivity, to be the way out of the predicaments of late capitalism. I will now point out—in the spirit of Habermas's own appeal to internal critique—several "enlightened" elements of his thought that could have been reflected on more carefully.

As I just indicated, when the subterranean crises of advanced capitalism surface, two distinct political alternatives emerge: democratization and totalitarianism. It can be well-documented historically that popular uprisings often lapse into totalitarianism; Nazi Germany serves as the paradigm for Habermas's concern with this possibility. Insofar as this is obviously undesirable, some form of initial direction is necessary if responses to late-modern crises are not to turn into postmodern nightmares. Enter the enlightened social analyst.[17] Habermas develops the model for this in an early essay, "On Systematically Distorted Communication," (which I will discuss in chapter 3) and seems to uphold it in his more recent work as well. I want to be quite clear that the model, as I am construing it, is an *interpretation* of the perspective from which the theory of communicative action is constructed; it is not a critique of the theory itself, nor is it a contention that Habermas would describe his own view of social science as I do in my interpretation. My concern is to show that when the relationship between analyst and analysand is based on this quasi-medicinal (Habermas himself comments on the oddity of using medical terminology) model, the normative implications of that analysis will be skewed by an imbalance of power. The analyst tacitly purports to have a more enlightened perspective and as such can legitimately prescribe curative measures for social-political ills. This may or may not cause difficulties in the case of the simple relationship between a psychoanalyst and her/his patient. When magnified to the dimension of the relationship between the social analyst and the social body, however, a different problematic emerges.

While in the analyst's eyes the source of crisis is systematically distorted communication that prohibits meaningful political participation, in the eyes of the general public (according to Habermas) the only indication of crisis will be a failure on the part of the state to ensure that all of their wants and needs are met. This indicates that the standards of legitimacy are different from the perspective of enlightened science and from that of the average consumer. The analyst's task is to demonstrate that substantive democracy, not the potential to accumulate exorbitant wealth, or even to merely subsist, is where the *true* wants and *true* needs of the populous reside. If this can be accomplished, the transition toward a society defined by communicative action will begin. As a result, the general interest will become increasingly manifest, which in turn contributes to the establishment of universal norms of action.

A theoretical projection of this sort, however, relies on two questionable assumptions that reflect Habermas's Enlightenment orientation. The first assumption is that the scientific sphere of society (upon which the analyst depends) can gain objective distance from the political and economic spheres, enabling an accurate analysis. While Habermas quite clearly recognizes the degree to which distorted communication and strategic action have infected the economic and political systems, he fails to consider the possibility that the sciences reflect these problems as well. His rebuttal to this would be that the sciences are by definition formally in the realm of disinterested discourse and as such have the potential for making objective pronouncements without becoming completely detached from specific interests.[18] In taking this stance Habermas is attempting to defend one of the most contested planks of the Enlightenment platform.

Such an assumption is problematic in two specific respects: First, the gap between the standards of legitimacy adhered to by the enlightened scientist and the average consumer is obvious and can only be narrowed if the predicted economic crisis occurs. As will be evident shortly, however, Habermas's most recent analysis of the late modern condition—and the type of problems it generates—is less committed to the inevitability of economic collapse. While he continues to be interested in the economic dynamics that could lead to substantial political change, he likewise acknowledges that capitalism has a remarkable ability to survive. This places additional pressure on the embedded Enlightenment premise that the only happy, healthy society is one in which the citizenry actively contributes to the determination of patterns of collective activity. The fact that public demand for this is not exerted when the economy is operating smoothly indicates that there is a serious bifurcation between the ideals of the Enlightenment and the standards of consumer societies. Second, it fails to take into account the degree to which the economic and administrative systems in advanced capitalist societies can infiltrate the spheres of scientific—including social scientific in the form of ideology—research. In the same way that workers can be politically neutralized by higher wages, and so on, the scientist can be co-opted by government-sponsored grants that steer research in the direction of strictly economic interests, high-paying private sector jobs that place the scientist in settings where scientific discovery is subordinated to corporate profit, and the general consumer ethos that prevails in advanced capitalist societies. In other words, the production of truth can easily be reduced to the production of commodities.

The problem in general is this: there is a gap between the ideals of enlightened science and the objectives of consumer societies. It is possible that if this gap is to be narrowed, enabling Enlightenment ideals to play a more important political role, then there will have to be some type of economic crisis. Unless this takes place, enlightened science won't have any social-political impact. The other direction in which this gap can narrow is toward what I referred to as the consumer ethos of advanced capitalism. This seems to be the more likely case given the survivability of the capitalist economy. Under such an arrangement, science is assimilated by economic imperatives that render it potentially dangerous. While I disagree with Habermas as to the exact role played by science in a theory of social-political change, I do agree that obtaining relevant social-scientific knowledge contributes to the process of social-political transformation. Nevertheless, it must be dealt with cautiously or science (including social science) will contribute to the domination, rather than the liberation of humanity. This is precisely the concern of Horkheimer and Adorno. "Knowledge, which is power, knows no obstacles: neither in the enslavement of men nor in compliance with the world's rulers" (DE, 4).

The communicative practices that have constituted the modern sciences that Habermas depends upon are bound up in the same general discourse as their economic and political counterparts: the discourse of modernity. Habermas would contend that the sciences accommodate a moment of internal reflection. This, however (as he points out), was the ideal of the modern state as well. In both cases these ideals are subject to corruption: a corruption that I would argue is the product of the way that power and knowledge interpenetrate under the rationality paradigm of capitalism. The consequence for action is that the already empowered continue to define emancipation in terms of their own interests. As such, a democracy as vacuous as bourgeois democracy is likely to obtain.[19]

The second enlightenment assumption that is apparent, and problematic, in Habermas's solution to the crisis conditions of advanced capitalism emerges in his characterization of the potential for communicative action. For Habermas this is rooted in the development of linguistic capabilities. As rationality develops, and becomes sedimented in natural languages, communicative practices tend to reflect a tacit reliance on the regulative principles of ideal speech. In turn, human coexistence moves toward a corresponding ideal that is rooted in communicative rationality and action.[20] This view follows from the universal pragmatic theory of language and communication (which is heavily dependent on sciences such as linguistics and psychology), a formal reconstruction that abstracts from concrete historical and political realities. Guided by the assumption that humanity evolves progressively and that reason is ultimately the driving force of this movement, Habermas conflates the formal model of linguistic development with social-political evolution. As both his empirical assessment, and Horkheimer and Adorno's critique, reveal, human reason does not exhibit a discernible developmental pattern that verifies this. In fact the power-knowledge model suggested by Horkheimer and Adorno seems to be based on more concrete evidence.[21]

This does not establish that the authors of *Dialectic of Enlightenment* are right and Habermas is wrong. It merely redefines their points of contention. Further, Habermas has carefully revealed the paradox that in his judgment freezes Horkheimer and Adorno in their tracks: you can't use reason to completely obliterate reason.[22] Nevertheless, if the anticipatory-utopian dimension of Habermas's theory is to succeed (even on a strictly theoretical level), so must the theory of language and communication, which, as I will argue in chapter 3, is bound up with the normative theory of modernity in a problematic fashion.

I have raised these concerns at the present juncture to introduce the idea that there are radical discrepancies between the normative content of modernity and the practices that define it socially, politically, and economically. This leads to further questions pertaining to what it means to say we live in a modern society and can tap into its enlightenment resources for the sake of bringing about emancipatory transformations. I will argue that Habermas's more recent analysis of contemporary Western societies pushes him in the direction of concessions to the descriptive claims of postmodernists such as Lyotard and Jameson. This in turn, I will claim, has further implications for the status of his normative theory.

I will discuss, too, some of Habermas's more recent work, concentrating on the second volume of *The Theory of Communicative Action* (TCA, 2) and an essay titled "The New Obscurity: The Crisis of the Welfare State and the Exhaustion of Utopian Energies" (TNO). Habermas's latest assessment of modernity in general and advanced capitalism in particular takes as its point of departure a critical reformulation of the system-theoretic model of society (a model that dominated Habermas's work in the '70s). Systems theory views society in terms of functions that are coordinated with respect to the social system in general. This model,

Habermas argues, fails to account for the role played by the lifeworld in the process of rational differentiation that is necessary for a functionally organized society to evolve in the first place. He proposes, in response, a bilevel theory of society: one that recognizes the relations that exist between system and lifeworld and the extent to which they have developed and been damaged during the modern epoch.

Habermas takes careful note, in this context, of the paradox that emerges with respect to action motivation in the modern period. On the one hand, due to rationalization, secularization, and differentiation within the lifeworld, modernity meets the conditions necessary for consensus formation to coordinate social action. On the other hand, due to the huge need for coordination in a social order that has grown increasingly complex, nonlinguistic "steering media" (money and power) play a more dramatic role. As efficiency is of paramount importance to the capitalist economy, it is the latter mode of action coordination that comes to dominate, relegating the lifeworld to subsystem status.

My primary concern will be with Habermas's recognition of the way that subsystemic units interact with one another via steering media and the degree to which this subdues available lifeworld resources. This analysis, I will suggest, conflicts with the view that language has as its telos intersubjective communication. In response I will continue to argue that language merely has the potential for numerous other communicative and action-coordinating modes. This critique will be developed largely in chapter 5. Habermas has adequately demonstrated the potential for intersubjective communication (explanatory-diagnostic) and has convincingly argued that a society based on communicative action is desirable (anticipatory-utopian). Between these two theoretical propositions, however, is a huge gap that is filled with the tangled bureaucracies of advanced capitalism (which are particularly void of communicative action coordination). My argument here, and in the remainder of this book, will be that Habermas's theory doesn't allow for a praxis that can bridge the gap between communicative potential and a communication-based social reality. Another way of putting this would be that Habermas fails to allow for a politics of enlightenment that is adequate to the task of dealing with the adversity-plagued aftermath of modernity.

Habermas's aim in his conceptualization of the lifeworld is to avoid the pitfalls of the phenomenological model developed by Schutz and Luckmann.[23] They, in line with traditional phenomenology, start from the standpoint of the abstract subject. "Like Husserl, they begin with the egological consciousness for which the general structures of the lifeworld are given as necessary subjective conditions of the experience of a concretely shaped, historically stamped, social lifeworld;" (TCA, 2:129). The strength of this position is that the lifeworld is conceived as a sociohistorically developed backdrop for action. The chief problem lies with the assumption that the acting subject is fundamental. In contrast, Habermas argues, the subject is always formed in contexts of intersubjectivity that are rooted in the communicative structures of the lifeworld (TCA, 2:126–35).

As conceived by Habermas, the lifeworld serves as the "horizon and backdrop of communicative action," a pool of already given resources that can be readily thematized within contexts of discourse. His characterization begins with a description of three actor/world relations. Each time a speech act is uttered, one of three world domains is explicitly thematized: the objective world, which is the domain of external things; the subjective world, which is the domain of internal experience; and the social world, which is the domain shared in common by a community of actors. In addition to the explicitly thematized relation, the other two relations are implicitly thematized, thus creating in each act a network of overlapping worlds. It is this network that constitutes the above-mentioned pool of resources, situating a communication dynamic that proceeds by defining and redefining the communicative possibilities available at any given time. "These redefinitions are based on suppositions of commonality in respect to the objective, social, and each's own subjective world. With this reference system, participants in communication suppose that the situation definitions forming the background to an actual utterance hold intersubjectively" (TCA, 2:120–22).

In each specific communication situation, pertinent content is drawn from the lifeworld. This points to the variability of lifeworld contexts relative to the situation being defined. Habermas accounts for this in terms of three lifeworld dimensions that correspond with the above-mentioned actor/world relations. The spatiotemporal dimension, which corresponds with the relation to the objective world, varies relative to the world that is available to the actor. This is delimited by such things as communication opportunities and transportation technology. The social dimension, which corresponds with the relation to the social world, varies relative to the specific collectivity of which the actor is part. This is delimited by the role of the actor and the scope of the world in which he/she acts (this might be a neighborhood for one person, a country for another, and the entire world for another). The personal dimension, which corresponds with the relation to the subjective world, varies relative to personal background or experiences of actors. This is delimited in terms of the social dimension to which an actor is bound. Themes of action, and their attendant plans, will shift with respect to context variability. These shifts affect both the focal point and the boundaries of the lifeworld (TCA, 2:122–24).

As general background the lifeworld is relatively trivial, gaining significance only when thematized in a specific situation. Habermas states this as follows:

> From a perspective turned toward the situation, the lifeworld appears as a reservoir of taken-for-granteds, of unshaken convictions that participants in communication draw upon in cooperative processes of interpretation. Single elements, specific taken-for-granteds, are, however, mobilized in the form of consensual and yet problematizable knowledge only when they become relevant to a situation. (TCA, 2:124)

The lifeworld should be conceived as a reserve of patterns that facilitate the interpretation of specific scenarios. These interpretive patterns are conveyed via cultural traditions and are organized linguistically. It is the view that the lifeworld is linguistically ordered that distinguishes Habermas's account from the phenomenological version. By positing semantically determined boundaries that are grammatically regulated, the "egological" problem is solved. Language, rather than the abstract subject, serves as a transcendental primitive. It (language) is the medium of exchange for content that can be thematized into communicative situations (TCA, 2:124–25).

In summary, the lifeworld is comprised, fundamentally, of a bank of knowledge that is located in the capacity to utilize ordinary language with the aim of reaching consensus (understanding). This is the unproblematic, unproblematizable resource that accommodates shifts in the horizon of the lifeworld yet makes transgression impossible. While the boundaries of the objective, social, and subjective worlds can be problematized and overcome, the lifeworld always constitutes the intersubjective acts that generate movement of this sort.

> The lifeworld is, so to speak, the transcendental site where speaker and hearer meet, where they can reciprocally raise claims that their utterances fit the world (objective, social or subjective), and where they can criticize and confirm those validity claims, settle their disagreements, and arrive at agreements. In a sentence: participants cannot assume in actu the same distance in relation to language and culture as in relation to the totality of facts, norms, or experiences concerning which mutual understanding is possible. (TCA, 2:126)

With this in mind I will proceed to Habermas's discussion of the way that the lifeworld is effectively subdued by "the system" in mature capitalist societies (TCA, 2: 124–26).

This aspect of Habermas's analysis is entrenched in the theory of social evolution that I commented on above. The general sequence of social evolution proceeds from tribal (organized by kinship) to traditional (organized by a central state) to modern (organized by steering media). Differentiation is the active mechanism in this sequence: within the lifeworld (rationalization), within the system (functionalization), and between the system and the lifeworld.[24] Habermas's main concern is to identify the developmental trends that lead to both the positive and negative consequences of differentiation in the modern epoch.

> As we shall see, modern societies attain a level of system differentiation at which increasingly autonomous organizations are connected with one another via delinguistified media of communication: these systemic mechanisms—for example, money—steer a social intercourse that has been largely disconnected from norms and values, above all in those subsystems of purposive rational economic and administrative action that, on Weber's diagnosis, have become independent of their moral-political foundations. (TCA, 2:154)

In spite of the "delinguistification" process within the system, and the degree to which this effects the lifeworld, Habermas contends that the lifeworld remains fundamental to the fabric of society. As such, it is within the structures of the lifeworld that emancipatory energy is located. While generally sympathetic to this position (with certain reservations concerning Habermas's account of the lifeworld), I will argue in the concluding chapter of this book that a lifeworld-based politics of enlightenment has to break with certain key standards to which Habermas adheres.

The first state of social evolution (tribal) is relatively undifferentiated. There is no distinction drawn between objective, subjective, and social worlds; the system itself is premised on kinship and gender relations rather than functional operations; and there is no distinguishable difference between system and lifeworld (TCA, 2:156–64). It is not until the phase of traditional (state-organized) society develops that differentiation begins to appear. "It is in societies organized around a state that functional specification first encroaches upon the very way of life of social groups" (TCA, 2:169). Membership in traditional societies is determined on the basis of a criterion other than kinship. One is acknowledged by virtue of legal status, acceptance (in principle) of the state's validity, willingness to participate in group activity by proxy, and submission to centrally administrated executive procedures. The significant difference between tribal and traditional societies lies in the amount of functional differentiation and the degree to which social action is centrally orchestrated (TCA, 2:169–71).

The transition into the modern phase is marked by decentralization of action orchestration through the development of both governmental and nongovernmental subsystems. This is due primarily to the emergence of a capitalist economy and the standardization of a monetary currency that serves as a medium of exchange between subsystems. The economy, as such, functions both as a subsystem and as an interconnective substrata that coordinates relations within the subsystemic network. The state comes to rely on this coordinating mechanism, leading it to restructure its own method of directing activity. "The state apparatus becomes dependent upon the media-steered subsystem of the economy; this forces it to reorganize and leads, among other things, to an assimilation of power to the structure of steering medium: power becomes assimilated to money" (TCA, 2:171). Hence, political power (administrative capacity) and economic power (money) converge. On the positive side, the shift into the modern epoch does away with traditional (that is to say, unquestionable) norms, creating an environment in which legitimation can be rooted in rational discourse. On the negative side, the type of economic system that emerges, and the efficiency that is demanded therein, leads to the above-mentioned delinguistified mode of action coordination. Rather than discourse (as Habermas is defining it), late modernity has steering media: money and power (TCA, 2:171–72).[25]

The prominence of steering media as coordinative devices weakens the capacity of the lifeworld to provide social integration. In Habermas's terms, the system is uncoupled from the lifeworld in modern societies: "The social system definitively bursts out of the horizon of the lifeworld, escapes from the intuitive knowledge of everyday communicative practice, and is henceforth accessible only to the counterintuitive knowledge of the social sciences developing since the eighteenth century" (TCA, 2:173). While structural differentiation within the lifeworld (due to increased rationalization) delineates the domains appropriate to the three validity claims raised in consensual communication (objective/truth, subjective/truthfulness or honesty, and social/rightness or justice), it likewise gives rise to increasingly complex systemic structures that tend to rope off or "colonize" the lifeworld: "the lifeworld seems to shrink to a subsystem," restricting its role as the social foundation. From the former aspect of rationalization follows an abstract system of law and an increase in demand for political legitimation that has a communicative basis. From the latter aspect follows a propensity to allow the steering media, which are reflections of the capitalist economy, to infringe upon the institutional domains (political, legal, etc.) that depend on highly developed communication structures (TCA, 2:173–78).[26]

The dilemma alluded to here can be thought of in terms of a process of clarification. During earlier stages of social evolution the spheres of communicative and strategic action were not clearly delineated. In contrast, the modern epoch is defined by its ability to draw distinctions between the two. Habermas characterizes this in terms of two modes of motivation: rational, which is premised on consensus formation, and empirical, which operates on the basis of coercion through the use of steering media (money and power). The former of course is grounded in the differentiated lifeworld structures; the latter, however, is detached from the lifeworld altogether.

> The way these media function differs according to whether they focus consensus formation in language through specialization in certain aspects of validity and hierarchizing processes of agreement, or whether they uncouple action coordination from consensus formation in language altogether, and neutralize it with respect to the alternatives of agreement or failed agreement. (TCA, 2:183)

As a consequence of the tendency during the modern epoch to rely on steering media rather than linguistic modes of action coordination, the lifeworld has been effectively subordinated. This results in the replacement of language games with symbolically determined behavior. Habermas refers to this trend "as a technizing of the lifeworld," the outgrowth not of modernity in general but of the specific economic mode (capitalism) that has determined systemic formation and, consequently, social integration (TCA, 2:179–83).

More recent developments in the capitalist economy (specifically the emergence of the welfare state) have only contributed to the problem. The "utopian energies" of modernity have grown increasingly suspect[27] while the media of money and power have become more and more dominant. Habermas labels this "the new obscurity" (which I will argue is tantamount to saying "the aftermath of modernity"), which "is part of a situation in which the program of the social welfare state, which still feeds on the utopian energy of a laboring society, is losing its capacity to project possibilities for a collectively better and less endangered way of life" (TNO, 3–5).[28]

The welfare state, Habermas contends, is compensation oriented; its main task is to offset class conflict by utilizing administrative mechanisms (which function under the guise of democratic consensus while actually operating on the basis of power) to dampen the "quasi-natural" evolution of the economy. In theory this enables capitalism and democracy to felicitously coexist, even if in a compromised fashion. Two important questions, however, must be addressed in light of this: Can the welfare state sustain itself? And does administrative intervention provide a path toward emancipation? (TNO, 5–7).

In response to the first question Habermas identifies a number of barriers that the welfare state must face. These can be viewed in terms of the complexity of international capitalism and the antagonisms that arise as a consequence of its administration. The outgrowth is a system of political blocs, each reflecting special interests (e.g., big businesses), that vie for positions of power. This is destabilizing and potentially debilitating. In response to the second question, the welfare state is always on the defensive, gearing itself more toward preservation than emancipatory transformation. As such, a dense bureaucratic network develops that impinges upon the remaining autonomous spheres of the lifeworld with purposive-rational patchwork strategies.[29]

> In short, inherent in the project of the social state is a contradiction between goal and method. Its goal is the establishment of forms of life which are structured according to egalitarian standards and which at the same time open up arenas for individual self-fulfillment and spontaneity. But apparently this goal cannot be achieved directly through a legal and administrative transformation of political programs. *Producing new forms of life is beyond the capacities of political power.* (TNO, 9—my emphasis)

The answer to both questions is negative. Welfare state capitalism, like liberal capitalism, needs to be protected from itself (TNO, 7–12).

Habermas proposes as a solution to this problem that existing channels be viewed with suspicion as their communicative structures are distorted by power relations and economic interests. The subsystemic media steered spheres must be bypassed by autonomous collectivities that emerge out of what remains of the lifeworld. Of the existing means for social regulation—money, power, and solidarity—solidarity needs to be positioned above the other two. This entails drawing upon the communicative capacity that is latent in the structures of the lifeworld. Habermas maintains that doing so will "influence the boundaries between communicatively structured areas of life, on the one hand, and the state and economy, on the other" (TNO, 14–17).[30]

A number of important developments take place in Habermas's analysis of modern society between the '70s and the '80s. First, he reconceptualizes the paradoxical situation of modernity, concentrating on the lifeworld as the pivotal element. Second, he defends a theory of the operations of modern societies that focuses on the dynamic of subsystemic relations. Third, he acknowledges that rationalization in the lifeworld is a necessary condition not only for communicative action but also for the type of strategic action, guided by steering media, that dominates social intercourse during this epoch. Finally, he notes that given the fragmented distribution of power in the later phases of modernity, remedial discourses must spring up locally in the form of grassroots solidarity movements. Given this, I will sketch out the reasons why these developments are incompatible with Habermas's communicative-evolutionary theory of social change. This in turn necessitates a reassessment of the diagnostic dimension of critical theory, which unavoidably leads to an encounter that I will construct between Habermas and certain key postmodernists.

The implication of Habermas's position is that differentiations in the lifeworld are the product of a dialectical process of social evolution. As a result of increased differentiation, two distinct and incompatible modes of social discourse emerge. This leads to intolerable incompatibility, resulting in one or the other gaining the upper hand. In the case of advanced capitalist society, the strategic mode is clearly dominant. Insofar as this is problematic, its opposite (pure intersubjectivity) is posited as the only acceptable solution. For Habermas, there is apparently no middle ground—even for transitional purposes. This is due partly to his overly narrow view of the potential that resides in ordinary language. The position that I will come to argue for is that ordinary language is susceptible to a number of different normatively structured formations and that the contextual circumstances of a "discourse" (and I intend to expand the meaning of this term) will vary quite dramatically. The demands of the early modern period gave rise to consensus-oriented and purposive-oriented discursive practices. The latter has subsequently become dominant, giving rise to the crises or pathologies (as Habermas has more recently labeled them) of late capitalism. I will argue that this calls for a reconceptualized notion of the politics of enlightenment: a type that is willing to break down, rather than repair, the discursive arrangements of late modernity.

This is suggested by Habermas's account of the degree to which purposive discourses have fragmented the social system and infiltrated every dimension of social life. Nevertheless, he continues to insist, albeit in more localized forms, that the appropriate practices in light of this predicament are the formation of collectivities of solidified consciousness that can establish patterns of communicative action within their subsystemic regions. This stance denies the revelations of his own analysis. Whether or not reform represents a viable way of altering existing patterns of social-political interaction is questionable. The alternatives seem to be either to capitulate to the standards of the system or to expand the vision of emancipation—the utopian energy of the theory—such that more substantive notions of transformations will factor into the normative content of critical social theory. Part of developing such a theory entails thinking through—practically—ways that existing channels of social coordination can be broken down. Only then does the utopian energy of communicative action begin to have political viability.

Habermas's response to my suggestions would be that theoretical knowledge provides the kernel of potential that will facilitate efforts to deploy consensus-oriented discourses. Picking up on the point I made earlier, I will argue that the normative terrain of modernity is inextricably intertwined with the political and economic systems, thus leaving no virgin soil for the growth of enlightened dialogue. If my assessment is correct, these views follow directly from Habermas's own analysis. Yet he fails to acknowledge the huge gap between his communicative ideal (which I subscribe to wholeheartedly) and the communicative reality that his analysis discloses. In order to substantiate this position, I will now turn to the work of Jean-François Lyotard and Fredric Jameson.

MODERNITY VS. POSTMODERNITY: NORMATIVE AND EMPIRICAL QUESTIONS

As I indicated in the introduction, postmodernism has replaced positivism as the archenemy of critical theory in recent years. Habermas's concern with postmodernism has been centered around the political implications of a mode of thought that insists upon undermining "established" normative structures simply for the sake of showing that they can be undermined. Further, he is concerned that this leads to an ambivalence with respect to regenerating normative standards that can provide the grounds for emancipatory action. Finally, he is distressed by the celebratory posture of reckless postmodernist who revel in a bacchanalian disdain for the progress that has been made in the quest for universally valid social, political, and ethical standards. The fact that the "post" in postmodernism situates his "debate" with central thinkers of that movement in either/or terms provides Habermas with an important opportunity to defend his attachment to *the* Enlightenment. In this section I will attempt to complicate this dichotomy—one to which Habermas strongly adheres.

Before proceeding to this it is useful to gain a sense of the genealogy of thought, as Habermas reconstructs it, that leads to the current modernity versus postmodernity debate. In *The Philosophical Discourse of Modernity* (PDM), Habermas provides a sophisticated historical analysis of the two main strains of antimodernist thought that have followed from Nietzsche's critique of modernity. The strain that develops from Heidegger to Derrida takes up Nietzsche's critique of the Western metaphysical tradition; the strain that develops from Bataille to Foucault assimilates his erotic Lebensphilosophie and his genealogical approach to the study of history. Habermas focuses his criticisms of the antimodernists upon the "paradox" of attacking modernity while still relying on modern philosophical suppositions. This is developed into an analysis of the problems that he associates with the "boundary-obliterating" postmodern thinkers: specifically, that once the distinctions that have traditionally delineated various modes of discourse are blurred, the substantive fields (such as scientific or political discourses) will have no basis for claiming their hierarchical superiority over expressive (literary or artistic) modes. Habermas concurs with the postmodern thinkers on one point: that the modern philosophy of the subject has run its course (see the above discussion of lifeworld theories). His proposal for transforming subjectively based philosophy, however, is different in two crucial respects: (1) Habermas contends that in order to break from the philosophy of the subject the modern project of enlightenment must be completed; and (2) that a critical component of this project is to theoretically rope off domains of discourse in terms of the validity claims that they raise. This, as I have been arguing (and will continue to argue), restricts a theory of social-political action, thereby perpetuating the gap that exists between real and ideal communication.

The fundamental question raised in PDM is: What is the significance of modernity? In addressing this question Habermas identifies two strains of antimodernist thought that have emerged in the twentieth century: neoconservatism and anarchism. Both developed a conception of modernity based on Weber's observation that the constitutive elements of modern society are secularization and rationalization—features that are systematically manifest in "the organization cores of capitalist enterprise and the bureaucratic state apparatus" (PDM, 1). The antimodernists de-historicize Weber's observations, which are still Marxist enough to be framed in the context of universal history. Breaking from the tradition of metanarrative historical theory enables two key moves pertinent to the epoch question: (1) the necessity of closure or completion of modernity is done away with; and (2) as a result, the shift into postmodernity can be posited without an identifiable historical referent. Hence, one merely has to declare the death of God, the death of metaphysics, the death of philosophy, the death of art, and in general the death of Enlightenment as sufficient grounds for claiming that a new age has arrived.[31] Habermas is suspicious of this. His suspicions focus on whether attempts to make this break are not always determined by a conceptual and historical linkage with modernity. "We cannot exclude from the outset the possibility that neoconservatism and aesthetically inspired anarchism, in the name of a farewell to modernity, are merely trying to revolt against it once again. It could be that they are merely cloaking their complicity with the venerable tradition of counter-enlightenment in the garb of post-enlightenment" (PDM, 5).

Modernity runs into none of these problems. It is qualitatively distinguishable from its predecessor epochs. "Modernity can and will no longer borrow the criteria by which it takes its orientation from the models supplied by another epoch; it has to create its normativity out of itself" (PDM, 7). Modernity developed along with historically determinate events such as the Reformation, the Enlightenment, and the great bourgeois revolutions. Hence, the primary characteristics of modernity have a traceable evolution. The attempted break from modernity does not, leaving it paradoxically dependent on categories that it no longer recognizes. It is this "paradox" that leads to the discussion that I will now pursue.

While, as I mentioned in the introduction, the term postmodernism has been around for quite some time, it was the publication of Jean-François Lyotard's *La Condition postmoderne: Rapport sur le savoir* (PC) that transformed it into a term with wide circulation in academic circles. Originally designed as a report for the government of Quebec on the current status of knowledge in advanced societies, it has become the postmodern bible for a generation of literary critics, philosophers, and specialists in cultural studies. Lyotard defines postmodernism as "incredulity toward metanarratives" (PC, xxiv). This, of course, situates postmodernism in a precarious position vis-à-vis the tradition of the Enlightenment from the outset. For instance, Kant's theory of enlightenment is deeply embedded in a historical metanarrative, as are the theories of Hegel and Marx as they attempted to reformulate the idea of enlightenment such that it met the demands of a rapidly changing world. Furthermore, even radical critics of the enlightenment—most notably Horkheimer and Adorno—rely on a metanarrative theory to "ground" their analysis. Finally, Habermas retrieves the tradition of metanarrative in his theory of social evolution, which as I showed above is central to his theory of emancipation. In short, without a metanarrative, it would appear that the very idea of enlightenment, regardless of one's perspective, starts to lose shape.

This immediately pits Habermas and Lyotard against one another on a very important issue: the possibility for emancipatory politics. The following claim further clarifies their points of contention:

> Thus, the society of the future falls less within the province of a Newtonian anthropology (such as structuralism or systems theory) than a pragmatics of language particles. There are many different language games—a heterogeneity of elements. They only give rise to institutions in patches—local determinism. (PC, xxiv)

In other words, a systematic theory of society such as Habermas's reconstructs social and political arrangements in a manner that enables the determination of where power resides and what forces operate at the heart of the system. In Habermas's case this tendency manifests itself as an analytic schema that places "language games" into two distinct categories: those that are coercive, and those that are enabling or emancipatory. In Lyotard's judgment, this denies the fundamental disorder that society finds itself in:

> The decision makers, however, attempt to manage these clouds of sociality according to input/output matrices, following a logic which implies that their elements are commensurable and that the whole implies that the whole is determinable. They allocate our lives for the growth of power. In matters of social justice and of scientific truth alike, the legitimation of that power is based on optimizing the systems performance efficiency. The application of this criterion to all of our games necessarily entails a certain level of terror, whether soft or hard: be operational (that is commensurable) or disappear. (PC, xxiv)

In denying this disorder, a disservice is done to those social agents—embroiled in their own heterogeneous matrices of language games—that is tantamount to annulling their (we might say) autonomy.[32]

While these passages represent a not-so-veiled polemic against Habermas, the next remark states their differences in straightforward terms:

> Is legitimacy to be found in consensus obtained through discussion, as Jürgen Habermas thinks? Such consensus does violence to the heterogeneity of language games. And invention is always born of dissension. Postmodern knowledge is not simply a tool of the authorities; it refines our sensitivity to differences and reinforces our ability to tolerate the incommensurable. Its principle is not the expert's homology, but the inventor's paralogy. (PC, xxv)

Under this description Habermas's discursive approach to a politics of enlightenment is both impossible and violent: impossible in the sense that it tries to bring order to that which is fundamentally chaotic; and violent in that in trying to achieve the impossible, differences between incommensurable groups of social actors are destroyed.[33] Furthermore, Lyotard suggests that there are emancipatory possibilities within the postmodern condition. This is where, as I will argue in the final section of the present chapter, his postmodernism becomes normative. From this perspective it is possible to discuss whether a politics of enlightenment that has as its fundamental aim the toleration of incommensurability is really worth anything.

In the main body of *The Postmodern Condition* Lyotard develops his positions in considerably greater detail. He extends his discussion even further in *Just Gaming* (JG) and *The Differend* (TD). My aim here is to situate Lyotard vis-à-vis Habermas's discursive view of the politics of enlightenment. This politics, as I have shown above, and will portray more formerly and abstractly in the next chapter, is rooted in the normative force of ordinary language within specified forums of discourse. Under conditions of discourse, claims Habermas, it only makes sense to communicate if we hold common presuppositions about the purpose of communication. For him this includes the general agreement that we will proceed in the direction of truth, that we will express our interests with sincerity, and that we will engage our interlocutors as equals.[34] Normatively this implies that linguistic discourses are governed by movement toward consensus. Lyotard, on the other hand, holds that consensus is not a viable candidate as the standard for validating claims concerning truth or justice. Holding such a position involves an anthropological mistake in that it holds false assumptions about subjectivity—such as that subjects are self-possessed agents of knowledge and that they are governed by their own wills—and also propagates the notion that history is moving in the direction of emancipation.[35] These ideas, according to Lyotard, are rendered *invalid* (and here the need to use normative language is once again significant) by the postmodern condition. "For this reason, it seems neither possible, *nor even prudent*, to follow Habermas in orienting our treatment of the problem of legitimation in the direction of a search for universal consensus through what he calls Diskurs, in other words, a dialogue of argumentation" (PC, 65—my emphasis). Habermas's view, Lyotard claims, assumes the possibility for universal agreement, whereas, in fact, language games are heteromorphous. It likewise assumes that the telos of discussion is agreement whereas in fact, Lyotard suggests, it is paralogy (PC, 60–65).

In *The Differend*, Lyotard claims that Habermas's insistence on consensus-building dialogues is Platonic. "You are preferring dialogue to differend. You are presupposing, first of all, that univocality is possible; and second, that it constitutes the healthiness of phrases" (TD, 84). He continues by raising questions about two key issues pertaining to Habermas: first, whether the idea of healthy versus sick discourses is addressing the nature of language; and second, whether there is a predifferentiated dynamic to the circulation of phrases that is lost in discourse analysis. This, for Lyotard, is the differend: "the unstable and instant of language wherein something that must be able to be put into phrases cannot yet be" (TD, 13). The question that Habermas would raise at this point would concern the ontological status of the differend. Is this a transhistorical category that takes its final shape within the postmodern condition? Or is it merely a symptom of a colonized lifeworld that has been stripped of its ability to serve as a historically developed linguistic resource? This is at the core of the normative/empirical question, as well as the modern/postmodern question. These in turn, are at the heart of the possibility for a politics of enlightenment in the aftermath of modernity.

Turning now to the broader context in which Lyotard situates his claims concerning language games, paralogy, and the differend, the distinction between modern and postmodern is designated as follows: "I will use the term modern to designate any science that legitimates itself with reference to a metadiscourse of this kind making an explicit appeal to some grand narrative, such as the dialectics of Spirit, the hermeneutics of meaning, the emancipation of the rational or working subject, or the creation of wealth" (PC, xxiv). All of these categories are rendered obsolete by the postmodern condition, which represents a "maturity" that enables us to see beyond the great ideological constructs of modernity.[36] In order to demonstrate this, he turns to the work of the later Wittgenstein. For Wittgenstein, language usage is constituted within distinct forms of life. These forms of life are in turn framed by rule-governed language games. Such games are composed of syntax, grammar, vocabulary, and a performative context. Hence, they are heterogenous—being contingent upon the form of life out of which they emerge and in turn which they help to form and reform. Language games, for Wittgenstein, are not universal, but rather are related to one another through the exhibition of certain family resemblances.[37]

Lyotard characterizes his appropriation of Wittgenstein as follows:

> What he means by this term is that each of the various categories of utterance can be defined in terms of rules specifying their properties and the uses to which they can be put—in exactly the same way as the game of chess is defined by a set of rules determining the properties of each of the pieces, in other words, the proper way to move them. (PC, 10)

Lyotard's aim is to show that discourses are not self-legitimating; they are based on ad hoc contracts of sorts. This leads to the establishment of tacit rules, without which there is no game. In turn, to alter the rules is to alter the game. Within this game context any particular linguistic act is analogous to a particular move in a given game. The main idea that Lyotard wants to convey in his appropriation of Wittgenstein is that language usage is fundamentally agonistic. It is not about establishing reciprocal relations with other speakers; rather, it is a question of gaining position vis-à-vis an interlocutor that will define relations of power. To speak is to fight. Such interaction leads to the composition of networks of social relations in the postmodern world.[38]

Up to this point Lyotard's discussion sounds perfectly modern. Metaphysically grounded norms are no longer valid so legitimation must assume a different form. In this case that form is provided by the tacit rules that govern language games. Another version of this is Adam Smith's invisible hand theory, which claims that economic activity is motivated and orchestrated by interests that at the intentional level are purely self-oriented but collectively assume a logical coherence. In other words it is a war of all against all by different means—one of the trademarks of post-Hobbesian political thought. What is distinctly postmodern about the language games that Lyotard describes pertains to their indebtedness to new technological developments that fundamentally alter the modes of circulation. The postmodern society is increasingly ordered by mechanistic means, primarily due to the advent of highly sophisticated computer technologies and the languages that are developed such that they can operate in the absence of centralized modes of administration. This results in the disabling of key modern categories such as the nation-state, democracy, truth, and most importantly for Lyotard, the "self." "The self does not amount to much, but no self is an island; each exists in a fabric of relations that is more complex and mobile than ever before" (PC, 15).

Lyotard's view of the self is an extreme version of the "decentered" subject that has been characterized by various poststructuralist thinkers. In his judgment, the subject is a nodal point within a matrix of linguistic operations. Together, these points create a linguistic circuitry that give rise to ever changing social formations. The model for this is a computer language and the programs that can be generated through its implementation. In any given program the status of individual lines in that program is contingent. When one line is changed, the matrix itself is altered. As the matrix is altered, so too are all of its constitutive parts. Hence, nodal points, represented by subjects within the matrix are flexibly (not reflexively) related to one another and are only as stable as the matrix itself. The question of the stability of the matrix is crucial here, for in order to characterize this "description" as fundamentally different from the modernist system-theoretic approach it must be demonstrated that the matrix or matrices in question are relatively unstable. While the demonstration for this is scant, it seems to be Lyotard's assumption (and to a certain extent a correct one). Given this, the status of the subject is reduced to that of a post through which messages pass. This leads Lyotard to the understanding that while the circulation of power in postmodern societies is increased—that is to say, the category of power plays an expanded role—the prospect for subjects' being empowered is virtually annulled. Instead of drawing normative distinctions between freedom and slavery, emancipation and domination, or coercion and communication, the normative delineations are based on degrees of performativity.

Lyotard sums this up as follows:

> It may even be said that the system can and must encourage such movement to the extent that it combats its own entropy;[39] the novelty of an

> unexpected move with its correlative displacement of a partner or group of partners, can supply the system with that increased performativity it forever demands and consumes. (PC, 15)

Hence, the distinction between manipulation and reciprocity dissolves into the postmodern mélange. It no longer makes sense to talk about truth, freedom, or justice, for all of these immature modern categories have been invalidated by the flexible positionality of contemporary social, political, economic, and legal institutions. At the same time, however—and this is where the incoherent normative structure of Lyotard's thought coalesces somewhat with Horkheimer and Adorno's, as well as my own—the potential for total administration is also eliminated. The postmodern society has too many points of slippage for any particular point to be the locus of power. To the extent that Lyotard is taking a position—and in fact I think he is taking a rather strong position that factors importantly into the descriptive aspect of his theory—it is that modernity totalizes. Postmodernity, on the other hand, recognizes the "truth" of the fundamental indeterminacy of all things. In this realization, which must be accompanied by the proper acceptance or resignation, we are *liberated* from the dangerous tendency to pursue totalities, whether they be social, political, or ethical.

As I have been hinting at all along in my discussion of Lyotard, there seems to be a philosophy of being lurking in the backdrop of his cryptic analysis of the postmodern condition. I find this most clearly expressed in his notion of paralogy and the differend. Paralogy, loosely defined, is false reasoning. In his appropriation of this term, Lyotard attempts to utilize it as a critical foil against the grand rational schematizations of the metanarrative tradition. His notion of paralogy is rooted in the microdynamics of "mini-narratives" that constitute what I will risk calling postmodern lifeworlds. Mini-narratives (or possibly regional lifeworlds) are paralogical due to internal limitations determined by their radical temporal and spatial contingency. This leads to confusion, paradox, and perpetual reconfiguration as the rules that govern these systems are grounded only in terms of their referential relationship to one another. Since these relations are not governed by a principle of coherence, the discourses that they produce are essentially arbitrary. As such, knowledge production, social organization, and political legitimation are inherently unstable: they are practices in paralogism, the point of which is not to progress or generate consensus but rather to undermine previous establishments.

If we situate this in terms of Habermas's characterization of the difference between the lifeworld and discourse (see chapter 5 for more details on this), paralogy would be located at the level of discourse.

More fundamental than this, however, is the level of the differend, which I see as being similar to the lifeworld in the broadest sense—not in the sense of regional lifeworlds, as I called them above, but rather in the sense of a postmodern lifeworld that corresponds to Habermas's modern lifeworld. Lyotard characterizes the differend as follows:

> The differend is the unstable and instant of language wherein something that must be able to be put into phrases cannot yet be. This state includes silence, which is a negative phrase but it also calls upon phrases which are in principle possible. This state is signaled by what one ordinarily calls a feeling: "One cannot find the words," etc. A lot of searching must be done to find new rules for forming and linking phrases that are able to express the differend disclosed by the feeling, unless one wants this differend to be smothered right away in a litigation and for the alarm sounded by the feeling to have been useless. What is at stake in literature and for philosophy, *in a politics perhaps*, is to bear witness to differends by finding axioms for them. (TD, 13)

The differend is the inexpressible that is basic to expressibility. It always exceeds that which can be put into phrases. As such, it provides for the generation of new, even if inadequate, modes of expression. In other words, the differend is an anti-metatheory of the impossibility of a self-contained discourse outside of parochially limited spheres. It likewise serves as the ontological precondition for the postmodern condition.

In brief summary, for Habermas, the lifeworld represents the possibility for discourses that tend toward the transformation of society through emancipatory practices. For Lyotard, the differend represents the impossibility of unified language games that tend toward totalities. Paralogy is the ontic state that demonstrates this ontologically rudimentary condition. For Habermas, the advanced capitalist system confounds these possibilities by literally imprisoning the semantic resources that undergird the potential for liberation. For Lyotard, postmodern capitalism is the coming to fruition of the repressed undercurrent of modernity, hence "freeing" us to recognize the radical contingency of the human condition. For Habermas, the modern lifeworld offers us the last hope of a politics of enlightenment. For Lyotard, recognition of the differend annuls the desire for a politics of enlightenment.

For readers of Horkheimer and Adorno's *Dialectic of Enlightenment*, their reactions are similar to those of readers of Aldous Huxley's *Brave New World*: it seems either self-evidently right or outrageously wrong. The interpretations differ, I believe, along political lines—depending on the readers position vis-à-vis the neoconservative "revolutions" of the 1980s. In this light, Fredric Jameson makes the following remark:

> Here at length, in this decade which has just ended but is still ours, Adorno's prophecies of the "total system" finally came true in wholly unexpected form. Adorno was surely not the philosopher of the thirties (who has to be identified in retrospect, I'm afraid, as Heidegger); nor the philosopher of the forties and fifties; nor even the thinker of the sixties—those are called Sartre and Marcuse, respectively; and I have said that, philosophically and theoretically, his old-fashioned dialectical discourse was incompatible with the seventies. But there is some chance that he may turn out to have been the analyst of our own period which he did not live to see, and in which late capitalism has all but succeeded in eliminating the final loopholes of nature and the Unconscious, of subversion and the aesthetic, of individual and collective praxis alike, and, with a final fillip, in eliminating any memory trace of what thereby no longer existed in the henceforth postmodern landscape.[40]

In other words, Adorno is the first modernist to theorize the postmodern condition. What Habermas recognizes, but tries to steer around with normative theory, and what Lyotard recognizes and tries to make into a "normative" theory, Adorno saw in advance. This is far from saying that Adorno just had it all right and that we need not look farther in our attempts to grapple with the present and forge a new future (Adorno is particularly weak on the latter). Rather, it is to say that Adorno anticipated what I am calling capitalism without Calvinism: a consumer society that has lost track of its material base and that possibly doesn't have enough consciousness left to maintain hope of regenerating visions of enlightenment. This is crucial for my argument as the issue hinges on whether or not the lifeworld has been irretrievably colonized by the system. Habermas thinks not (and in fact I agree). His own analysis, however, suggests otherwise. The difficulty, then, as I have alluded to above, lies with how to square the idea of a colonized lifeworld with a lifeworld-based politics of enlightenment. For Habermas, the *modern* lifeworld contains all the necessary possibilities. In my judgment (and as I will argue in chapter 5), to the extent that the lifeworld is modern, it has exhausted its possibilities. Hence, the return to Adorno, and hence my appeal to Jameson.

If Lyotard's *The Postmodern Condition* has become the postmodern bible, then Jameson's essay "The Cultural Logic of Late Capitalism"[41] should at least be assigned the status of one of the lost gospels. In the book-length version of the essay, Jameson provides a series of analyses of the contemporary social, theoretical, political, and economic scene; or, more generally, postmodern culture. The title essay sets the stage. It demonstrates the way that various cultural products of late capitalism grovel nostalgically for the past without even entertaining the possibility of a future. In doing so a sort of depthlessness is admitted that doesn't merely preclude emancipatory political practices but goes a step further by precluding even the thought of "enlightenment." Jameson situates this in terms of a metanarrative (in spite of Lyotard) of capitalist development. Informed by Ernest Mandel's *Late Capitalism*, Jameson identifies three distinct phases of capitalism's evolution. The first he deems market capitalism, the second, monopoly capitalism, and the third, multinational or postmodern capitalism. To each of these corresponds a particular technological innovation. For the first it was the steam engine and the revolutionary changes that it made possible in the industrial world; for the second it was electricity that enabled a qualitative departure from the classical period of capitalist production—one that led to imperialism; for the third it was the computer, which enabled capital to achieve the sort of liquidity that made the whole world its backyard. Jameson claims that this final, postmodern, phase of capitalism is the purest. In a sense it represents the destiny of capitalism.[42]

This is one of the points that I was attempting to make in my discussion of Lyotard: that the postmodern condition is a highly developed—if not quite inevitable—stage of capitalism. This, once again, seems to square with Habermas's analysis. Reading Lyotard's description of the postmodern condition leads one almost immediately to the conclusion that what postmodernity is about is economies. That is to say, the postmodern world is a grand circulatory system in which sign value is exchanged at the same pace, and on the same level, as commodities. Or, to put this in Habermasian terms, we live in a world that is steered by forces—money and power—that have systemic lives that range well beyond the control of individuals or collectives of individuals. As such, the ideas of autonomy and emancipation really are reduced to the nodal politics of Lyotard's matrix. For Jameson, who remains attached to the base/superstructure model of Marxian fame, this is best explained in terms of ideologies of the market. As such, I will turn to the chapter in *Postmodernism* titled "Postmodernism and the Market."

Jameson begins his discussion by identifying the market as one of the great "ideologemes" of the modern period. It represents a transcendental force that rescues us from our futile attempts to order our own lives, rationally determine our material wants and needs, and corrects our tendencies toward excessiveness by defining limits in terms of consumer power. Jameson's objective is to show how the market, as ideologeme, cannot be separated from the political economy of capitalism:

> So also with the attempt to separate ideology and reality; the ideology of the market is unfortunately not some supplementary ideational or representational luxury or embellishment that can be removed from the economic problem and then sent over to some cultural or super-

> structural morgue, to be dissected by specialists over there. It is somehow generated by the thing itself, as its objectively necessary afterimage; somehow both dimensions must be registered together, in their identity as well as their difference. (CLC, 260)

His view is that the idea of the market lies at the very heart of the possibilities for the radical transformation of society (or in my terms a politics of enlightenment). Once we have thoroughly internalized the idea that the market is an economic constant that reflects human nature, we will have effectively eliminated a whole range of other possibilities.

As one reads through Jameson's analysis—which is based on section 1 of Marx's *Grundrisse* (to which I will return in chapter 3)—one begins to wonder what this has to do with postmodernity. He returns to this theme, however, precisely where his argument concerning the idea of the market reaches a point of transition. "The representational consequences of a view like this will now lead us belatedly to pronounce the word postmodernism for the first time" (CLC, 268–69). What distinguishes the modern market from the postmodern market is effectively a shift in pace and volume. In other words, it is a classic case of a quantitative change becoming qualitative. Whereas the modern market was underpinned by a frugality—rooted in the Protestant work ethic (which was both an ethic of production and an ethic of contained consumption)—the postmodern market is consumption gone berserk. "We must therefore posit another type of consumption: consumption of the very process of consumption itself, above and beyond its content and the immediate commercial products" (CLC, 276). For Jameson this shift is rooted in the new technologies that he identifies with multinational or postmodern capitalism: electronic technologies such as computerized information systems and mass media. This metaconsumption can be explained in terms of the evolution of modern market economies. In order for capitalism to work there has to be ever increasing consumption. Yet consumer needs are finite—you can only need so much. As such, in order for the economy to continue to operate, mechanisms need to be introduced so as to trump up consumption. Hence, the economy becomes dematerialized: exchange for exchange's sake. Without stating this in so many words, what Jameson implies is that the postmodern market has created a sort of consumptive ethos that has permeated to the core of consciousness in advanced capitalist society. This is not to say that metaconsumptive urges can be fulfilled under these conditions. In fact, needs are never fulfilled: whether one lives in abject poverty or in extravagant luxury. The market, Jameson seems to claim, has moved qualitatively from the base of modern economics to the metaphysical superstructure of postmodern economies. This development must be confronted if a politics of enlightenment is to take shape. "What is wanted is a great collective project in which an active majority of the population participates, as something belonging to it and constructed by its own energies. The setting of social priorities—also know in the socialist literature as planning—would have to be part of such a collective project. It should be clear, however, that virtually by definition the market cannot project at all" (CLC, 278).

NORMATIVE VERSUS DESCRIPTIVE POSTMODERNISM: TOWARD A CRITICAL THEORY OF THE AFTERMATH OF MODERNITY

The focus of this chapter has been Habermas's account of advanced capitalist societies. I identified a shift in his thinking from *Legitimation Crisis* to *The Theory of Communicative Action*. This shift, in my estimation, makes important concessions to a certain type of postmodernism. A good indication of this is the way in which he appropriates the language of "steering media." That his description is of *postmodern capitalism* is testified to by the way that he shows how money and power have become those media. The modern dream of self-determination has been surpassed by the systemic imperatives that are at the heart of the capitalist mode of production. The fact that Habermas has significantly toned down the language of legitimacy in this more recent analysis indicates that the notion of political legitimacy has come to play a much smaller role. This suggests that he is making major concessions to the critique that started with *Dialectic of Enlightenment*; it is conceptually incoherent to forecast a legitimation crisis when illegitimacy has been internally accepted. This analysis is augmented by Lyotard's and Jameson's. Lyotard, it could be claimed, has a micro-analysis of steering media. While he wouldn't want to accept Habermas's systematic totalization of the situation, his own account resonates strikingly with the notion that all of social life is determined by systems of exchange. Jameson makes this point more explicitly. His claims are more economic than political, but in the final analysis so are Habermas's. He (Habermas) shows quite conclusively—without any sophisticated economic analysis—that a material base rooted in market economies that are premised on the high-speed exchange (money) of commodities leads to the exchange of political power in a similar fashion. What drops out of the analysis for all three theorists is the notion of collective agency under such conditions. In each case some mechanism, or set of mechanisms, have kicked in which diminish significantly the social, political, and economic role of the modern subject. This, in my judgment, adds up to a qualitative change, if not a determinate rupture.

Does this mean, then, that we now live in a postmodern world? Further, does it mean that we are beyond the point of establishing movements aimed at collective emancipation? Both of these questions depend to a certain extent on how we define our terms. This is particularly the case with the former. As such, I would like to conclude this chapter by distinguishing more clearly between normative and descriptive postmodernism and to show why I prefer to revise the terminological debate.

Let me begin with descriptive postmodernism. This side of the distinction is relatively self-explanatory. A descriptive postmodernist is one who characterizes various contemporary scenarios as being postmodern without making value judgments about that condition. Jameson falls easily into this category as he explicitly claims that postmodernity is an advanced phase of capitalism. I have also suggested that to a certain extent Habermas falls into this category. His is a more difficult case as he would deny this at all costs. His reasons for this denial are sound, as for him, the politics of enlightenment are bound up in normative structures that are distinctly modern. As I indicated above, however, there are key shifts in his analysis that place him closer to Lyotard than he himself would be comfortable with. This leads to an empirical/normative dualism that plays itself out as incompatibility. In other words (and as Jameson points out) you can't wish for a modern politics of enlightenment if we now live in a postmodern world.

Habermas's response to this would be that if we concede the postmodern condition we can't talk about a politics of enlightenment at all. Jameson equivocates on this question while Lyotard seems to agree with Habermas and celebrates this point of no return. As Christopher Norris puts it, Lyotard propounds a "rock-bottom cynical outlook" (and in quoting this I am agreeing with it). Citing a passage in which Lyotard lampoons virtually all the ideals of modernity, Norris states the following:

> This passage is the center-piece of Lyotard's argument that we have now lived on into a postmodern epoch when it is no longer possible to attach any credence to those old "meta-narrative" schemas (truth, enlightenment, progress and so forth) which once lent support to such grandiose ideas. Henceforth it can only be a matter of "phrases in dispute," piecemeal items of evidential witness which claim no privileged epistemic status (much less any access to the master-code of history), and which thus submit themselves to the nominalist tribunal of isolated facts, dates, or events. Any theory that attempts to do more—to situate those facts within some larger, more ambitious explanatory paradigm—is ignoring the weight of de facto evidence that composes the sad chronicle of history to date.[43]

Lyotard fails, however, in his attempt to be a cool positivist, simply laying out the facts. As I pointed out in my analysis of *The Postmodern Condition* Lyotard's vocabulary is laced with terminology that celebrates the postmodern condition that we find ourselves in. We have been liberated from the myth of autonomy; we are emancipated from the responsibility to pursue our own destinies; we have matured beyond the point that universally valid values are even thinkable; and we are no longer responsible for making history. Lyotard doesn't simply describe postmodernity; he prescribes it as well. In what might seem a paradoxical formulation, Lyotard is a straightforwardly normative postmodernist. His description is an admonition to be resigned to a world in which we are no longer expected to think and act for ourselves and with others.

The cynicism of this, as Norris put it, is more blatantly expressed in Lyotard's *Just Gaming*. This text, a dialogue between Lyotard and Jean-Loup Thebaud, is supposed to be a postmodern version of Plato's *Republic*. It is a playful attempt to think through the question of justice in an age that has no basis for distinguishing between legitimate and illegitimate action. The thesis is that in a standardless world we are limited to the expression of preferences. In their defense of this position they turn to Kant's *Critique of Judgment*.[44] I won't rehearse the views that they articulate as they are generally weakly defended and of no great interest to critical social theory (unlike *The Postmodern Condition* and *The Differend*, which I think are very important). Rather, I will turn to a passage that illustrates both the normative status and moral and political vacuity of Lyotard's stance:

> Yes, it is quite broadly a politics of capital, actually. That is true. And I think that what interested me, was to see it at work within capital, to make it appear in its affirmative force. Except that, insofar as one is a political thinker, one cannot do without justice. But the question is: What is this horizon? Which horizon are we determining? (JG, 90–91)

This remark is prefaced with a parenthetical laugh "(laughter)." It seems to be an attempt at irony. 'We used to believe in the abolition of capitalism, the goals of 1968, but now we are simply defending the status quo. Isn't it ironic?' Lyotard realizes, in a moment of self-reflection, that his postmodernism has brought him full circle. Since all of the ideals that factor into a theory of justice have been obliterated, we are right back to square one: only better or worse, depending on one's perspective. Better if the return to capitalism, in its postmodern form, is the sign of maturity; worse if it represents the lost hope that Kant identified with maturation. Lyotard, while loathe to judge positively on this issue, seems to come down squarely on the side of postmodernity, which as he seems to recognize is to advocate what Jameson calls postmodern capitalism.

Having roughly sketched the normative/descriptive distinction, I would now like to problematize it. Habermas seems concerned that to concede the descriptive point is to border on accepting the normative point. Lyotard's irrepressible use of normative language seems to illustrate this problem. Jameson makes the strongest effort to keep the two separate but ultimately runs into similar problems.[45] A possible solution to this difficulty would be to dispense with postmodernity as a descriptive term and refigure it as a normative term. It is interesting to note that the first time Habermas uses the term *postmodern*, in *Legitimation Crisis*, he does so with the intent of affirmatively expressing a possible future. I don't think too much should be made of this in terms of attributing to Habermas postmodern tendencies. It is, however, quite significant in the framework that I am developing. If, as I claim, the project of enlightenment cannot be fulfilled in modern terms, then it only stands to reason that we should look toward something postmodern. What is currently described as postmodernity holds some of the answers; but as I have been trying to show, it culminates in a cynical resignation to what is worst about modernity. As such, I prefer to call what is being characterized as the postmodern condition, the aftermath of modernity: a phase in the evolution of modernity that is qualitatively distinguishable from early phases, but does not represent a radical departure.

In defense of this terminological shift, it is important to note once again the reasons for labeling the present as "postmodern." The most sophisticated advocates of this view point to important cultural, social, and economic changes that indicate the end of modernity. It is not precisely an end, however, but rather a slipping back and forth—into and out of—modern forms and conditions. As such, the distinctive feature of postmodernity is ultimately its fuzziness. This is most obvious in modes of cultural expression; rather than the clean detached radicalism of "high modern" art, architecture, prose, and poetry, postmodern expressions integrate elements from diffuse traditions while at the same time disintegrating the notion that they comprise a totality. Socially, postmodernity is defined by crises in identity; gender roles, racial identities, and sexual orientation have all become question marks rather than handed-down truths. Economically, postmodernity is marked by radical liquidity; capital, in the atmosphere of leveraged buyouts, multinational/multidimensional conglomerates, and mazelike corporate structures, has in a sense lost its determinateness and as such is vulnerable to radical redistribution. These I take to be some of the more positive aspects of the postmodern condition—those that afford important possibilities.

The common factor in each of these spheres of postmodernity is the emergence of radical difference and conglomeration. I question, however, the authenticity of these features. In the cultural sphere they seem subjectively contrived; in the economic sphere they cloak and preserve the very worst of modern capitalism (alienation and exploitation) while expunging that which is desirable (efficiency and productivity); in the social sphere they provide the framework for a political myth that deflates contestation and reifies existing hegemonies. In fact, then, the conditions of advanced capitalist societies are not postmodern at all. Rather they represent the aftermath of modernity, or modernity in struggle with itself: still modern but at a point where modernity runs up against its own contradictions. At its best, postmodernity is a projection—one that must be thought through in terms of political strategies that are appropriate to bringing it about. Hence the need for a politics of enlightenment in the aftermath of modernity.

As I indicated above, Habermas might possibly agree with this up to a point. He certainly wants to deny that advanced societies are postmodern. It is his view that all necessary emancipatory structures have developed during modernity and that this must be the point of departure for a politics of enlightenment. This, however, ignores the radical deformation of these structures in their present state—a condition that Habermas describes with piercing insight. In the following chapter I will focus on the value structures of modernity and argue for my claim that they are inextricably intertwined with the capitalist mode of production.

CHAPTER 3

Modern Normativity and the Utopian Ideals of Discourse

In chapter 1 I examined the problem of enlightenment from a conceptual point of view. In chapter 2 I discussed the same problem in sociological terms. In the present chapter I will be approaching the question from a normative perspective. The primary concern can be stated as follows: Do the normative structures of modernity have a relationship to enlightenment that is unambiguous enough to ground a politics of enlightenment? I have suggested thus far that this is not the case. Here I will undertake the task of providing a more substantial defense of my position. In doing so I will begin by examining Habermas's theory of language and communication. This may, on the surface, seem odd; but for Habermas this is the most important place to explore the pure normative content of modernity. It is within the structures of modern languages that we find the embedded moral content that provides us with a foundation for criticizing the aberrations that mark advanced capitalist societies. My critique of this will take as its point of departure Marx's analysis of bourgeois categories such as freedom and truth in the *Grundrisse* and will proceed to an analysis of Habermas's central categories: truth, freedom, and justice.

HABERMAS ON LANGUAGE AND COMMUNICATION

As I noted in chapter 1, most of the questions that occupy postwar social thought are addressed, albeit haphazardly at times, in *Dialectic of Enlightenment*. A careful reading of this text indicates that language, and the uses to which it is put, should be a central concern of social theorists. Horkheimer and Adorno's analysis of the similarities between mythical and scientific language is provocative but lacks the empirical evidence needed to verify their thesis. Their critique is considerably more convincing when applied to the specific manipulations of language that facilitate the proliferation of fascist propaganda.[1] Habermas's concerns with language are apparently molded by Horkheimer and Adorno's analysis of the operations of fascist discourse. He is guided by two fundamental questions: What are the social-structural constitutives of the type of distorted communication that enabled the rise of fascism? And what are the necessary conditions for a social structure premised on discursive clarity? These questions lead Habermas deeply into theories of language and communication. According to Thomas McCarthy, this provides the foundation for his entire project:

> The theory of communicative competence is decidedly not a theoretical luxury in the context of critical social theory; it is a concerted effort to rethink the foundations of the theory-practice problematic. The success or failure of this effort cannot be a matter of indifference to a social theory designed with a practical intent. As we shall see, Habermas' argument is, simply, that the goal of critical theory—a form of life free from unnecessary domination—is inherent in the notion of truth; it is anticipated in every act of communication.[2]

This states the importance of language and communication analyses for Habermas's formulation of critical theory. In the following section I will discuss the development of his views on this topic, keeping in mind the role that they play in his notion of a politics of enlightenment.

Communicative Distortion

Fred Dallmayr points out that while Habermas's work did not take an abrupt "linguistic turn," at a relatively well-defined point it became necessary for him to undertake a careful study of language and communication theories. In 1970 two articles, "On Systematically Distorted Communication" and "Towards a Theory of Communicative Competency," appeared in consecutive issues of *Inquiry* that for the purposes of this discussion will serve as an introduction to Habermas's theories of language and communication.[3] The first utilizes Freudian psychoanalytic methods to evaluate communication breakdown caused by systemic linguistic discrepancies; the second draws upon Chomsky's theory of generative linguistics, as well as Austin's and Searle's speech-act theories, to substantiate the view that in discourse, validity claims can be raised to the levels of truth, truthfulness, and rightness. These essays state the fundamental problem, and provide the framework for a solution that has guided Habermas's critical theory in the '70s and '80s. I will here explicate their main features, highlighting the themes that are developed more completely in subsequent writings.

In "On Systematically Distorted Communication" (SDC), Habermas identifies two types of communication irregularities: the first he associates with psychosis—communicative behavior that is completely out of synch with social reality; the second, which he labels "pseudo-communication," is a form of communicative neurosis, causing distortion that is not noticeable in the context of communicative practice. It is the latter form of deviance that concerns Habermas, as it has a significant effect on everyday discourse. Pseudo-communication is detectable only by a neutral observer who can then trace distortion to an elemental point of crisis. Habermas uses the Freudian analyst as a model for the neutral observer. By evaluating communication patterns in terms of established criteria, the analyst can identify the problem and provide counsel that will contribute to the reconstruction of communicative behavior such that systematically embedded deviances are eliminated.[4] Habermas argues that there are norms of communication that ensure communicative clarity. These are instantiated in a language system shared by a community of speakers. When the rules of the system aren't adhered to, communicative practice will be distorted. Habermas summarizes as follows:

> No matter on which level of communication the symptoms appear, whether in linguistic expression, in behavioral compulsion, or in the realm of gestures, one always finds an isolated content therein which has been excommunicated from the public-language performance. This content expresses an intention which is incomprehensible according to the rules of public communication, and which, as such, has become private, although in such a way that it remains inaccessible even to the author to whom it must nevertheless be ascribed. There is communication obstruction in the self between the ego which is capable of speech and participants in intersubjectively established language-games, and that "inner foreign territory" (Freud), which is represented by a private or primary linguistic symbolism. (SDC, 205–7)

Habermas's intention is to use psychoanalysis as a model for examining communicative distortion. He asserts that incomprehensible communicative practice is infected with a sort of neurosis of the language system. This results in semantic incongruity, causing defective meaning representation. The process of tracing this back to a point of critical breakage in the sequence of linguistic development is analogous to the psychoanalyst's probing of the patients past experiences in search of a crisis that will account for some behavioral disorder. Like the psychoanalyst, the communication analyst attempts to reconstruct the developmental process in line with normative standards, enabling the communication participant to regain access to public discourse (SDC, 207–9).

The theoretical basis for this rests on three propositions: (1) that we have a preconceived notion of undistorted communication; (2) that distortion can be traced to a specific breakdown in the developmental sequences of symbolic organization; and (3) that in order to explain communication distortion a theory of interactional patterns and personality structures must be utilized (SDC, 209–10).

Habermas's objective can be understood more clearly by taking into consideration the point I made earlier concerning his interest in the role of propaganda in the rise of fascist regimes. Propaganda is the archetypical form of distorted communication: it is monological and semantically inconsistent, and it appeals to emotions rather than reason. Insofar as language plays an important role in action coordination, a linguistic system premised on propaganda will lead to corporate action that is unreflective, unpredictable, and irrational. Given the obviously undesirable nature of such activity, remedial action should be aimed at distortion in the communication system(s). How this can best be accomplished is an entirely different matter. The approach suggested by Habermas is problematic in several crucial respects.

First, the analogy between psychoanalysis and social analysis is weak. There are radical differences between a patient on the analysts couch and an aggregate of subjects that share a communication system. How can a communication community be interrogated in such a way that the corporate soul is laid bare? Who is qualified to conduct the analysis? To what degree is the analyst a product of the distorted communication patterns of the community? Habermas would argue that the answer to all of these questions is located in the social-scientific hermeneutic that is applied by the psychoanalyst. This simply needs to be adapted to the circumstances faced by a social analyst.

Another important objection is issued in by this response. The assumption fundamental to Freudian analysis is that behavioral disorders can be linked to a traumatic moment in the past. Once this moment is identified and brought to the level of patient consciousness, the "cure" can begin to take shape. Disregarding the questions that can be raised concerning this approach to psychoanalysis, the notion of an origin to which communicative distortion can be traced is highly problematic. Language, and the formations it assumes in communication, is the product of a complex of historical phenomena. To isolate a particular phenomenon, label it the primary cause of distortion, and begin to therapeutically reshape communication from this point of original transgression is a dubious task. The example that seems to be in the back of Habermas's mind—communicative distortion in Nazi Germany—is a case in point. A number of interwoven and overlapping phenomena facilitated the proliferation of fascist propaganda. To isolate a point of origin in this causal mishmash would be difficult if not impossible.

Finally, the claim that a set of communicative rules can be used as a standard of normalcy is problematic. If discursive practice is distorted, why would discourse rules be any less distorted? This ties into the question raised in my first objection concerning the relationship between the social analyst and the "patient." If the analyst operates within the same network of communication as the "patient" (which is necessary if there is to be intelligibility), then analysis will reflect the distortions that permeate the communicative system. Habermas's assumption seems to be that the analyst is enlightened above and beyond the average participant; and that this illumination provides access to ideal rules of communication. If the analyst is bound by distorted discursive rules, the proposed remedy will only contribute to the existing predicament. Habermas would claim that there are metasystemic rules that can be grasped and used as standards against which discursive practices are measured. I will indicate some problems with this view shortly.

While this is not Habermas's most sophisticated version of his theory of clear and distorted communication, it does contain several elements that figure prominently in later formulations. Specifically, the notion of an originary communicative form, the claim that intersubjectivity has a natural primacy over other discursive patterns and the use of hermeneutic social science to grasp and repair problems. As they stand, the objections I have raised are merely questions. I will develop these more completely in terms of Habermas's latest work in the final chapter of this book. For now it suffices to say that "On Systematically Distorted Communication" is a problematic, yet crucially important, phase in the evolution of Habermas's theory of communicative action.

The main tenets of this essay are drawn together with a view to its sequel. Semantic analysis in general depends upon a well-formed notion of communicative competence between native speakers (participants in a communication community). In order to detect and remedy distortion, a theoretical understanding of communicative competence is essential. As such, this essay leads directly into the theory of communicative competence.

Communicative Competency

In "Towards a Theory of Communicative Competence" (TTCC), Habermas moves out of Freudian psychoanalytic theory and into Chomskyan linguistics. His focus is on Chomsky's view that linguistic experience is disproportionate to linguistic knowledge; we know more than can be accounted for by our experiences. Chomsky explains this in terms of the following assumptions: (1) speakers rely on an abstract linguistic system that is composed of generative rules; (2) this system of rules is innate; (3) the innate structure shapes all natural languages (universally); and (4) specific instances of language usage are a manifestation of deep linguistic structures that surface through the application of transformation rules. The competent speaker is one who has sufficiently mastered these rules—

derivatives of the innate linguistic mechanism (TTCC, 360–61).

While impressed with Chomsky's focus on speaker creativity, the grammatical structures of language, and the asymmetry between experience and knowledge, Habermas finds fault in his "monological" characterization of linguistic competence. The only model of intersubjectivity that can be derived from this is mechanistic; shared meaning is merely a function of similarities between the linguistic program of speakers. "Speech, the actual language behavior, would then have to be explained as the result of interaction between linguistic competence and certain psychological, as well as sociological, peripheral conditions which restrict the application of competence" (TTCC, 362). This monological model of communication is accompanied by an aprioristic semantic theory that neglects the "pragmatic dimension of language performance," denying the potential for meaning development in the context of reciprocal communication (TTCC, 361–62).

Habermas attempts to counter these flaws by developing a semantic theory that recognizes both a priori and a posteriori universals. A priori universals provide the foundation for communicative and interpretive schemas. A posteriori universals are contingent but apply transculturally. The difference between the two can be understood in terms of the difference between intersubjectively and monologically determined semantic structures: "Therefore, we differentiate between semantic universals which precede all socialization and semantic universals which are linked to the condition of potential socialization (monological/intersubjective)" (TTCC, 363). This theory generates four classes of semantic universals: dialogue-constituent universals, which include personal pronouns, imperatives, interrogatives, assertives, and so forth; cultural universals, which include organizational signifiers such as words that designate kinship relations; universal cognitive schemes of interpretation such as substance, causality, and space and time; and universals of perceptive and motivational constitution, which are a function of basic drives—such as the sex drive, hunger, and thirst—and patterns of emotional expression. The first two are respectively intersubjective a priori and intersubjective a posteriori; the second two are respectively monological a priori and monological a posteriori (TTCC, 363–64).

Habermas seeks to develop his theory of communicative competence on the basis of intersubjective universals. While Chomsky's monological universals have a valid function, their theoretical usefulness is limited by an inability to go beyond an "elementaristic meaning-analysis" (TTCC, 365). This excludes all complex semantic relations and meaning development. Speaker competency must be defined in terms of situations of linguistic application that depend on an intersubjective linguistic structure.

> This structure is generated neither by the monologically mastered system of linguistic rules, nor by the extralinguistic conditions of its performance. On the contrary, in order to participate in normal discourse the speaker must have at his disposal, in addition to his linguistic competence, basic qualifications of speech and symbolic interaction (role-behavior), which we may call communicative competence. Thus communicative competence means the mastery of an ideal speech situation. (TTCC, 367)

In order to clarify this position, Habermas turns to the speech-act theory of Austin.

Austin, in his analysis of the usage of performative verbs, draws a distinction between locutionary and illocutionary meaning. Locutionary meaning is solely a function of the propositional content of an expression; illocutionary meaning is a combination of propositional content and the general notion of a speech situation.[5] Habermas, following Austin, labels this "illocutionary force." Any expression of illocutionary force depends upon an a priori knowledge of the structures of intersubjective communication. This, for Habermas, establishes the existence of "the universal pragmatic power of utterances" (TTCC, 367). The theory of communicative competence must therefore be premised on this notion of universal pragmatics (TTCC, 366–67)

Habermas's claim is that at the foundation of any linguistic utterance lies an intersubjective a priori semantic structure that is itself, in a sense, linguistically determined; the speech situation is composed of reflexive relations. This is not, however, to be understood as an empirical generalization. Rather, in order to generate data for empirical observation, "the structure of potential speech" must be in place. "It is the dialogue-constitutive universals, as we now prefer to say, that establish in the first place the form of intersubjectivity between any competent speakers capable of mutual understanding" (TTCC, 369). The basis, then, of communicative competence is the ideal speech situation. In order to engage in communicative acts the speaker must have a mastery of intersubjective a priori universals.

Habermas's objective is to identify a number of symmetrical relations that exist in the ideal speech situation.

> Pure intersubjectivity is determined by a symmetrical relation between I and You (We and You), I and He (We and They). An unlimited interchangeability of dialogue roles demands that no side be privileged in the performance of these roles; pure intersubjectivity exists only when there is complete symmetry in the distribution of assertion and dispute, revelation and concealment, prescription and conformity, among the partners of communication. (TTCC, 371)

Maintaining these symmetries enables subjects to reach consensus through open-ended discussion, provides for genuine interpersonal rapport through honest self-representation, and facilitates the establishment of universalizable norms through the explication of common expectations. These three symmetries, Habermas contends, are the linguistic correspondents of the ideas of truth, freedom, and justice (truth, truthfulness, and rightness): truth in the sense that propositional content is universally intelligible; freedom in the sense that there is genuine, undisguised self-representation between speaking subjects; and justice in the sense that correct courses of action can be determined (TTCC, 371–72).

Habermas acknowledges that pure intersubjectivity is unrealizable—that the ideal speech situation cannot be established. Nevertheless, the achievement of communicative competence does indicate the presence of these ideal structures in the communicative practices of speakers. As such, a competent speaker is able to conceptualize truth, freedom, and justice independent of any existing socio-political system. The model of ideal speech also provides a standard against which asymmetries that distort communication can be measured. With this addition to the theory of systematically distorted communication, Habermas provides a model for rehabilitating communicative abnormalities. The claim that intersubjectivity is a standard form (or normal), however, is not defensible on these grounds. Language can be applied in asymmetrical discourse just as readily as in symmetrical contexts without deviating from metalinguistic rules. For example, the fact that the system of personal pronouns in a modern language allows for clear identification of dialogue roles among participants does not standardize participatory equality. It is just as likely that participants will be distinguished in terms of subordinate and superordinate roles.

My point is that, given the analysis of linguistic competence that Habermas provides, there is no reason to accept the implicit (later to be made explicit) claim that intersubjective communication is the natural end or telos of linguistic practice. That language can be applied in a number of discursive contexts for numerous purposes is a more plausible conclusion to draw. If this were Habermas's conclusion, the method of identifying distortion and rehabilitating deviances would need to be revised. Communicative, or discursive, patterns would have to be analyzed in terms of the way that metasystemic rules translate into discursive rules. This would allow the social theorist to dispense with the notion of an original point of distortion and concentrate on existing discursive practices that promote deception, domination, and injustice. In the case of fascist propaganda, the specific relations between this form of communication and the intolerable practices that follow would be analyzed in terms of the discursive rules that operate in specific communicative contexts. The ideal situation could still serve as a standard of sorts. But not as one that represents the core or original mode of language usage. Habermas recognizes that these two essays represent a rudimentary "first attempt to grasp communicative competence in terms of linguistic theory" (TTCC, 372).

Communicative Pragmatics

In "Towards a Theory of Communicative Competence," Habermas suggests that both linguistic and communicative competence are susceptible to rational reconstruction in universal terms. In order to reconstruct communicative competence, careful attention must be paid to the universal pragmatic foundations of the ideal speech situation that are presupposed by all speakers in communication communities. Habermas's most detailed attempt at reconstructing communicative competence is found in "What Is Universal Pragmatics?" (UP), a lengthy and extremely complex essay that is a benchmark in the development of his theory of communication. In this section I will discuss this essay in terms of the way that it develops the ideas forwarded in "On Systematically Distorted Communication" and "Towards a Theory of Communicative Competence."

In "What Is Universal Pragmatics?" Habermas focuses on the validity basis of speech: "I shall develop the thesis that anyone acting communicatively must, in performing any speech action, raise universal validity claims and suppose that they can be vindicated (or redeemed)" (UP, 2). In communication that seeks understanding, the following validity claims are unavoidably raised: (1) that the utterance is understandable; (2) that the utterance has propositional content; (3) that the speaker is representing his/her self authentically; and (4) that intersubjective agreement can be established. Corresponding to these are four requirements: (1) that speech is intelligible; (2) that the propositional content is true; (3) that the speaker presents him/her self truthfully; and (4) that rightness can be agreed upon by subjects. This is of course essentially the same as the criteria for communicative competence (intelligibility is an embedded criterion in the earlier account). The purpose of the present analysis is to determine the way in which ambiguity infiltrates communication and to provide a discursive model of rectification. Without this, communication becomes strategic: that is, manipulative and domineering.[6] In order to isolate the point at which communication becomes opaque, Habermas contends, distinctions must be established between the situation that allows for validity claims to be raised, the actual content of the validity claims, and the means by which validity claims are redeemed (UP, 2–4).

Habermas writes at some length on the similarities and differences between the universal pragmatic approach and competing analyses of language and communication. It is not necessary here to go into these questions in detail. The conclusion drawn is that speech-act theory is most compatible with his project. As such, I will direct my discussion toward his appropriation of Austin's work.[7]

As was noted previously, Habermas is influenced by Chomsky's generative linguistics. It was also noted that he detected flaws in generative linguistics that limited its usefulness for his theory. In order to define the object domain of universal pragmatics, linguistics (which analyzes sentences in terms of grammatical rules) must be supplemented with speech-act theory (which analyzes utterances in terms of communicative rules). The domain of linguistics is sentence production; the domain of speech-act theory is sentence utterance. Combined, they cover the four mandates of communicative competence: comprehensibility (linguistics) and truth, truthfulness, and rightness (speech-act theory). Insofar as it is speech-act theory that moves analysis closest to the domain of intersubjective communication (by focusing on utterances rather than sentences), it will provide a theoretical point of departure (UP, 26–34).[8]

Habermas identifies the following as the objective of speech-act theory: "the principle task of speech-act theory is to clarify the performative status of utterances" (UP, 34). As was noted above, Austin's analysis of illocutionary utterances proved useful for Habermas's theory of communicative competence. His primary interest is not in the way that this analysis characterizes utterances as always interrelational (as opposed to sentences which can be analyzed in the abstract). Rather, Habermas is concerned with the generative power of utterances, which "consists in the fact that the speaker, in performing a speech act, can influence a hearer in such a way that the latter can take up an interpersonal relation with him" (UP, 35). At this level, speech-act theory can enter into an analysis of the conditions of intersubjectivity or communicative action (UP, 34–40).[9]

In "Towards a Theory of Communicative Competence" Habermas suggested that the a priori structures of communication are already linguistic in that they represent a set of reflexive relations. This, he now claims, is due to the double structure of speech. All speech acts have semantic content on two levels: locutionary and illocutionary. At the former level is propositional content that can be utilized in any number of speech acts. At the latter level is intersubjective content that contributes to understanding in a specific context of employment. Recognition of this double semantic structure identifies a fundamental feature of natural language: reflexivity. "Thus the peculiar reflexivity of natural language rests in the first instance on the combination of a communication of content—effected in an objectivating attitude—with a communication concerning the relational aspect in which the content is to be understood—effected in a performative attitude" (UP, 43). As such, linguistic theories that attempt to abstractly analyze the way that propositional content is transmitted are undercut; they are incapable of accounting for the process of understanding content. In this light, Habermas defines the direction of universal pragmatic analysis:

> As opposed to this, I consider the task of universal pragmatics to be the rational reconstruction of the double structure of speech. Taking Austin's theory of speech acts as my point of departure, I would like now to make this task more precise in relation to the problems of meaning and validity. (UP, 41–44)

Habermas begins by identifying the semantic categories of universal pragmatics. Following Austin's distinction between meaning (locutionary) and force (illocutionary), he delineates pragmatic and linguistic meaning. Pragmatic meaning, that of an utterance, is contingent and flexible; linguistic meaning, that of a sentence, is stable. The fundamental difference between pragmatic and linguistic meaning can be characterized as the difference between an intersubjective and a subject/object relation. In the former, meaning is shaped by an illocutionary context; while in the latter, meaning is determined by the relationship between component words and sentence structure. Habermas considers his formulation to be superior to Austin's in that it attributes semantic content to contexts of employment. Any consistent theory of meaning must take this into account (UP, 44–50).

The significance of the transformation of Austin's semantic distinction is demonstrated by the light it sheds on the relationship between communicative modes and the thematization of validity claims. Insofar as the distinction between locutionary and illocutionary modes of communication cannot be drawn on the basis of the difference between meaning and force, neither can it be drawn on the basis of the difference between constative and performative acts. Under this schema only locutionary acts can be evaluated as either true or false; illocutionary acts are merely either happy or unhappy. Austin came to realize this error and replaced the class of locutionary acts with "(a) the propositional component contained in every explicit performative utterance, (b) a special class of illocutionary acts that imply the validity claim of truth—constative speech acts" (UP, 50). Austin understood the class of constative speech acts to be unique in their ability to render universal validity claims. Habermas, on the other hand, contends that this applies to the whole range of speech acts:

> It is easy to see the reason for this; the validity claim of constative speech acts is presupposed in a certain way by speech acts of every

> type. The meaning of the propositional content mentioned in nonconstative speech acts can be made explicit through transforming a sentence of propositional content, "that p," into a propositional sentence "p"; and the truth claim belongs essentially to the meaning of the proposition thereby expressed. Truth claims are thus a type of validity claim built into the structure of possible speech in general. *Truth is a universal validity claim; its universality is reflected in the double structure of speech.* (UP, 52)

Truth content is a function of propositional content; propositional content is built into the semantic structure of every speech act. Therefore, the truth claim embedded in the meaning of all utterances enables the specific claim of an utterance to be universalized (UP, 50–52).

Austin ultimately abandoned the constative/performative distinction. Habermas, however, chooses to reconstruct it in more suitable terms. In communication, he asserts, participants engage one another on two distinct levels that can be characterized in terms of intersubjective and propositional meaning. The former represents a predominately interactional use of language, while for the latter, language usage is fundamentally cognitive. Depending on the context, one or the other of these modes will be dominant. It appears on the surface that the nature of the validity claim established in a given context will be shaped by the dominant mode. This is in fact the case, but the difference, Habermas claims, is one of degree, not of kind. If the context calls for an interactive use of language, then interpersonal relations are thematized and validity is construed in terms of rightness. The thematic difference determines *which* universal aspect of speech is emphasized, not *whether* the claim is universalizable. By retaining the constative/performative distinction, albeit in highly revised form, Habermas feels that he has successfully broadened the range of universalizable validity claims, enriched the concept of truth and certified the notion of rightness. Comprehensibility is presupposed in any mode of communication. If a breakdown occurs at this level, a hermeneutic discourse is utilized in order to establish intelligibility. The fourth speaker mandate—truthfulness—is a function of expressive mode of communication and is thematized in terms of speaker intentions. It also has universal implications insofar as it plays a role in all illocutionary acts (UP, 53–59).

The problems that I have alluded to thus far are to a certain extent dealt with through the clarification of the double structure of speech and the introduction of an intersubjective semantic theory. These developments ground communication in contexts of usage. They don't, however, overcome my two main objections: the implicit claim (1) that there is an originary form of communication, and (2) that one particular type of linguistic practice is in line with the purpose or natural end of language usage. To suggest that because every validity claim has propositional content it aspires to universality ignores the contextual embeddedness of patterns of communication established by the intersubjective semantic theory. And to claim that because meaning is formulated in discursive contexts it is grounded in intersubjectivity ignores other modes of communication that operate in discursive situations. Habermas's analysis is more advanced in this version and seems to move in the direction of discourse analysis. He nevertheless clings to the "universal" at the expense of the "pragmatic."

In the remainder of "What Is Universal Pragmatics?" Habermas attempts to ground his analysis in a theory of rationality. This is dealt with more effectively in subsequent work and will be addressed in the following section. The significant contribution of this essay is the detailed explication that it provides of the basic notions outlined in "Towards a Theory of Communicative Competence." It constructs a necessary bridge between the early writings and *The Theory of Communicative Action.*

Communicative Action

At this point it is worth pausing for a moment to note the amazing breadth of Habermas's social theory. Working under the immediate influence of the revisionist Marxism of the Frankfurt School of critical theory, his studies span a range that is bound by Vienna Circle positivism on one end and French poststructuralism on the other. His own philosophical project settles in somewhere between German philosophical hermeneutics and Anglo-American speech-act theory. Habermas's work in the '80s draws all of these diverse influences together into one magnum opus, *The Theory of Communicative Action.* In this section I will discuss the development of his theory of language and communication in this text. I will concentrate on the way that developments in the present context lead into a theory of social action, which will be the main topic in chapter 4.

In the third major part of *The Theory of Communicative Action* (TCA), "Intermediate Reflection: Social Action, Purposive Activity and Communication," Habermas attempts to articulate his analysis of linguistic communicative structures to a normative theory of social action. Taking as his point of departure Weber's theory of action (TCA, 1:279–84), Habermas develops a typology of action that is based on a distinction between nonsocial and social action. Nonsocial action is purely instrumental; its only objective is to achieve a desired consequence.[10] (For example, if I wanted a window shut I would simply get up and shut it.) Social action can be subdivided into two main categories:

action oriented to success and action oriented to reaching understanding. Success-oriented "strategic action" is based on what Horkheimer and Adorno called "instrumental rationality" (see chapter 1). It aims at influencing rational agents in order to secure some advantage for the actor. (For example, the way that a capitalist uses workers in order to secure profit for her/himself.) Understanding-oriented "communicative action" is Habermas's primary concern:

> By contrast, I shall speak of communicative action whenever the actions of the agents involved are coordinated not through egocentric calculations of success but through acts of reaching understanding. In communicative action participants are not primarily oriented to their own individual successes; they pursue their individual goals under the condition that they can harmonize their plans of action on the basis of common situation definitions. In this respect the negotiation of definitions of the situation is an essential element of the interpretive accomplishments required for communicative action. (TCA, 1:286)

This can be pursued in terms of a theory of the rationality of action informed by speech-act theory.

Habermas begins by developing a schema that can be used to determine whether an action is strategic or communicative. Rather than depending on an analysis of psychological states, this schema relies on knowledge of the structural foundations of "reaching understanding."[11] Understanding can be simply defined as agreement between speakers. The process of reaching understanding involves a rationally driven movement toward consent with respect to the propositional content of an utterance. Habermas stresses the point that understanding cannot be imposed in any way; it must be mutually achieved. This, for him, is "the inherent telos of human speech." In order to defend this claim Habermas turns once again to speech-act theory (TCA, 1:286–88).

In addition to the original categories of locution and illocution, a third category adopted from Austin, perlocution, now enters into the analysis. A perlocutionary utterance is one that brings about an effect or change in the world. These effects can either be trivial or significant. Trivial effects are merely unforeseen side effects of interaction; significant effects are the function of strategically designed interactional contexts. "The effects ensue whenever a speaker acts with an orientation to success and thereby instrumentalizes speech acts for purposes that are only contingently related to the meaning of what is said" (TCA, 289). The relation between illocutionary and perlocutionary acts, and communicative and strategic action should be clear. As such, distinguishing between illocution and perlocution will contribute to the task of categorizing action (TCA, 1:288–90).

Habermas proposes the following set of criteria for drawing this distinction:

1. Illocutionary acts clearly aim to convey meaning through reciprocal understanding, while the aim of perlocutionary acts is unclear and context dependent.
2. Illocutionary success can be achieved without achieving locutionary success, while perlocutionary acts must achieve locutionary success.
3. Illocutionary results are regulated by internal meaning, while perlocutionary results are regulated by external meaning.
4. Successful illocutionary acts make intentions explicit, while successful perlocutionary acts leave intentions unknown.

In contrast to the distinction between locutionary and illocutionary acts, the distinction between locutionary and perlocutionary acts is not analytic. Perlocutionary acts are structurally dependent upon illocutionary acts. If the speaker cannot transmit meaning to the hearer, the effect will not obtain. This, for Habermas, confirms the claim that communication is originally and essentially illocutionary. Perlocutionary communication is an exploitative parasite (TCA, 1:290–93).

The basic conditions of communicatively coordinated interaction include the utterance of a speech act by a speaker and the reception and affirmation by a hearer. This grounds the speech act in an interpersonal relationship that is structured by propositional content, a speaker guarantee, and obligation on the part of the hearer (truth, truthfulness, and rightness). The speech act can be responded to on three levels: yes or no, accept or decline, and action in accordance with the obligation (truth, truthfulness, and rightness). Insofar as semantic content is a function of the process of understanding, the speech act has the authority to coordinate interaction. "The pragmatic level of agreement that is effective for coordination connects the semantic level of understanding meaning with the empirical level of developing—in a manner dependent on the context—the accord relevant to the sequel of action"[12] (TCA, 1:294–300).

In order to raise this analysis to the level of validity claims, Habermas draws a distinction between simple imperatives and complex normative imperatives. The simple imperative relies on the above-stated conditions; the complex normative imperative, which takes the form of a command or order, involves the additional conditions of an established norm and institutionally based authority. Also, some threat of sanction is generally included. Determining whether a validity claim is raised with a simple imperative is relatively easy; it depends on whether the conditions of interactional understanding are intact in the specific context of communication. In the case of a complex normative imperative, whether or not a validity claim is raised depends on the nature of its foundation. If it is based on rationality, can be subjected to argumentation, and is accepted or rejected on these grounds (as opposed to power-motivated acquiescence), then in fact the complex normative imperative raises a validity claim (TCA, 1:300–5).

As I have noted, there are three criteria for determining whether a validity claim should be redeemed or rejected: truth, truthfulness, and rightness. Habermas formulates this in a number of ways and summarizes as follows: "the fact that the intersubjective commonality of a communicatively achieved agreement exists at the levels of normative accord, shared propositional knowledge, and mutual trust in subjective sincerity can be explained in turn through the functions of achieving understanding in language" (TCA, 1:308). Illocutionary meaning is the focal point for testing any validity claim as all speech acts have a cognitive, expressive, and regulative dimension. The cognitive content indicates something about the objective world; the expressive content indicates something about the speaker's internal or subjective world; and the regulative content indicates what type of action is legitimate in the social world. Habermas's main claim is that by studying the structures of language and communication we can develop a method for categorizing the different types of social actions and determining which of these are legitimate (TCA, 1:306–10).

The remaining question pertains to how this highly idealized structure can be translated into the "real world." Habermas suggests that a model for this can be developed by connecting formal and empirical pragmatics. Doing so involves adapting the formal conception in a number of ways. The analysis of basic modes of communication needs to be supplemented with illocutionary models that account for culture-specific interpersonal communication. In addition to a set of standard forms of speech acts, a method for realizing speech acts is required. The fact that the greater part of communicative practice does not plug neatly into a universal pragmatic category is problematic. The scope of analysis has to be broadened tremendously in order to accommodate the complex networks of communication and the overlap of ideally distinguished performative attitudes and their corresponding "worlds." An operable model of planning, based on the concept of communicative action, must be developed. And finally, further consideration needs to be given to the existing networks of norms and background institutions. As such, the ideal speech situation is still an unrealizable abstraction; and universal pragmatic distinctions break down when the ideal meets the real (TCA, 1:328–30).

This is not to say that the formal pragmatic analysis is without merit:

> An empirical pragmatics without a formal-pragmatic point of departure would not have the conceptual instruments needed to recognize the rational basis of linguistic communication in the confusing complexity of the everyday scenes observed. It is only in formal-pragmatic investigations that we can secure for ourselves an idea of reaching understanding that can guide empirical analysis into particular problems—such as the linguistic representation of different levels of reality, the manifestation of communication pathologies, or the development of decentered understanding of the world. (TCA, 1:331)

The ideal model provides a solid backdrop for identifying communication-related social problems (which for Habermas includes virtually all social problems). It likewise establishes a rational foundation for what I consider to be Habermas's primary objective: to develop a discursive theory of social-political action that is premised on participatory consensus. In short, then, what Habermas establishes—albeit not unproblematically—is that there is a direct connection between normative structures and patterns of language usage.[13]

In chapters 4 and 5 I will concentrate on Habermas's effort to develop this theory into a politics of enlightenment. In his efforts to do so, the gap between ideal speech and communicative problems in the real world is narrowed. Habermas situates his theory of language and communication within the context of the modern lifeworld (as noted in chapter 2). This establishes an historical context for, and practical application of, the formal normative structures discussed in this section. The problems that I have identified are likewise carried into this aspect of his theory. While in the final formulation of the theory of communicative action (which I have just discussed) Habermas is more conscious of the importance of actual communicative contexts, the difficulties that I have alluded to throughout are heightened. Habermas states specifically that his theory establishes the claim that all language usage can be referenced to an "original mode" and that its natural end or "telos" is intersubjectivity. These problems will factor importantly into the remainder of my analysis in this chapter and will carry on into the chapters 4 and 5. The most significant development at this stage is the relationship that Habermas has established between modern linguistic systems and modern normativity. This is of crucial importance in that it gives a historicist twist to universal ethical standards. I would like to twist the historicist point a bit more at this time—moving it in the direction of classical Marxism. The assumption that ethical standards and linguistic development can emerge independent of concrete economic conditions strikes me as being mistaken. As such, in order to provide the basis for my argument against this I will take a short detour through Jameson's analysis of Marx's *Grundrisse*.

A MARXIST INTERLUDE: MODERN IDEALS AND THE CAPITALIST MODE OF PRODUCTION

In order for Habermas's normative positions to be viable, it is necessary that the standards of truth, truthfulness, and rightness, or, alternately, truth, freedom, and justice, can be cleanly separated from the capitalist mode of production. As we saw in chapter 2, that mode of production has lead to the distortion of values and the reduction of communicative interaction to the steering media of money and power. His attempt to make this separation is ingenious. If, Habermas surmises, we can show how modern modes of communication are inherently dependent on these norms, then it can be established that, qua values, they are independent of the capitalist mode of production. His attempt to make this determination is enticing, if not ultimately compelling. Where it fails, as I have indicated, is in its inability to contend with the specific ways in which value structures are in fact distorted in the late modern world. As I put it above, Habermas focuses too much on the formal and not enough on the pragmatic. Another way to put this would be that Habermas's theory of language and communication is excessively abstract. In the following sections of this chapter I will argue this point conceptually. In chapter 4 I will argue the same point from a historical and political perspective.

In chapter 2 I concluded with a brief discussion of Fredric Jameson's account of postmodern economics. His critical foil in this analysis is the classic section on money in Marx's *Grundrisse*. I will now follow his analysis, paying particular attention to the remarks on Habermas in this context, in preparation for my critique of modern normativity.

Marx's discussion in the *Grundrisse* takes the form of an attack on "utopian socialist" views on economics. One can simply summarize his point as being that the utopian socialists (the Proudhonists in this instance) seem to think that one can get rid of money without getting rid of the exchange system. The general idea here is that we can have it both ways: exchange economies without the "evils" of money. Marx's claim is that when one is adopted, the other will return, not so much as comedy or farce, but rather as business as usual. Jameson summarizes as follows:

> So also with the attempt to separate ideology and reality: the ideology of the market is unfortunately not some supplementary ideational or representational luxury or embellishment that can be removed from the economic problem and then sent over to some cultural or superstructural morgue, to be dissected by specialists there. It is somehow generated by the thing itself, as its objectively necessary afterimage; somehow both dimensions must be registered together in their identity as well as difference. (CLC, 260)

This is precisely the case that I wish to make against Habermas: that modern norms such as truth, freedom, and justice, are figured in such a way that they cannot be cleanly separated from the modern mode of production. This is not to say that they are valueless; in fact, I will argue they are invaluable. It is to claim, however, that if they are to have emancipatory content they need to be refigured in terms of a politics of enlightenment that is as independent of the modern mode of production as possible. This is to say that a normative appropriation of these values must be characterized in terms of the aftermath of modernity—not as a defense of modernity.

Returning briefly to Jameson and Marx, I will cite a passage from the *Grundrisse* to which Jameson appeals and then show vis-à-vis Jameson's interpretation how this pertains to my problem.

> Exchange value, or, more precisely, the money system, is indeed the system of *freedom and equality*, and what disturbs (the Proudhonists) in the more recent development of the system are disturbances immanent to the system, i.e., the very realization of equality and freedom, which turns out to be inequality and unfreedom. It is an aspiration as pious as it is stupid to wish that exchange value would not develop into capital, or that labor which produces exchange value would not develop into wage labor. What distinguishes these gentlemen from the bourgeois apologists is, on the one hand, their awareness of the contradictions inherent in the system, and, on the other, their utopianism, manifest *in their failure to grasp the inevitable difference between the real and the ideal shape of bourgeois society*, and the consequent desire to undertake the superfluous task of changing the ideal expression itself back into reality, whereas it is in fact merely the photographic image of this reality. (CLC, 261–62—my emphasis)

Jameson's analysis goes as follows: What Marx is criticizing is a sort of naive realism in the Proudhonist socialists. They believe that the status of values such as freedom and equality is to be found, free of ambiguity, within the established framework of bourgeois society. While the reality of the situation doesn't bear this out, all that needs to be done in terms of concrete social change is to "improve the model and make freedom and equality appear for real" (CLC, 262). This sounds amazingly like Habermas's own account of the retrieval of modern normativity. The question that I will approach in the concluding section of this chapter concerns whether Jameson and Marx are right that the only way to realize these ideals is to abolish them along with the reality that brings them about.[14]

The issue of modern normativity is addressed most directly by Habermas in lecture XII of *The Philosophical Discourse of Modernity* (PDM). This discussion is situated by his analyses of thinkers ranging from Nietzsche, to Horkheimer and Adorno, to Foucault and Derrida. He distinguishes between the "cryptonormativity" of, for instance, Foucault, and the clear and distinct "normative content of modernity" to which he appeals. In my discussion of this text I will flesh out the position that I have been developing throughout this book: that the normative content of modernity is at best ambivalent and at worst in complicity with the very system that Habermas denounces. And in line with my claim in chapter 2, I will argue that Habermas's own assessment of late modern society provides some of the most convincing evidence in support of this position.

The Spectre of Postmodernism

Three thinkers and three methods of analysis that have developed during the twilight of modernity are indicted by Habermas as the greatest threats to modern normativity: Adorno and negative dialectics, Derrida and deconstruction, and Foucault and genealogy. Insofar as each defies the boundaries that separate the constitutive discourses of modern knowledge production, without acknowledging any debt to premodern tradition (such as the neoconservatives have done), they are left without an analytic base. "They cannot be unequivocally classified with either philosophy or science, with moral and legal theory, or with literature and art. At the same time, they resist any return to forms of religious thought, whether dogmatic or heretical" (PDM, 336). In other words, they subscribe to no standards—making up the rules as they go along and monitoring their development only in terms of analytic efficacy. This, Habermas would maintain, along with their characteristically flamboyant rhetoric, has earned them a following analogous to the patronage of outrageous late-modern art: obscurity provides a shelter from the demands for normative justification.

In their haste to condemn modernity the late-modern "anarchists" have suspended the primary modern virtue—rationality—which while dangerous when misused, is nevertheless inexpendable. The two abuses of rationality, aptly analyzed by the above-mentioned critics, are instrumentalism and totalism; the critique of instrumental reason was most adamantly pursued by Adorno, while the critique of totalistic reason was and is the pet project of Derrida. Foucault, it could be said, combines the two in his genealogical studies of discourse formations and power relations. Habermas wouldn't deny the value of these critiques, as he too is a critic of modern forms of reason. His critique is distinguished from the others, however, as it points to an alternative form of reason—communicative rationality—that while rooted in the normative content of modernity is not vulnerable to modern abuses. Foucault and

Derrida, he claims, revert to irrationalism. The assumption that undergirds this pronouncement is that the above-mentioned critics view rationality as something that is inherently warped: that there are no good forms of reason. Hence, as the opposite of rationality is irrationality, and these critics oppose reason in totalistic fashion, they must be irrationalists.

It would be difficult to find conclusive evidence in the writings of these thinkers supporting the claim that they advocate irrationalism. Habermas confuses their renunciation of certain forms of rationality with an all-encompassing "obliteration" of reason. He himself recognizes that the forms under analysis are not the only possible manifestations of reason. What he fails to see is that there is quite conceivably more than one alternative and that forms of rationality have to be tailored to the historical (social, economic, cultural, political) circumstances within which they are developed. Habermas argues that communicative rationality has universal applicability and that the differentiated structures of the modern lifeworld facilitate its development. I will argue that while communicative rationality needs to be one element in the complex normative structures that take shape in the aftermath of modernity, it is not in and of itself sufficient for grounding a politics of enlightenment: it is not sufficiently forceful to solicit changes in late modern societies that will lead to the establishment of the communicative society that Habermas tacitly advocates. In order to grasp the rational for Habermas's claim, it is necessary to observe the relationship that he identifies between communicative reason and the cultural reserve that gives rise to its production.

For Habermas, modern lifeworld differentiations correspond to the components of speech acts (as discussed above). The cultural sphere corresponds to propositional content; the societal sphere corresponds to illocutionary content; and the personal sphere corresponds to intentional content. The structures of language and the structures of the lifeworld are functionally interdependent:

> Cultural reproduction ensures that (in the semantic dimension) newly arising situations can be connected up with existing conditions in the world; it secures the continuity of tradition and a coherency of knowledge sufficient for the consensus needs of everyday practice. Social integration ensures that newly arising situations (in the dimension of social space) can be connected up with existing conditions in the world; it takes care of the coordination of action by means of legitimately regulated interpersonal relationships and lends constancy to the identity of groups. Finally, the socialization of members ensures that newly arising situations (in the dimension of historical time) can be connected up with existing world conditions; it secures the acquisition of generalized

> capacities for action for future generations and takes care of harmonizing individual life histories and collective life forms. Thus, interpretive schemata susceptible of consensus (or "valid knowledge"), legitimately ordered interpersonal relationships (or "solidarities"), and capacities for interacting (or "personal identities") are renewed in these three processes of reproduction. (PDM, 343–44)

This can be summarized as follows: the lifeworld serves as a text that is the source pool for the three linguistic components that are thematized in speech acts (I will develop this extensively in chapter 5). The first ensures that there is semantic consistency with respect to objects in the world: so that when *I* say "dog" you envision a creature with four legs and a tail instead of one with wings and a beak. The second provides for continuity between spheres of action through mutual understanding: *we* can make the transition from one mode of collective activity to another. The third ensures that the concept of *I* that is produced in the contexts of *we* will endure and develop from generation to generation.

Habermas openly acknowledges that this is an idealization, one that must contend with masses of evidence indicating that modern societies don't reproduce themselves in this manner. The following, however, is the important question: Does this characterization of the modern lifeworld have an actual correspondent in any form, and if so, how can it be drawn upon to move in the direction of a society that coordinates action through consensus?

Habermas argues that, formally, everything is in place to begin conducting social life on the basis of these lifeworld differentiations. Modernity is no longer strapped by mythologically legitimated knowledge; rather, what is constituted as knowledge hinges on consensus among the appropriately empowered figures (such as a community of scientists). There is also greater leeway available for personality development, enabling increased individuality. Finally, the *idea* of universal legal and moral structures has developed, providing formal protection against arbitrary changes based on power shifts. Habermas attributes this to the realization in lifeworld structures of the inherent qualities of language that correspond to the essential values of truth, freedom, and justice.

Central to Habermas's argument is the notion that at no time in the history of the West (or any other civilization) has there been so much potential for intersubjective communication. Truth, freedom, and justice are defined in terms of democratic equality, hence providing for a consensus-oriented public sphere that could produce in practice something similar to the "public will." "The procedures of discursive will formation established in the structurally differentiated lifeworld are set up to secure the social bond of all with all precisely through equal consideration of the interests of each individual" (PDM, 346). Stating this in more linguistic terms: the system of personal pronouns that provides the referential basis of modern languages finds its home in the modern lifeworld; insofar as there is potential for direct interchange between "I" and "I" (ego and alter) the establishment of a well-conceived "we," one that reflects the social, economic, and political concerns of its referent, is possible. This also contributes to the process of secularization as the power of discourse overrides that of tradition.

The question that I would raise in light of this is whether the power of modernity is located in either tradition or discursive will formation. Certainly there has been a trend away from traditional modes of justification (divine rights of royalty or papal primacy). But has this in fact been replaced with a rationally determined, consensus-oriented type of legitimation? Modern theory clearly moves in this direction; and there is evidence that these theoretical developments have been translated into constitutional discourses. My concern is whether these discourses in fact contribute to the establishment of consensus-oriented polity or whether they merely cloak the dominant modern practices that are justified in between the lines. Do the modern concepts of justice, freedom, and truth have a conceptual foundation in democratic equality or in the steering media of the modern mode of production—money and power (force)? If, as I will argue, the latter is the case, then the normative content of modernity is an ambiguous "pseudonormativity." The dominant normative content, that which guides practices and serves implicitly as the justification for those practices, resides within the motivational structures of the capitalist mode of production. To state this explicitly, and in fairly conventional Marxist terms: the normative foundation of modernity is not freedom, truth, and justice, in any universalistic sense; rather it is these ideals, conceived relative to production, profit, and technical proficiency. The modern Enlightenment concepts of freedom, justice, and truth are simply traditional ideals (and worthy ones at that) that are tailored to support the systemic norms that certify modern activities. Further, as Horkheimer and Adorno, Habermas, and Foucault have carefully detailed, these activities take on a distinctly negative tone in the late phases of modernity.[15]

Habermas accounts for this by suggesting that rather than operating within the boundaries of modern normativity, modern practices have deviated from the normative standards to which they are accountable. Consequently, three types of pathologies develop in late modern societies: loss of meaning (a semantic pathology), social anomie (an interpersonal pathology), and personality disorders (a pathology of the individual). These correspond to the structural differentiations of the modern lifeworld (objective, social, and subjective). In effect, what Habermas is stating is that sociopolitical developments (grounded in the modern lifeworld) that distinguish modernity from previous periods are susceptible to both enlightened or pathological practices—that the problems of the late modern period are in fact native to modernity. This, I would argue, is due to the bilevel normativity of modernity. Rather than accounting for the above-mentioned "pathologies" as deviances, I would suggest that the are actually in conformity with a more pronounced, although less visibly expressed, normative base. I will stress here that my argument rests on the notion of two levels of normativity and the interplay that exists between them; it is not my position that there is simply one exclusively dominant level (this would merely reverse Habermas's position).

As I noted in chapter 2, Habermas's most recent assessment of late modern society takes note of a bilevel societal structure: system and lifeworld. He further notes that increasingly the system infringes upon the lifeworld, isolating it as a subsystem and squeezing from it the type of communicative patterns that meet late-modern economic and political needs. In doing so, the normative content is marginalized; it is replaced with system imperatives that are directed via steering media—money and power. By insisting on a rigid system/lifeworld distinction (that recognizes normative content only in the lifeworld), Habermas can keep intact his psychomedicinal model for social change. If the essence of normalcy is located in some all-but-lost social-political foundation (one constructed under the auspices of an emerging bourgeois society—see chapter 4), then in fact the appropriate course of action is to bring this concept of normalcy to the fore and measure sociopolitical practices against it. By doing so, rampant late-modern pathologies can be diagnosed and "cured."[16] If, however, the system/lifeworld distinction is questioned while the bilevel theory of society is retained—focusing on the interplay between, rather than the distinctiveness of the two levels—a new picture emerges that calls for a different remedial strategy. As I mentioned above, the two levels that I am referring to both factor into the normativity of modern society: the explicit, but weak, ideal dimension corresponds to Habermas's lifeworld, while the implicit, but more powerful dimension corresponds to Habermas's system.[17] Characterized as such, grounding efforts to bring about social-political change in modern normativity will be dubious. Doing so stands to solicit the recurrence of existing problems. I will now provide a defense of this position and point to some further repercussions.

The Late Modern Condition

To begin, it is important to clarify what I mean by normative. I use this term, as does Habermas, to refer to the standards against which social, economic, and political practices are measured. If the bilevel or pseudonormative foundations of late modernity are to be determined, then it is necessary to consider the practices that are prevalent in late modern society. Insofar as Habermas provides an excellent account of those practices, I turn once again to his analysis.

Habermas develops his critique in terms of the communication theory that serves as the basis for his entire system. Summarizing my earlier discussion: the central problem of late modern society is the lack of substantive communication. Human interchange is driven by economic imperatives that are coordinated through the steering media of money and power. As a result, the system has overtaken almost every sphere of human life. It has infiltrated the objective, subjective, and intersubjective worlds of modern individuals. "The deformation of a lifeworld that is regulated, fragmented, monitored, and looked after are surely more subtle than the palpable forms of material exploitation and impoverishment; but internalized social conflicts that have shifted from the corporeal to the psychic are not therefore less destructive" (PDM, 362—here Habermas exhibits still too much faith in the welfare state). Habermas goes on to recognize Foucault as the master analyst of this phenomenon. "The legal-administrative means of translating social-welfare programs into action are not some passive, as it were, propertyless medium. They are connected, rather, with a praxis that involves isolation of facts, normalization, and surveillance, the reifying and subjectivating violence that Foucault has traced right down into the most delicate capillary tributaries of everyday communication" (PDM, 362). Clearly such practices are not in line with the principles of freedom, truth, and justice unless these concepts are defined relative to some other form of normativity: production, profit, and technical power.

But are these flaws the mark of failure or a rather warped form of success? Do they deviate from or refine the normativity of modernity? Habermas raises this question as follows: "In the utopias painted in the old romances about the state, rational forms of life entered into a *deceptive symbiosis* with the technological mastery of nature and the ruthless mobilization of social labor power. This equation of happiness and emancipation with power and production *has been a source of irritation for the self-understanding of modernity from the start*—and it has called forth two centuries of criticism of modernity" (PDM, 366—my emphasis). My point is this: given Habermas's own analysis of late modern society, his recognition of the dominant modes of communication and sociability, the normative content of modernity (as he clearly points out) becomes questionable. Late-modern problems such as "isolation of facts, normalization, and surveillance, the reifying and subjectivating violence" may in fact correspond to, rather than deviate from, the complex bilevel normativity of the modern period. With these doubts about the modern program on the table I will turn to my conceptual argument.

Freedom, Justice, and Truth

Freedom is not a concept that is unique to modernity. It gains attention in almost every political theory from Plato to Rawls. The important questions that surround this concept include: (1) What does it mean to be free? (2) To what extent should freedom be limited? And (3) who should be free? In the modern epoch the focus has been placed on the third question. The official response has been: everyone. Habermas latches on to this aspect of modern freedom—the claim to universality. This, for him, is representative of an implicit consensus among modern individuals. While I would certainly not want to deny that universal freedom has been a focal point of modernity, it is quite clear that universal freedom has not been the norm.[18] Further, the most pervasive forms of nonfreedom—the subjection of women, the incarceration of ethnic minorities in ghettos and housing projects, the exploitation of wage laborers, and so on—have been justified on the basis of the formal concept of freedom, with all its universalistic abstraction, that is native to modernity. When forms of "enslavement," such as I have mentioned, are pointed out, a common response is (and I say common here as common sense seems to reflect the sort of normative ideals to which Habermas's theory aspires): What prevents people in these situations from liberating themselves? They are not determined by law to live under such conditions (this is the more sophisticated version of the "Get a job" argument).

These of course are the obvious cases; ones that I think can be accounted for within the framework of modern normativity via Habermas's "illness" model. The more difficult cases are those identified by Habermas only in his later work (as mentioned above) and that have been the focal point of Foucault's research since the late '50s: the use of power strategies to permeate all spheres of human life for the sake of achieving and maintaining a distinctly modern form of *productivity*. This activity relies upon institutions of pedagogy, mental health, manufacturing, administrating, and rehabilitation. And, as Foucault has carefully pointed out, all of these institutional practices have been justified on the basis of humanistic values that repeatedly appeal to the concept of universal freedom that Habermas considers to be fundamental to modernity. In light of this, the following points can be made:

1. Habermas is in agreement with Foucault concerning these modern practices and quite openly acknowledges that what they amount to is domination.

2. The rhetoric of freedom, as defined in the modern period (an idealistic abstraction), is deployed in the service of the aforementioned practices of domination.
3. The real justification for these practices (which is the way that Habermas defines normativity) is a distinctly modern form of productivity: one that produces not only material products but also the various types of subjects that are needed to maintain this productive mode.

My suggestion is that given Habermas's recognition of these practices in late modern societies it becomes increasingly difficult to claim that the solution to the unique forms of domination that prevail will be found in the ambiguous modern notion of freedom. The *ideal* of freedom has been shaped to serve the *norm* of productivity.[19] This is not to say that freedom isn't a modern norm in any sense; rather, to the extent that freedom is normative, it is defined and institutionalized relative to the norm of production.

The norm of productivity has endured during modernity, and flourished during late modernity, because the ideal of freedom that was formulated in the early stages failed to address explicitly the other two questions that are central to conceptualizing a notion of freedom: What is the nature of freedom and what sorts of limitations should be placed on free activity? These questions were implicitly addressed within the economic sphere, allowing the quest for productivity to shape the modern concept of freedom and to use the explicit appeal to universality in justification of practices that can (and are by both Habermas and Foucault) be viewed as domination rather than liberation. This being the case, it seems unlikely that these problems can be solved on the basis of a clear and distinct modern normativity, as modern normativity has neither of these qualities. Movement toward a solution cannot be retrogressive. Rather, in order to begin refiguring the ideal of freedom, its rootedness in the modern norm of production must be carefully analyzed.

The second important component of modern normativity, in Habermas's account, is justice. This takes form in the modern legal system. The modern system of law purportedly ascends to universal standards of action that are rationally determined (as opposed to being determined by some religious principle). As was the case with freedom, the feature of the modern system of law that appeals to Habermas is its universality: it is supposed to be applicable across the range of individuals—recognizing no special cases or exceptions. By objectifying these principles within a durable legal structure, the contingencies of shifting regimes and arbitrary manipulation of law and order are eliminated. The central feature of this system is a stable center of political power—some form of republic—that can administer justice independent of the interests of particular administrators. Hence, equality before the law is the slogan of modernity.

As was the case with freedom, modern theorists were not the first to be interested in the concept of justice. Nor were they the first to conceive of a universal law; the Romans also had a notion of universal natural law that was rooted in the common human capacity to reason. The assumption was that on the basis of this common capacity, rationally determined law receives tacit consent from all of humanity. It would not be generally agreed, however, that Roman society was a paradigm of justice. A simple example would be that while in the abstract it was considered intolerable to maintain any form of slavery, in actuality slavery was central to the Roman economy and was justified by Roman law. As such, it would be safe to say that this ideal was tenuously applied as a norm.

If, during the modern epoch, the ideal principle of universal justice has been clearly raised to normative status, then an analysis of practice should confirm this by showing that deviations are in conflict with, not supported by, the conception of justice that is distinctly modern. Practices such as slavery (in the United States), exploitation of child labor, and sexual discrimination and cases of unfair treatment due to race, gender, or lifestyle preference in courts of law, can be accounted for in this manner: as practices in exception to, rather than legitimated by, the modern concept of justice. These are not conceptual problems but rather stem from residual biases that can be increasingly filtered out as "we" become more enlightened.

The harder cases are those that prevail in the late-modern period (not that the others have gone away). These fall into two general categories. The first concerns sectors of society that regardless of legal reform—both systemic and individual—are not dealt with justly. I would include in this category people who are homeless, a high percentage of single parents, numerous ethnic minorities, and the bulk of working women (where average salaries are consistently lower than those of men with comparable training). These are problems that Habermas associates with the welfare state in "crisis": incongruities that persist after legal adjustments have been made to provide for greater amounts of social and economic justice. There are no legal reasons why the aforementioned groups cannot achieve social, economic, and political status equal to those from notably different circumstances. It is the very fact that formal legal justice is achieved that movement toward substantive justice is halted. The argument would once again be: "What is prohibiting them from changing their status? They simply need to show some initiative." (This is of course not Habermas's argument.) My point is that these problems cannot be accounted for as deviations from modern standards of justice; rather, they are supported by the pseudonorm of justice that is conceptualized relative to the principle underpinning these practices. I will return to what I consider this principle to be after discussing the second category.

The second category concerns those aspects of the law that provide advantage to sectors of the population that possess a great deal of power. I would include in this tax laws that favor the affluent (both corporately and individually), criminal laws that almost encourage (by virtue of leniency) white-collar crime, laws that allow for unsafe levels of contaminants to be put into the environment (legitimated on the grounds that it is necessary in order to remain competitive), as well as putting unsafe additives into food products (naming only a few). The fact that laws have been enacted to deal with these problems (under the guise of reform) serves to cloak the abusive practices that ensue. My point once again is that the rhetoric of equality before the law (justice) complies with the principle that undergirds these practices.

The normative principle that perpetuates the aforementioned practices is profit. From the very beginning of the modern period an ethic of profit has been central: virtually any activity is justified if profit is the consequence. When stated so bluntly this is of course offensive. Hence it is necessary to equate the pursuit of profit with some principle of justice. This, I would argue, is the principle of justice that has developed during the course of modernity. When pressure for legitimation becomes intensive (for instance, during the civil rights movement in the United States or during the student movements in both the United States and Europe), adjustments are made that are formally satisfying and have enough substance to quiet unrest. They don't, however, lead to the kind of social change that is needed to eliminate the problem (witness the regressions of the '80s and '90s). It could be argued that when justice comes into conflict with the principle of profit, the powerful sectors of society that thrive on profit exercise their force to preserve their favored position. Habermas would in fact accept this argument on the basis of his own analysis of modernity. He would contend that this deviates from a more genuine sense of justice that is distinctly present in the modern lifeworld. My position is that this "genuine" level of justice is not as distinct as Habermas claims—that an analysis of late-modern practices reveals a conceptual interrelationship between the Enlightenment ideal of justice and the profit-oriented imperatives of capitalism. As such, movement toward a more substantive form of justice shouldn't be in the direction of a clear and distinct normativity that is already in place. Rather, the task of theory is to reconfigure the notion of justice such that it is independent of the subterranean normative standard of profit.[20]

The third component of modern normativity, in Habermas's account, is truth. Truth is primarily the product of science during the modern period and there is little doubt that science has flourished. The question, however, is whether it has been the quest for truth, or some other force, that has driven modern science. Once again it is important to take note of the fact that the modern sciences emerged at essentially the same time as the modern economy. As a result, the pursuit of truth has often been guided by production and profit in the form of technical prowess.[21] In the realm of the hard sciences, theoretical research is funded on the basis of potential for technical application. The proliferation of truth in this sphere has brought us to the point where we are dealing with the greenhouse effect and mutually assured destruction (see Habermas's remarks on this in PDM, 366–67). In the realms of the human sciences, technologies have been developed to shape subjects into individuals that are useful in the quest for production and profit. The truth of social-scientific discourses is measured in terms of their efficacy; if they do the job, they are true. As a result, we now have layer upon layer of these discourses reforming the practices of modern individuals. Given this it can be argued that the dominant norm in question is technique—truth conceptualized relative to technical efficacy. I am not claiming that science has been driven exclusively by technical motives. Nor am I claiming that scientists are not motivated by the pursuit of truth. Rather, my point is that given the type of truth that feeds the modern "system," the norm that guides scientific research (when viewed broadly) is indelibly linked to technique (at the expense of research that might produce truths that are actually more in line with enlightened ideals). If this is correct, then returning to some untainted modern notion of truth simply runs the risk of reinscribing the distortions that are prevalent in modern sciences as currently practiced. My claim is that the norm of truth (lifeworld) cannot be separated from technical imperatives (system).[22]

The arguments that I have presented are not completely incompatible with either Habermas's assessment of modernity or his general theory that modern society has a bilevel structure. They are, however, in opposition to Habermas's claim that the two levels of modern society (system and lifeworld) are distinct from one another and that the lifeworld contains the last remaining kernels of unperverted modern normativity. My position is that the two levels of modern society both factor into modern normativity and that the interplay between the two cloaks the operational motivation of late-modern practices. If Habermas's view is accepted, a theoretical model of a politics of enlightenment must hark back to the pure normativity conceptualized early in the modern period. The desire for an unperverted primitive origin that can be tapped into and applied in present conditions is exactly the sort of thing that he accuses the critics of modernity of yearning for. His claim is that they long for a prerational impulse, Dionysian in tenor, that will liberate humanity from the oppression of rationality. My point is that Habermas seems to be making a similar move, with the exception that the origin he appeals to is modern rationality prior to its capitalistic corruption: a form of reason that was originally a product of the modern lifeworld but that has been twisted into the service of system imperatives. I have tried to show that the two are inextricably intertwined and that a contemporary theory of a politics of enlightenment should not yearn for the originary pristinity of enlightened (as opposed to corrupted) modernity.

While my argument here is not definitive, I hope that it raises serious questions about the normative structure that is at the base of Habermas's model for a politics of enlightenment, or what we can infer concerning a politics of enlightenment. The strength in his position is his ability to link normativity with modern standards of communicative competence. This contextualizes his position historically without succumbing to relativism. The theory of language and communication, however, also serves as a weak link in that if, as I have attempted to show, the norms of modernity—rooted in the lifeworld—cannot be separated sharply from steering imperatives—rooted in the system—then neither can communicative action. In chapter 4 I will continue to deal with the first of these issues. In chapter 5 I will address the latter.

CHAPTER 4

The Politics of Enlightenment and the Aftermath of Modernity

At this point I feel it will be helpful to recapitulate the main positions that I have developed thus far. I introduced the problem that I am concerned with in terms of the modern/postmodern debate that Jürgen Habermas has participated in over the years. The purpose in using this as my point of departure was to establish that this debate is at the crux of my concern with a politics of enlightenment. Typically the enlightenment/anti-enlightenment split has located thinkers in one of the camps of the modern/postmodern dichotomy. My suggestion is that this need not be the case.

In chapter 1 I examined the historical development of the concept of enlightenment from Kant through Horkheimer and Adorno, to Foucault, Habermas, and Derrida. In doing so I aimed not so much at drawing particular conclusions, but rather to suggest some of the possible ways that the concept of enlightenment could be elaborated.

In chapter 2 I turned to Habermas's theory of advanced capitalist societies. Contained within his critique is a strong defense of modernity: a modernity that he argues has been deformed by the steering media of advanced capitalism. From there I turned to a discussion of postmodernism that focused on a distinction between normative and descriptive postmodernism. My objective here was to show that one could waver a bit on the modern/postmodern question without hesitating with respect to the question of enlightenment. My suggestion was that we consider referring to the contemporary condition as the aftermath of modernity: a condition that is inherently unstable, yet one that is fraught with possibilities.

In chapter 3 I turned to Habermas's theory of language and communication. My aim here was to show how Habermas has extracted a normative theory from his analysis of language and discourse. Further, I showed how this analysis is deeply linked to his understanding of the normative content of modernity. Finally, I argued that the normative content that he associates with modernity is not as cut-and-dried as he sometimes holds it to be. This advances the theme that I have been developing concerning the relationship between modernity and enlightenment.

In developing the three central points that constitute my analysis of Habermas—the concept of enlightenment, the status of advanced capitalist societies, and the normative content that is basic to the modern condition—within the framework of the modern/postmodern debate, an interesting convergence begins to take shape that moves toward a theoretical conception of a politics of enlightenment appropriate to the aftermath of modernity. It is, I believe, necessary to understand these three strains in Habermas's thought as providing the framework for a theoretical conception of a politics of enlightenment. In order to reflect upon the possibilities concerning emancipation, participatory government, self-determination, and community formation, these three points must converge with one another. What Habermas has achieved, I would argue, is a social theory that has as its basic concern the question "What lies within the realm of possibilities for a politics of enlightenment?" In this chapter I will attempt to address this concern directly and somewhat more concretely. In order to do so I will return to the theory/practice problem that has always been central to critical social theory, as well as to Habermas's earliest work, which I believe suggests clearly what he could mean by a politics of enlightenment. Further, I will follow some of the recent literature that has concerned itself with the political aspects of Habermas's work—focusing on politically significant debates in which Habermas has participated. Finally, I will argue that while the terms of these debates are quite modern in nature, other issues concerning questions of emancipation, participation, and societal transformation are less amenable to Habermas's modernist politics of enlightenment. This will provide the groundwork for my reconceptualization of Habermas's theory of the lifeworld and discourse ethics in the concluding chapter.

CRITICAL THEORY AND THE PUBLIC SPHERE

The translation into English of Habermas's *The Structural Transformation of the Public Sphere* has revived interest among American critical theorists in the political use and abuse of the idea of a public sphere of political discourse (or, in my terms, a modernist politics of enlightenment) that developed in the early modern period. As Craig Calhoun points out: "Habermas task . . . is to develop a critique of the category of bourgeois society showing both (1) its internal tensions and the factors that led to its transformation and partial degeneration and (2) the element of truth and emancipatory potential that it contained despite its ideological misrepresentation and contradictions."[1] My concern here will be to discuss Habermas's analysis in terms of critical theory's focus on concrete political possibilities and to ultimately argue that this is unsuitable for a theory/practice model that is legitimately concerned with the conditions of the aftermath of modernity.

The development of critical social theory has as one of its constitutive features a close relationship to contexts of political action. During the early, formative, days of the Frankfurt School, the concerns of socialist and communist party movements in Germany were a central issue of theoretical debate.[2] These concerns came to bear importantly on what might be called the manifesto of critical theory: Max Horkheimer's "Traditional and Critical Theory" (TCT). In this essay Horkheimer distinguishes between a type of theory that has dominated the modern scene and an alternative type that breaks from this mold.[3] "The traditional idea of theory is based on scientific activity as carried on within the division of labor at a particular stage in the latter's development. It corresponds to the activity of the scholar which takes place alongside all the other activities of a society but in no immediately clear connection with them" (TCT, 197). In contrast, critical theory focuses on "a definite individual in his real relation to other individuals and groups, in his conflict with a particular class, and finally, in the resultant web of relationships with the social totality and with nature" (TCT, 211). In other words, Horkheimer's distinction marks the difference between theories that tacitly prop up the status quo and those that call it radically into question.

It is not altogether clear, however, whether this formative feature of critical theory has had a lasting legacy. Due to perceived weaknesses in the German leftist parties, a coming to awareness of the logic of Soviet communism, and a profound experience of the totalizing effects of European fascism, the work of Horkheimer and Adorno, and to a certain extent Marcuse, began to move away from the theory-practice nexus that they inherited from Marxism.[4] While critical theory did not return to more traditional approaches, the shift in emphasis indicates a recognition that what it means to be critical is more ambiguously related to concrete political struggles than was previously suspected. Adorno, for example, denied the possibility of an identity relationship between theory and practice.[5] This is not to say that critical theory began to ignore altogether concrete political movements; Marcuse, for example was a major source of inspiration for the student movement in the '60s. Rather, the point is that this connection came to be problematized in such a way that theory seemed to take priority over practice.

Habermas's work developed under the influence of these important considerations. There is a sense in which he attempts to rethink the relationship between theory and practice: not by returning to the original

Frankfurt program, but rather by reconsidering the ideological constraints placed on science as well as the potential for change in advanced-capitalist societies.[6] Habermas frames the relationship between theory and practice as follows: "On the one hand, it (theory) investigates the constitutive historical complex of the constellation of self interests, to which the theory still belongs across and beyond its acts of insight. On the other hand, it studies the historical interconnections of action, in which theory, as action-oriented, can intervene" (*Theory and Practice* [TP], p. 2). His attempts to comply with this imperative involve "extended reflections on the nature of cognition, the structure of social inquiry, the normative basis of social interaction, and the political, economic, and sociocultural tendencies of the age" (TP, 4). Theory must be directly linked to the aspirations of social actors concerned with bringing about a world that will enable them to flourish as autonomous individuals within the spheres of a community that provides economic stability, cultural cohesiveness, and social solidarity. In other words, the theory/practice problematic is about the theorizing of a politics of enlightenment.

While critics of Habermas have argued that his work has slid back in the direction of what Horkheimer referred to as "traditional theory,"[7] there is a strong sense in which he has brought critical theory back down to earth. This is exemplified in his analyses of the student movement in the sixties, as well as more recent work on neoconservatism, the Historikerstreit, and the collapse of Eastern block communism. My concern here will focus on whether Habermas's work offers analytic, as well as practical, insights that illuminate the problems of contemporary political struggles. The focus of this analysis will be *The Structural Transformation of the Public Sphere*. I will concentrate on the way that public spheres are constituted and whether a politics of enlightenment should work within established public spheres or attempt to negate these spheres and constitute alternative forums. This is a particularly important concern when there is a pervasive "end of history" sentiment occluding much of what masquerades as public discourse. This, I will contend, is a symptom of the aftermath of modernity, and one that must be mitigated against in an enlightened social theory.

Critical theorists concerned with the theory/practice issue outlined above have been most interested in Habermas's work on the public sphere.[8] This interest makes perfect sense, as a concern with the possibilities for radical democratic social-political formation entails addressing the problem of how public discourse comes to be constituted. It is not entirely clear, however, whether Habermas's discussion of the public sphere should be the source of inspiration or the object of criticism in this context. His analysis has been characterized as valorizing the liberal conception of democracy without being attentive enough to its exclusive character.[9] While this is true, and will be discussed shortly, it is also the case that Habermas attempts to get at what is radical about liberalism and, in a sense, develop a normative perspective from which liberal ideals can be used against liberal realities. Clearly this was the issue at stake in chapter 3. I will, in this more concrete setting, take seriously Habermas's aim to pit liberalism against liberalism while at the same time pointing out some of the shortcomings of this approach.

While Habermas is, to a certain extent, ideologically allied with liberalism in *The Structural Transformation of the Public Sphere* (STP), his approach is clearly informed by Marxist social science. His concern is to provide a careful account of the economic factors that gave rise to the bourgeois public sphere. In doing so, Habermas focuses on the way in which the relative opening up of economic markets necessitated the opening up of forums of rational discourse that were in principle accessible to all members of society. Initially this impulse was prompted by the need for news that pertained to expanded market relations. It was also necessary to establish a vantage point from which attempts by the state to impinge upon economic activity could be criticized and effectively fended off. The objective was to develop forums within which critical discussion could unfold with the intent of exerting indirect influence over governmental policy. These forums became informally instituted in the French salons, the German table societies, and the English coffeehouses. Without explicitly affirming this development, Habermas clearly feels that the emergence of these democratic ideals more than compensates for their flawed character in reality.[10]

I want to highlight the point that Habermas extracts from the socioeconomic fundaments of liberal society a radical dimension that has had considerable impact on the arousal of a democratic consciousness in bourgeois society. While keeping in mind (to a certain extent) that gender, social status, and economic class could effectively exclude one from what was in principle a participatory arena, he illuminates empirically a dimension of early modern society that seems to have considerable normative importance. In other words, regardless of the actual exclusiveness of the bourgeois public sphere, "with the emergence of the diffuse public formed in the course of the commercialization of the cultural production, *a new social category arose*" (my emphasis). As such, Habermas's appeal to the egalitarian "spirit" that played a key role in the development of modern society has radical significance, in spite of its exclusive constraints.

Habermas's aim is to show how this democratic spirit, which flourished in the eighteenth century, could have issued in a new era of substantive democracy. It was a forum in which protest against government policy could be articulated, as well as a medium through which popular opinion could percolate up. It is important to note that the market economies of the seventeenth and eighteenth centuries were not really capitalistic in the strong sense. By the nineteenth century, however, full-scale capitalism, complete with heavy industry and mass production, began to dominate the urban landscape in most of Europe. This development, and the consequences that obtained for the markedly larger working classes, rendered explicit the contradictions of a universal sphere of discourse being dominated by a single economic class. Further, the economic trauma experienced by the working classes, which ultimately was neutralized through welfare state interventions, lead to a different conception of publicness—one that resonated with the mandates of post–laissez-faire capitalism.

In order to defuse the politically volatile implications of class conflict, the media through which public opinion is shaped and disseminated had to be radically altered. On this score Habermas's analysis is masterful. He demonstrates with precision a twofold dynamic that effectively annuls public debate. On the one hand, the bourgeois family is transformed from a private sphere for existential retreat to an essentialized domain that serves as a "conduit for social forces channeled into the conjugal family's inner space by way of a public sphere that the mass media have transmogrified into a sphere of cultural consumption. The despecialized province of interiority was hollowed out by the mass media; a pseudo-public sphere of a no longer literary public was patched together to create a sort of superficial zone of familiarity" (STP, 162). This, Habermas contends, leads to an ascetic aversion for both reading and political argumentation. In addition, the media form is itself transformed by the mandates of commodity exchange.

> Today the conversation itself is administered. Professional dialogues from the podium, panel discussions, and round table shows—the rational debate of private people becomes one of the production numbers of the stars in radio and television, a salable package ready for the box office; it assumes commodity form even at 'conferences' where anyone can 'participate.' Discussion, now a 'business,' becomes formalized; the presentation of positions and counter-positions is bound to certain prearranged rules of the game; consensus about the subject matter is made largely superfluous by that concerning form. (STP, 164)

As such, the free debate of the liberal public sphere is shifted into management complexes that serve to control critical appraisals of the system and to conform behavior to the imperatives of welfare state capitalism.

Taking these points into account, it is important to consider whether Habermas's interpretation of the bourgeois public sphere is acceptable. Should we, with Habermas, interpret it radically—taking it seriously as a normative feature of modern society, if not an empirical reality? Or should we view it as part and parcel of bourgeois ideology—a sphere that was from the outset simply exclusive and supportive of a repressive economic mode? These are essentially the questions that I addressed in chapter 3, only now from a more historically informed perspective. Once again, the primary issue is whether or not the normative developments that Habermas associates with modernity are separable from the economic developments that also factored prominently into the emergence of modern society. These questions are heightened by the direct relationship that Habermas identifies between economic freedom and the bourgeois public sphere. If we take the position that the radical interpretation is correct, the deterioration of this sphere can be viewed as a deviation from a *core value* of modern society: a value that under altered socioeconomic and political conditions could flourish. If we take the position that the bourgeois public sphere is always already in complicity with capitalism, what Habermas describes as deterioration, and implicitly deviation, is nothing less than the outcome of the fundamental logic of an inherently exclusive public sphere. As should be clear from chapter 3, I lean strongly toward the latter interpretation, and will attempt to show how this pertains to constituting public spheres in atmospheres hostile to opposition. At the same time I do not want to dismiss too quickly the normative importance of the former interpretation. If we are interested in formulating theories that illuminate the problem of constituting public debate, we need to take seriously the models that are at our disposal.

This interpretive debate has more than theoretical importance. While it is true that the public sphere is a social-theoretic concept, and its status as a concept doesn't have a great deal to do with contemporary political situations, it is also part of the worldview (web of ideas) that underpins most Western societies (this is precisely Habermas's point about the modern lifeworld). Evidence to this effect is presented in the constant appeal to public debate when controversial issues arise concerning governmental policies and action. What is important about these appeals is that their referent is the same idealized conception to which Habermas appeals. I will later discuss more directly the way that the rhetoric of public debate stifles real public debate. At present, however, I will focus on the question of interpretation as it pertains to the specific problem of constituting oppositional public spheres. If we can accept Habermas's interpretation, the following analysis can be developed: the public sphere in late capitalist societies has been thoroughly deformed—to the point that what it means to have public debate has all but evacuated the consciousness of the general populous or the average citizen.

What we have in place of public debate is media saturation, which is directly linked to the steering media that Habermas identifies with the system. What was once a vibrant living idea, albeit instantiated imperfectly, has been undermined by the imperatives that drive advanced capitalist societies: money and power. As such, the idea of public debate plays no role in the decision-making processes that shape institutionally based political practices.

This seems a plausible enough interpretation. Yet it strikes me as one that fails to take seriously the evolution and transformation of the *idea of public debate*, not as an empirical reality but as an *idea*—an element of a worldview—that is malleable enough to be put to ends that run completely counter to its original intent. Following the more skeptical interpretation, I will focus on the exclusive character of the public sphere rather than its principle of openness. Critics of Habermas's interpretation have pointed out that this idealization of the bourgeois public sphere is shot through with the empirical exclusions that were instrumental in establishing the political hegemony of a specific group of individuals. Nancy Fraser summarizes the work of these "revisionist historians" in her article "Rethinking the Public Sphere" (RPS).[11] She points out how the work of Joan Landes[12] illuminates the inherent gender biases that infiltrate the bourgeois ideal of public discourse that Habermas privileges. This analysis is supported and amplified in Geof Eley's "Nations, Publics, and Political Culture."[13] He shows how the ideal of public discourse was simply a devise for instituting a new elite. Rather than a model to which we should appeal for normative purposes, "it was the arena, the training ground, and eventually the power base of a stratum of bourgeois men who were coming to see themselves as a 'universal class' and preparing to assert their fitness to govern" (RPS, 60). Fraser summarizes the problem as follows:

> Now, there is a remarkable irony here, one that Habermas' account of the rise of the public sphere fails fully to appreciate. A discourse of publicity touting accessibility, rationality, and the suspension of status hierarchies is itself deployed as a strategy of distinction. Of course, in and of itself, this irony does not fatally compromise the discourse of publicity; that discourse can be, indeed has been, differently deployed in different circumstances and contexts. Nevertheless, it does suggest that the relationship between publicity and status is more complex than Habermas intimates, that declaring a deliberative arena to be a space where extant status distinctions are bracketed and neutralized is not sufficient to make it so. (RPS, 60)

With these observations in mind, I would suggest the following interpretation of the bourgeois ideal of publicity: Rather than fostering universal participation, the original idea of the public sphere served to forge a locus of power that could be used to conglomerate influence and protect economic interests.[14] The "talk" of publicness was simply a devise that facilitated the pursuit of these ends. If this be the case, it is reasonable to project that contemporary "talk" about public debate is used in a similar manner. What is interesting about this interpretation is that it indicates that the ideal of publicity that Habermas identifies as emerging in the seventeenth and eighteenth century actually plays an important role in contemporary discourse. While Habermas's normal/deviant model would suggest that most contemporary discussion departs from the bourgeois ideal, my interpretation suggests that this ideal continues to guide the conglomeration of influence and protection of economic interest. My point is that depending on how one reads the development of the idea of the public sphere, and the uses that it is put to, the role that it plays in current political struggles changes significantly. Rather than saying that the "ideal" has no bearing upon the real with respect to current political debates, I would suggest that this ideal still has currency and is used in manipulative ways that reflect its initial exclusive character.

With Habermas I want to argue that the ideal of publicness, which emerged, for whatever reasons, in conjunction with early modern society, should not be dismissed out of hand, as some of his critics seem to have done. Contra Habermas, however, I want to assert that rather than being in need of a normative revival, this malleable ideal needs to be reformed in such a way that it can be used to undermine hegemonic public spheres. I will return to this later in the present chapter. Before doing so, however, I will discuss some of Habermas's own attempts to participate in important debates. These debates, I believe, illustrate the sort of politics of enlightenment that his normative theory gives rise to. My questions will concern whether this sort of political action, if I can use those terms, really moves toward the goal of emancipation that needs to be basic to a critical social theory.

JÜRGEN HABERMAS: CRITIC IN THE PUBLIC SPHERE

The point that I have been leading up to in the first section of this chapter can be summarized as follows: For Habermas's work to be taken seriously as a project *within* critical theory, there has to be a practical dimension that is politically oriented, or, stated more strongly, politically motivated. If he is strictly interested in providing a foundation for a critical theory of society—as could be inferred from my discussion in chapter 3—then his own work is only a useful tool for critical theorists, not a critical theory itself. I think it is quite clear that Habermas has been, and probably remains, devoted to the idea of developing a critical theory that stands on its own. In order to do justice to this intent, however, it is necessary to interpret his recent work—such as the collection on discourse ethics—in light of the earlier work on the public sphere. This, at any rate, is the approach that I would contend his various projects dictate.

There has recently been several interesting monographs and collections of essays that support my position. I have already discussed Calhoun's collection on the public sphere. In addition to this a volume of Habermas's "political" writings, *The New Conservatism*, appeared in 1991. Finally, two books on Habermas, Robert C. Holub's *Jürgen Habermas: Critic in the Public Sphere*,[15] and Jane Braaten's *Habermas' Critical Theory of Society*, both deal at length with the politically significant dimensions of Habermas's writings. Holub's book in particular is relevant because he traces from early on in his (Habermas's) career what I would call Habermas's politics of enlightenment. He begins by laying out the relationship between Habermas's explicitly theoretical work—particularly the theory of communicative action—and the ideal of a distortion-free public sphere. Holub then shows how there has always been a practical side to these ideals that Habermas himself has exemplified in various debates that he has participated in, including the positivist debate, the Gadamer debate, debates with members of the New Left student movement, the debate with Niklas Luhmann, the debate over postmodernism, and finally the debate with revisionist German historians. I will take up the latter two of these debates presently—discussing each in terms of the strengths and weaknesses afforded by the approach that Habermas utilizes in tacitly propounding a politics of enlightenment. This will serve as preparation for my discussion of an important issue in progressive american politics that Habermas's approach—unmodified—has difficulty contending with.

The Historian's Debate

My primary concern with respect to the debates that Habermas has participated in will be the historians' debate. My emphasis on this particular debate is for two specific reasons: First, I think it shows Habermas—and what I am calling his politics of enlightenment—at his best; second, the case can be made that this debate involves a very interesting intersection between philosophy and politics that sheds light on the so-called postmodernism debate that I will discuss next. The texts that I will focus on in this discussion first appeared in English in the spring/summer 1988 volume of *New German Critique*. The two essays that will concern me here concentrate on the interpretation of Germany's Nazi past and the impact it should have on national identity. While the central aim of Habermas's analysis is to criticize the neoconservative political agenda that is in the backdrop of the historiographical method at issue, there is also a subtle connection made between the work of the historians in question and the philosophy of Martin Heidegger. Elsewhere Habermas has conducted careful investigations of the relationship between Heidegger's affiliation with the National Socialist movement and his philosophical work. His conclusion is that the connection is intrinsic, and that those he has influenced should be viewed with suspicion (hence the connection to postmodernism—particularly the philosophy of Jacques Derrida). That a school of historiography swayed by Heidegger aims at minimizing the significance of the worst aspect of Nazism—the Holocaust—seems to lend credence to this view. My aim here will be to provide an analysis of the relationship between Habermas's critique of revisionist historiography in Germany and his assessment of Heideggerian philosophy; the two exhibit striking similarities in both form and content. This will serve to illustrate the concerns that motivate Habermas's interventions into public debate as well as the relationship these debates have to his overall theoretical project. Once again, the objective is to determine whether it makes sense to claim that Habermas's theory contains within it a politics of enlightenment, and if so, to establish the basic principles and conditions by which it is grounded.

While I am interested in analyzing Habermas's work, not the Historikerstreit (Historian's debate) per se, a few words on the latter are needed to provide a context. According to John Torpey, the fundamental issue at stake in the debate surrounding the Historikerstreit is the way in which contemporary German national identity should be understood with respect to its past: "The Historikerstreit, which is in fact more political than historiographical, is principally concerned with the way in which the understanding of history shapes contemporary popular discourse" (Torpey 1988, "Habermas and the Historians," 6—hereafter HH). As should be clear from this passage, there is a specific political agenda attached to the sought after self-understanding—that of the German neoconservative movement. The central figures in the Historikerstreit don't attempt to deny the Holocaust;[16] rather, they seek to cast doubt on the responsibility that Germany, as a nation, should bear for this aspect of its past. Three basic strategies are employed: (1) questions are raised concerning the degree of atrocity; (2) efforts are made to reduce or neutralize the relative significance of specifically German atrocities; and (3) aspects of the German role in World War II that are more easily interpreted positively are highlighted (e.g., the stand on the Eastern front, which is presented as action against "communism"—the typical neoconservative bogeyman). The net result, according to critics such as Habermas, is that the negative standard against which constitutional Germany must continually measure itself is effectively weakened. This in turn serves the interests of the German right wing.

In his contributions to the Historikerstreit, Habermas suggests that the aim of the revisionists is to provide a historical backdrop for the admission of Germany into NATO. This takes the form of an abstract subsumption of the past with the intent of establishing an unambiguous national identity. In order to achieve such an objective, several questionable moves have to take place. Habermas notes the following:

> To start with, the memory of recent periods of history which is a predominately negative one and which inhibits identification has to be bulldozed clear; then, under the sign of freedom or totalitarianism, the always virulent fear of Bolshevism must be used to keep alive the correct image of the enemy. (Habermas 1988a, "A Kind of Settling of Damages," 27—hereafter KSD)

As a scholarly exercise, historiographical practices of this sort would be dubious enough. What concerns Habermas more, however, is the way that these positions have been publicly disseminated:

> Whoever has read Ernst Nolte's level-headed contribution in the last issue of *Die Zeit* and has not been following the emotional discussion in the *Frankfurter Allgemeine Zeitung* must have the impression that the argument we are involved in is about historical detail. In fact, it is concerned with a political conversion of the revisionism which has emerged in modern historiography and which has been impatiently demanded by politicians of the "Wende" government. . . . In the center of his deliberations stands the question: in which public consciousness? The increasing distance in time, he asserts, makes a "historicization" necessary—one way or another. (Habermas 1988b, "Concerning the Public Use of History," 40—hereafter CPH).

In light of these observations, Habermas's objection to the revisionists are directed at three aspects of their work: (1) their attempt to minimize specifically Nazi war crimes; (2) their attempt to solicit an uncritical appropriation of the German past; and (3) their efforts to articulate the first and second to a political agenda premised on national identity.

The first of these, the attempt to relativize Nazi atrocities, is accomplished by adopting an intimate hermeneutic perspective. Rather than assessing the events of World War II in retrospect, the revisionist assumes the position of participant. By doing so, the historian "wishes to put himself in the position of the fighters of the period who are not yet framed and devalued by our retrospective knowledge"—"the point of view of the courageous soldier, of the desperate civilian population and also of the 'tried and tested' leading Nazi functionaries" (KSD, 30).

This generates empathy for those who participated in activities that subsequently have been condemned as criminal. In an effort to reduce the significance of Nazi atrocities, and the impact that they have on German national identity, this period in general, and the specific crimes associated with it, has to be relativized. Nazism cannot be allowed to stand out as uniquely abominable. "Its significance has to be leveled out" (CPH, 46). Habermas's theoretical objection to this procedure notes that a hermeneutic of empathy is impossible; we always view the past in light of the present (KSD, 30). His more concrete objection will be discussed below.

Habermas's second major concern is the attempt by the revisionists to encourage the German people to uncritically appropriate their past. This is aimed at establishing a renewed sense of national identity—one free of guilt. Habermas finds this both absurd and dangerous. Concerning the dangers, he points out that there is a strong link between tradition and identity. When tradition includes a period of institutionalized criminality, then this too has to factor into identity. Only under conditions of preserving the memory of the victims, and with that an awareness of the capacity for horrible actions, can identity formation relate legitimately to tradition in the Federal Republic. Without the glare of Auschwitz, there can be no critical appropriation of tradition; any relationship to the past will be a matter of blind faith (KSD, 43–46). It is at this point that the concrete objections to the more abstract matter of historiographical procedure become important. By leveling Nazi atrocities to just another form of human violence, revisionist historiography warps the relationship between tradition and identity. By encouraging the public to internalize this perspective, "the scurrilous philosophy" of "neoconservative modern historians" enters into the political arena.[17]

Habermas's third concern is with the politicizing of activity that should be restricted to the scientific reconstruction of the past. The political agenda is clear: anti-communism and pro-NATO. By reducing the status of Auschwitz to that of just another unfortunate incident (and one that most likely has been "exaggerated"), emphasizing the anticommunist strain in National Socialism, and disseminating this view of history publicly, the historian in the Federal Republic becomes an ideologue. As such, Habermas claims, "knowledge" is used as a form of political power (CPH, 47).

These are the three main objections that Habermas levels against the revisionist historians. A fourth, less explicit, but, as I will attempt to demonstrate, rather significant, is the connection drawn between this form of historiography and Heideggerian philosophy. I will now take up an analysis of that connection.

Habermas makes two specific references to Heidegger in the articles that I have been discussing. The first, in "A Kind of Settling of Damages," pertains to Nolte's "philosophical historiography." Habermas notes that Nolte is a "former student of Heidegger" and that his historiographical theory employs a "curious use of Heidegger's concept of 'transcendence'" (KSD, 34). This notion of ontological transcendence provides the philosophical foundation for the leveling effect that is central to the revisionist project. Under such a schema, fascism and Marxism become similar responses to the failure of modernity. Hence, the pragmatics of modern progress are cast aside and replaced with a Heideggerian notion of identity. "In this dimension of profundity in which all cats are grey, he then solicits understanding for the anti-modernist impulses which are directed against an 'unreserved affirmation of practical transcendence'" (KSD, 34–35). The second specific reference to Heidegger is found in "Concerning the Public Use of History." The concern here is not with Heidegger's influence on revisionist historiography, but rather with the effect of revisionism on the way that Heidegger can be read.

> As long as the appropriating eye of the late-born observer is directed towards the ambivalence which reveals themselves to him through the course of history without personal merit, it will be impossible to make even outstanding figures immune to the retroactive power of corrupted historical reception. After 1945, we read Carl Schmitt, Heidegger, Hans Freyer, and even Ernst Juenger in a different way than before 1933. (CPH, 46)

At the same time, however, there is an implicit concern with the way that a Heideggerian notion of tradition gives rise to an historiological, rather than historical, reading of figures from the Nazi era.

Several less explicit references to Heidegger are made in the two articles. Habermas notes that the revisionists appeal to the centrality of Germany, both geographically and otherwise, with respect to Europe in general; he labels the revisionists antimodernists; and he identifies an element of nostalgia in their politics. More significant, however, is the similarity between Habermas's evaluation of revisionist historiography and his reading of Heidegger. I will argue below that the former is premised on the latter.

The same leveling tendency that Habermas detects in revisionist historiography is the point from which his critique of Heidegger in *The Philosophical Discourse of Modernity* departs. He notes that Heidegger's postwar philosophy is rooted in an ontological presupposition: that Being is the active "agent" in history. The movement of Being is reflected in the various metaphysical presentations of Western thought. This movement comes to its critical culmination in the totalitarianism of the twentieth century—a function of subjectively grounded modern metaphysics. As such, reason, which for Heidegger is indelibly bound up in subjectivity, must be condemned as a form of thinking that is inattentive to the call of Being. Habermas is concerned with the way that this assessment reduces all modern cognition to what he would prefer to call "strategic rationality."

> Heidegger hardly pays any attention to the difference between reason and understanding, out of which Hegel still wanted to develop the dialectic of enlightenment. He can no longer gleam from self-consciousness any reconciling dimension in addition to its authoritarian aspect. It is Heidegger himself—and not the narrow-minded Enlightenment—that levels reason to the understanding. (PDM, 133)

Hence, no distinction is made between good and bad rationality. Yet, Habermas claims, Heidegger remains indebted to an obscure normativity that depends on some form of post-metaphysical reason (PDM, 131–34).

The task of the post-metaphysical thinker is to return to the pre-metaphysical thought of antiquity in search for that which was concealed by metaphysical bracketing. This involves Being in its withdrawal: a feature of Being that is utterly ignored in modern philosophy. According to Habermas, Heidegger's ontological blinders prevent him from connecting his critique of metaphysics with the reality of everyday existence. This follows from his wholesale rejection of modernity, including modern science. As such, any insights from the social sciences that might supplement his historiographical critique are swept aside. "To make this claim of necessity, of a special knowledge, that is, of a privileged access to truth plausible, even if only superficially, Heidegger has to level the differentiated developments of the sciences and philosophy after Hegel in bewildering fashion" (PDM, 136).

This clearly indicates that Habermas's concern with leveling in revisionist historiography is likewise a point of contention with Heideggerian philosophy. More recently Habermas has argued that this leveling tendency in Heidegger's later writings serves as a mechanism for distancing himself from his Nazi past. Had Heidegger seen fit to comment on the crimes of Auschwitz, it is claimed, he would most likely have reduced these events to a particularly unfortunate revealing of Being in its final metaphysical hours. This in fact is how he dealt with Nazism in general. The operation that enables the revisionist historians to characterize the Holocaust as one among numerous manifestations of the current "will to power" is already well developed in the philosophy of Heidegger. "That is how it was in 1945, and that is how Heidegger always repeated it: abstraction by essentialization. Under the leveling gaze of the philosopher of Being even the extermination of the Jews seems merely an event equivalent to many others. Annihilation of Jews, expulsion of Germans—they amount to the same thing" (Habermas, "Work and Weltanschauung," 453—hereafter WW).[18]

Habermas's evaluation of Heidegger's appropriation of tradition is also a central feature of the critique sustained in *The Philosophical Discourse of Modernity*. While it is not as obviously linked to his assessment of the neoconservative traditionalism of the revisionists, a connection can definitely be made. In recalling Habermas's concerns in this context, two general points are worth noting: (1) that neoconservatism uncritically embraces tradition in its entirety; and (2) in doing so a uniform tradition is created by selectively editing that which doesn't fall neatly into the conceptual framework and political agenda that is at stake. In his reading of Heidegger, Habermas identifies these moves in reverse form: the metaphysical tradition is rejected in wholesale fashion; and in doing so, key elements that enable this move are covertly retained. This aspect of his thought became dominant at about the same time that fascism broke out in Germany. Habermas claims that during the early days of the Nazi period, Heidegger began to mix philosophy and ideology (WW, 439). The section of *Being and Time* that gives rise to this is number 6 in the introduction: "The Task of Destroying the History of Ontology."

In *Being and Time* Heidegger ran up against a dilemma. In his effort to break with philosophical subjectivity, Habermas claims, Heidegger merely stood Husserlian phenomenology on its head. As such, he is saddled with an egocentric concept of the world that ignores the networks of intersubjectivity that are fundamental to being-with-others. In order to preserve the radical voluntarism that, according to Habermas, lies at the heart of *Being and Time*, Heidegger needs the very transcendental ego that the philosophy of Dasein aimed at overcoming. Habermas argues that Heidegger recognized this dilemma and opted for an alternative notion of transcendence rather than a revised doctrine of being-in-the-world (constructed more intersubjectively). Hence, the "turn"—prompting a shift in the interpretation of destining from that of an active Dasein to a quietistic shepherd who, "hanging on in spite of fate yields to self-surrender to the destining of Being" (PDM, 149–52). This move finds its impetus in the destruction of the history of ontology. "According to the self-understanding of *Being and Time*, it belonged to the province of a phenomenological destruction of the history of ontology to loosen up rigid traditions and to awaken the contemporary awareness of problems to the buried experiences of ancients thought" (PDM, 153). As such, Heidegger's leveling of the history of metaphysics, and his renunciation of that tradition as a source pool from which appropriate responses to present conditions can draw, is rooted in this section of *Being and Time.*

The above characterizes Habermas's dispute with Heidegger concerning his rendering of a diffuse tradition in uniform fashion and judging it on the basis of sweeping generalizations. As was the case with the revisionist historians, doing so has an ideological function. It also requires some selective editing, which in Heidegger's case takes the form of covert appropriation rather than conspicuous denial. What he sneaks in from tradition, according to Habermas, is the philosophical subjectivity with which he attempts to break. Habermas notes this early on in his critique of Heidegger (PDM, 136) and attempts to substantiate it at a later point in the analysis (PDM, 151–52). As I noted above, Habermas contends that in his later works, Heidegger, in response to this dilemma, merely inverts "Ursprungphilosophie." Hence, the later writings are premised on the same subjectivism that stifled *Being and Time.*

At the heart of Habermas's assessment of revisionist historiography and his critique of Heideggerian philosophy is an implicit, but deeply felt, concern with nihilism (ungrounded or falsely grounded thought and action). Nowhere in his discussions of Heidegger does he explicitly accuse him or his thought of being nihilistic. Implicitly, however, this seems to be his concern (see WW, 448–56, and PDM, 155–60). By rejecting the modern tradition uniformly, while still relying on one of its most questionable features (subjectivity), Heidegger's thought is rendered inherently indeterminate. This sets the stage for the turns and denials that Habermas notes. As it is the ramifications of this for politics that are most disturbing, I will proceed to discuss the political agenda with which Habermas associates Heidegger, and implicitly the revisionist historians.

While the contrast between the political implications of Heidegger's thought and the work of the revisionist historians is notable (Heidegger's postwar politics was passive while the historians' is clearly active), it is the similarities that are most striking. In both cases, the fundamental problem is that of the meaning of the constitution of history. "The more real history disappeared behind Heideggerian 'historicity' the easier it was for Heidegger to adopt a naive, yet pretentious, appeal to 'diagnosis of the present' taken up ad hoc" (WW, 434). Habermas's criticisms are not aimed at Heidegger's Nazi alliances. Rather, he condemns Heidegger for his failure to make amends for this obviously mistaken association (WW, 435–36; PDM, 155–56). Further, Habermas claims, his reasons for not doing so are justified by an appeal to his own philosophical position. The development of that position is characterized in terms of three key moves. First, Heidegger the philosopher wrote the monumental *Being and Time.* This work, removed from the context of subsequent historical events, could have had a wide range of philosophical impacts. Second, Heidegger the philosopher/Nazi propagandist interpreted the main features of *Being and Time* such that they were compatible with National Socialism. This is most evident in *An Introduction to Metaphysics*. Finally, insofar as Heidegger had committed himself both politically and philosophically to National Socialism, he needed an escape that didn't threaten the integrity of his thought. This was the political factor that prompted the turn. Rather than address the issue of responsibility directly, Heidegger hid behind ontological generalizations. This preserved his significance as a philosopher and sidestepped the question of political accountability. The nihilistic implications of this should be clear: when responsibility is dismissed through an appeal to an abstract notion of the history of Being, then anything will be permissible and nothing will be learned from past errors. Habermas's implicit claim is that this is precisely what is taking place with the activist Heideggerianism of the revisionist historians.

The Postmodernism Debate

Rather than draw any substantive conclusions from this particular aspect of my analysis, I would like to move directly into a brief discussion of the so-called postmodernism debate. I want to stress here, however, that there is a continuity between the seemingly concrete debate over national identity and the apparently abstract concern with postmodernism. The bridge between the two, as I have attempted to show, is Heidegger: both politically and philosophically. Habermas's concern, then, should be clear: modernity provides us with resources that protect against the deviations that can lead to fascism. This is true both practically and theoretically; and it is a strain that I have tried to show runs through Habermas entire literary corpus. If enlightenment is the source of continuity, which I believe it is, and, if the politics of fascism represents the alternative to a politics of enlightenment, then Habermas's engagement in debates, both philosophical and political, have to be understood as enlightenment-informed interventions. If this isn't true, then it seems impossible to count Habermas as the most eminent *critical theorist* of his generation.

As I have been indicating all along, the most important nexus in Habermas's more recent work is that between his defense of the Enlightenment and his rejection of postmodernism. It should be clear by now that these are closely related aims. The Enlightenment, for Habermas, represents three basic values: truth, freedom, and justice. As I noted in chapter 3, each is associated with a particular relationship between a speaker and the world domain that is thematized in specific types of speech acts. Truth has to do with our orientation to the objective world; freedom has to do with our orientation to the social or intersubjective world; and justice has to do with our orientation to the world of responsible individuals or the subjective world. It is Habermas's aim to show that any possibility for emancipatory action has to be rooted in these values. Habermas finds these values grounded in the modern lifeworld, and figured in a specifically modern fashion; were this not the case his theory would amount to an ahistorical defense of values that are, by necessity in his analysis, linked to the Enlightenment.

The crucial point here, in linking his defense of the Enlightenment with his rejection of postmodernism, is the rootedness of these values in distinctly modern forms of life. Claims that we have moved beyond modernity seem to dismiss this point in rather cavalier fashion. This amounts to a celebration of the impossibility of emancipatory action. Being party to this, Habermas would claim, involves engaging in a performative contradiction. Beyond this rather superficial postmodernism, which is prevalent enough, there is a more sophisticated theoretical development—neither modern nor postmodern in any conventional sense of the terms—that wants to engage in a rigorous analysis of the values that Habermas sees as thoroughly intertwined with modern forms of life, that is, truth, freedom, and justice. It is the latter type of postmodernism that seems to bother Habermas the most; and it is with these thinkers—spanning from Nietzsche to Derrida—that Habermas has his "debate."[19]

The question that Habermas never really gets around to asking is whether or not these "postmodernists"—the more sophisticated types—are really postmodernists at all. With respect to those that celebrate postmodernism—most notably Lyotard and Baudrillard—Habermas is for all intents and purposes silent. The most vivid example of this is *The Philosophical Discourse of Modernity*. Where, for instance, is the chapter on Lyotard? Habermas ignores him with the exception of the following remark in the preface: "Its theme (the project of modernity), disputed and multifaceted as it is, never lost hold on me. Its philosophical aspects have moved even more starkly into *public consciousness* in the wake of the reception of French neo-structuralism—as has the key term 'postmodernity' in connection with a publication by Jean-François Lyotard." Beyond this not an explicit word on the most activist of the French thinkers associated with postmodernism. It could be claimed that the entirety of *The Philosophical Discourse of Modernity* is aimed at the repercussions of the condition that Lyotard assesses. Insofar as Lyotard has, in a sense, written two books on Habermas (*The Postmodern Condition* and even more so *The Differend*—see my discussion in chapter 2) with only a few veiled references to the subject of his critique, it is possible that Habermas is playing a similar game. But while Habermas isn't entirely above this, he seems more genuinely concerned with the implications of what he might call the really dangerous postmodernists: the lineage that leads from Hegel, through Nietzsche, to Bataille and Foucault on the one hand, and, more importantly, to Heidegger and Derrida on the other.

Why, then, do these thinkers concern Habermas more than the straightforward postmodernists? This question is particularly important in light of the fact that none of them write about postmodernism, or identify with it. Here is where the problem of the Enlightenment comes back into play. It is Habermas's point, I believe, that the work of these theorists throws into question the validity of values such as truth, freedom, and justice, without taking seriously the implications of doing so or even being aware that this is what they are doing. So the fact that these philosophers don't write about the postmodern condition does not make them less postmodernists in Habermas's view. They are, in one sense, substantive evidence for the point being made by Lyotard and others.

Kant's rather stern essay (as discussed in chapter 1) on the question of enlightenment seems to serve as a point of departure in Habermas's analysis of the "postmodernists" in *The Philosophical Discourse of Modernity*. This is most evident in his polemic against Derrida. He begins by accusing Derrida of being a unrepentant or "orthodox" Heideggerian. As he states in the very first sentence of "Beyond a Temporalized Philosophy of Origins": "Insofar as Heidegger was received in postwar France as the author of the 'Letter on Humanism,' Derrida is correct in claiming for himself the role of an authentic disciple who has critically taken up the teaching of the master and productively advanced it." This remark situates Derrida in two precarious positions vis-à-vis Heidegger: first, he is an immature follower of the pied piper of Nazism; and second, he has mimicked this dimension of the Heidegger "scene," cultivating his own network of followers. The main difference being that Heidegger yearns for premodern simplicity while Derrida strives for postmodern complexity. Habermas frames this in specifically political terms: "Whereas Heidegger decks out his history-of-Being fatalism in the style of Schultze-Naumburg with its sentimental homely pictures of a preindustrial peasant counter world, Derrida moves about instead in the subversive world of the partisan struggle—he would even like to take the house of Being apart and, out in the open, 'to dance . . . the cruel feast of which the *Genealogy of Morals* speaks.'" This characterization (and even Habermas would probably admit that it is more caricature than characterization) renders Derrida susceptible to an anti-Enlightenment reading: one which is, of course, somewhat plausible. As

Kant put it: "Enlightenment is man's emergence from his self-imposed immaturity. Immaturity is the inability to use one's understanding without guidance from another. This immaturity is self-imposed when its cause lies not in lack of understanding, but in lack of resolve and courage to use it without guidance from another." Plugging Habermas's account of Heidegger and Derrida into this equation, we come up with Heidegger representing pre-Enlightenment authority and Derrida representing post-Enlightenment playfulness. What washes out, for Habermas, is a mature concern for those Enlightenment values that, when dispensed with in either direction, turns into atrocity.

If we forgive Habermas for not really taking seriously Heidegger's important contributions to contemporary thought, and for taking a considerable amount of interpretive license with Derrida, the questions that frame the relationship between postmodernism and enlightenment come into focus. Taking these caricatures of Heidegger and Derrida as signs operating within a rather tense economy of meaning (which is, ironically, what I perceive Habermas to be doing in *The Philosophical Discourse of Modernity)*, Heidegger's character represents traditional conservatism while Derrida's represents young conservatism. Neither, as emblem, has the *maturity* to realistically address questions about the need for emancipation or the value of democratization, much less something as hopelessly "metaphysical" as revolution. As such, the former will nostalgically yearn for a higher-order authority structure, while the latter will rip away at any type of structure through an academically sedated version of terrorism. What Habermas hopes to show is that there are a lot more signs circulating in this economy than the "conservatives" would have us believe, and that under certain conditions these emblems, or values, could possibly be brought into the forefront of human-being. This leads into the other side of the "debate," one that has been carried out by "Continental" philosophers in the United States and England for the most part. These "interlocutors" hold up Habermas as a sign for the sake of protecting against a fearful encounter. Habermas's sign value, which is set up to a certain extent by his own rhetorical stylizations, is that of a staunchly traditional rationalist who can't quite keep pace with the fast-moving French scene. This caricature requires a selective, and often blatantly wrong, reading of Habermas's work. As is the case with Habermas's reading of postmodernism, however, there are strategic gains to be made in doing so. By writing off Habermas (and I will admit that he invites this on a certain level), it becomes a whole lot easier to write off his concern with questions of value. It is always uncomfortable for someone who prefers to wax poetic about "the political" to have to address questions concerning action oriented toward political emancipation. By simply dismissing this as a "Habermasian" (read metaphysical) or modern or enlightenment question, it is easier to pass on into the real business of praising Heidegger or imitating Derrida.

At the risk of being redundant, I would like to spell out explicitly the connection between the question of enlightenment and the view that is presented by the postmodern side of this debate. Both of these problematics are linked to what Habermas has termed the completion of the project of modernity. Two basic approaches are taken when attempting to philosophically engage the question of enlightenment. The first, which tends to be done in the name of Habermas, and up to a point by Habermas, appeals to clear and distinct principles of the Enlightenment that can be construed more or less independently of actual deviations that have emerged in the course of their development. At the center of this analysis is both the ideal, and the concrete, public sphere as the site of a politics of enlightenment. This approach, which advocates *the* Enlightenment, tends to seek closure on the question of enlightenment by theorizing its completion. The other approach tends to assume that the Enlightenment has been thoroughly discredited and as such we no longer need to talk about the question of enlightenment at all. This tact likewise appeals to a closure of sorts: enlightenment is a problem that has already been attended to. As I noted, the former approach tends to operate under the banner of Habermas; the latter, however, operates within the mainstream of Continental philosophy but needs Habermas—as the objective enemy—just as much as the former. Both ignore that impulse in Habermas's work that asserts that we simply cannot relinquish the question of enlightenment (I believe Habermas ignores this himself at times). Kant has a strong riposte to all of this: "Laziness and cowardice are the reasons why so great a proportion of men, long after nature has released them from alien guidance (naturaliter maiorennes), nonetheless gladly remain in lifelong immaturity, and why it is so easy for others to establish themselves as their guardians. *It is so easy to be immature.*"

Such is the state of the debate between postmodernism and Habermas. It is somewhat odd that schools of thought that are known for their intensive self-reflexive critiques (critical theory), and their rigorous denial of the possibility for final closure (deconstruction or, more generally, postmodernism) are so quick to sign, seal, and deliver the question of enlightenment. This in itself raises questions about the normative status of the public sphere from the perspective of both camps. I would like now to conclude this section with some general comments about the relationship between enlightenment and the public sphere with respect to these two key debates. This will serve the purpose of moving in the direction of a reformulated notion of the public sphere.

In this summation I want to stress the importance of context. I began my discussion of the politics of enlightenment in chapter 1 by placing at the heart of the problem Horkheimer and Adorno's *Dialectic of Enlightenment*. This text, I argued, is so important because of its thematization of the problem of enlightenment in terms of the rise of fascism in Europe. I argued further that this text, and its focus on fascism, offers an interesting interpretive perspective from which the development of Habermas's social theory can be engaged. This is most obvious in his theory of language and communication, which is at the core of his theory of society. Taking this interpretive perspective, once again, as our point of departure, a number of interesting theoretical and political moments begin to converge.

In analyzing the objective of the historians' debate, it seems clear that Habermas is concerned with recidivism. A neoconservative political climate obtained in Germany at that time that wished to formulate a post-Nazi nationalism that by necessity had to normalize the period of atrocities so as to factor them unproblematically into a renewed conception of national identity. Habermas intervenes against this by pointing out how the historiographical procedures are politically motivated. He in turn casts his objections in political terms: anti-neoconservative and pro-enlightenment. The point of engagement, or location of the debate, serves to enforce this claim. It was conducted within a literary public sphere that enabled the thematization of issues that resided at the heart of Germany's collective self-understanding.[20] A similar claim can be made about the other important debates that Habermas has participated in: the positivism debate, the Gadamer debate, the debate with Luhmann, and the debate over the student movement. Each was situated within a context that enabled either face to face communication—à la the coffeehouses or salons—or some form of literary exchange. Likewise, in each of these earlier debates we observe conditions governed by something like the enlightened discourse that is central to Habermas's normative theory.

The Historikerstreit, however, is somewhat more complex than the earlier debates. It is more infiltrated with power relations than are the others and tends to contain the potential for greater degrees of distorted communication. Habermas seems aware of this and notes himself how the debate more or less dwindled into a series of polemics.[21] His challenge here is that the historians whom he contested did not take up the substantive claims that he was presenting and that they resorted to politically motivated polemicizing. In my discussion of his role in the debate I argued that Habermas himself had a political axe to grind that lead him to link this specific sphere of discourse to another (the "debate" over postmodernism) via his frequent adversary Heidegger. This move, I would argue, brings his enlightened conception of proper political procedures down to a level that forces him to accept certain terms of debate that run contrary to his own normative statutes. In short, Habermas himself indulges in polemic and questionable associations (revisionism equals Heideggerianism equals fascism), which is part and parcel of attempting an enlightened form of discourse in unenlightened discursive arenas.

This is perpetuated by the association that he makes between revisionism and postmodernism. As I noted above, Habermas's discussions of the key figures that he attacks in *The Philosophical Discourse of Modernity* are sometimes little more than crude caricatures of complex thinkers—regardless of the political implications of, and motivations behind, their thought. Habermas feels compelled—I would argue politically compelled—to paint his "interlocutors" in the most reductionist fashion possible. As I also noted above, there are good reasons for developing the line of argument that he pursues in *The Philosophical Discourse of Modernity*. These are not, however, legitimate excuses for setting up a discursive forum that sets up straw opponents simply for the sake of blowing them over. This is a politics of enlightenment that defies its own leading principles: one that we might even say involves a performative contradiction.

This dilemma—which results in using enlightenment politics in unenlightened spheres, leading to doubly distorted communication—illustrates both the need for a rejuvenated politics of enlightenment and for a deep concern with the problem of the aftermath of modernity. Bill Martin refers to this condition as the impasse of postmodernity.[22] While I take issue with the designation of the present as postmodernity, this is primarily a question of terminology. Martin accounts for this impasse in terms of a flattening out of consciousness, or loss of the capacity for generating meaning. This condition is bound up in the very sorts of things that I have been associating with the aftermath of modernity: media saturation, metaconsumption, crises in identity, and a general feeling of malaise. Another way of putting this might be that the aftermath of modernity represents a profound sort of illiteracy. I don't mean this in the sense that less people are able to read and write. Rather, my point is that the critical acuity that is necessary for public discourse has somehow been transformed beyond the point at which it can be salvaged by a regenerated version of the traditional politics of enlightenment. This is a structural as well as a normative question. The normative side of the coin has been dealt with in chapter 3. I will now turn to the structural side, which I introduced in chapter 2, with a case study in failed enlightenment politics. The interpretive context for this is Habermas's recession into the polemicizing that he so adamantly opposes in "postmodernists."

A CASE STUDY IN POST-ENLIGHTENMENT PUBLIC SPHERES: THE ANTIWAR MOVEMENT OF 1991

In August 1991, the government of Iraq invaded its neighboring country Kuwait for the purpose of gaining both economic and military hegemony in the Persian Gulf. For various reasons—primarily, I would argue, to establish its military power in the Gulf region—the United States government swiftly moved large numbers of troops and armaments into the arena. This prompted an immediate response among political progressives in the United States that converged into an antiwar movement. In spite of the efforts of the antiwar movement, however, a very destructive war came about that temporarily elevated the United States to the status of international "protection" force. A primary objective of the movement had been to bring into forums of public debate issues that are crucial to the determination of what the war was about and whether the American people should have supported it. Unfortunately, access to existing forums, such as the mass media, was all but impossible to obtain and the constitution of alternative forums was met with systematic opposition. In effect, the antiwar movement confronted a carefully constructed and controlled public sphere, and was unable to gain an adequate hearing, either within the existing sphere or through the construction of alternative spheres. As such, the movement, in spite of being large and well organized, failed to have an appreciable impact on any of the policy decisions related to the war: decisions to send troops, to increase troop strength, to start the war, and to go to a ground war.

This is not to say that the movement went altogether unnoticed. On the one hand, the movement was unable to break into the public sphere constructed and engineered by the government in support of the war; nor was it able to construct an effective alternative public. On the other hand, the movement represented a potential to bring radically into question the status quo, a potential that conditioned the nexus in which all the decisions relating to the war were made. My analysis here will focus on the role played by the media or what might be referred to as the contemporary version of a literary public.

It is helpful to begin an analysis of the role played by the media in the Gulf War through a consideration of the media's role during the Vietnam era and the changes that have taken place in the intervening years. A commonly held view of the antiwar movement of the Vietnam era claims that the war was lost by the media. However, analyses of the antiwar movement of the Vietnam era must first consider that the popular recollections of the movement today are mediated by the same forces whose effects need to be analyzed, that is, the media influenced and controlled by governmental and economic interests (money and power in Habermas's analysis). In other words, the standard view of the protest movements of the Vietnam era itself needs to be called into question. While the popular recollection of this era has the media playing a role fiercely critical of government policy, a closer look reveals that it took the media a considerable amount of time to achieve this position of independence. It was not until after the January 1968 Tet offensive, many years into the war, that they began to present something other than the official version of the war's progress and, in order to back their side of the story, bring into the living room pictures and stories relating the full extent of the war and its destruction. When senior correspondents, and even anchors, found themselves reporting, from bunkers under siege in the middle of the Tet offensive, that American victory was close at hand, the media was confronted with the enormous distance between the official version and reality. The media faced a decision: to continue reporting the official version of the war and risk losing all credibility, or to adopt a critical stance. This was prompted by a critical attitude that was already relatively widespread among the American public: an attitude bolstered by the peace movement's reasoned analyses of the conditions that obtained in Vietnam, a growing revulsion for the carnage of the war, reports from returning soldiers, and openings that occurred in the media. These factors, along with the general state of social unrest prompted largely by the civil rights movement, effectively forced the media to become critical.

While it would be a mistake to discount the positive effect of the media, once it turned critical, it is equally important to disregard claims that it is the media that subdued the war effort. The media was only responding to social pressures that would otherwise have resulted in its becoming marginalized. In effect, the media had no choice but to become critical. Given this analysis, the Gulf War antiwar movement was naive in its surprise at the enthusiastic coverage conducted by the mainstream media; there was relatively little pressure to behave otherwise. One of the lessons of Vietnam is that the media, when covering the government, is a docile creature until forced by the public to take a critical stand; the subsequent development of the media makes this all the more true today. In one sense I think we could say that the Vietnam era antiwar movement represented an expression of the classical politics of enlightenment. Operating against the grain of the structurally transformed public sphere, opposition movements that formed within the textures of a repoliticized civil society gained a certain amount of control over information media—the twentieth century's version of a literary public. Dramatic changes, however, have taken place in the media since then. These changes correspond, I would argue, to the increasing forces that have moved us in the direction of the aftermath of modernity.

During the years between Vietnam and the Gulf War, the various media, as businesses, did for the most part what other businesses did: they grew enormously. Through fiercely competitive times, a long series of mergers and acquisitions has resulted in fewer people owning a much larger share of the media.[23] It has become far more likely "that the American citizen who turns to any medium—newspapers, magazines, cassettes—will receive information . . . controlled by the same handful of corporations, whether it is daily news . . . or a text book."[24] Newspapers and radio and television stations are no longer, for the most part, individually owned and operated but rather part of a conglomerate. These larger units are more appreciative of the perspective of the forces of money and power because they themselves operate within the spheres of these steering mechanisms (or, using more telling terminology, "media"). In other words, the media's critical stance has been undermined to the extent that it has become more of an interested player in what it was previously criticizing; their ability to threaten the system was diffused by pulling them into the system. I don't want to present this as some sort of conspiracy theory as it is strikingly nonconspiratorial. Rather, the shifts that I am noting seem to be on a continuum with the structural transformation of the public sphere, albeit in more contemporary forms.

The growth of the media was facilitated by governmental deregulation, the same factor acting in other sectors of the economy. But in addition to the changes in investment laws that permitted any large accumulation of wealth to grow all the more rapidly, the media were the beneficiaries of changes in a different body of laws—laws that had previously regulated who could own how much of the media. These laws had taken seriously the intentions of the Communication Act of 1934, which had declared the media a public good to be watched over by government regulators.[25] Such laws have since been considerably weakened.

Finally, beyond the economic and legal changes that brought about a fundamentally different point of view on the part of the media, there has been one very specific development relating to the ability of the media to cover a particular type of story: the advent of pool reporting to cover actions of the U.S. military. Pool reporting was the arrangement put forth by the Pentagon after the press protested being left out of the Grenada invasion. Field tested during the invasion of Panama, by the time the war in the Gulf was launched the restrictions placed upon the press had been highly refined.[26] Sydney Schanberg sums up the restrictions as follows:

> The only way a reporter can visit a front-line unit is by qualifying for the "pool" system. . . . Only a fraction of the reporters, mostly from the largest news organizations, can qualify. . . . The rest are permitted

> to forage on their own but the rules . . . warn that if they make the attempt (to go to the forward areas) they will be "excluded"—taken into custody and shipped back. By February 12, as this article went to press, at least two dozen journalists had been detained.[27]

Once assembled in a pool, typically six reporters and a camera operator, reporters could go only where the military escorts (Schanberg calls them "baby sitters") took them, and interview only those people chosen by the escorts while the escorts listened in. And then, the finished story had to be presented to military authorities where it was held, sometimes for days, for final "editing" before its transmission to the United States.

The restrictions governing where reporters can be and to whom they can speak amount to prior restraint; the requirement to submit all stories to military authorities for editing amounts to censorship. Why didn't the media react more strenuously than they did against these infringements on the First Amendment? One can only imagine how quickly these regulations would have disappeared in the following scenario. A relatively small number of players (e.g., the three major networks, the *New York Times*, *Washington Post*, and *L.A. Times*) simply announce, on the first day of the war, that they will use no pooled sources and, instead, will leave large sections of their papers and programs blank or, better, fill them with stories about the requirements of the pool system—presented in a critical fashion. There in fact was a lawsuit filed against the government's pool service by eleven small alternative news organizations and five writers charging infringement of the First Amendment. In spite of their knowledge of this suit, none of the major networks either joined it or lent it their support.[28] This further illustrates the extent to which the public sphere was occluded by systematic imperatives that convened against critical perspectives on the war. When conventional "Enlightenment" type oppositions were undertaken—such as appealing to rights or attempting to open up dialogue—these were thwarted by powerful political and economic structures that denied them access to potentially critical spheres of discourse. This, I would contend, represents a further structural shift from the already transformed, but nonetheless latent, bourgeois public sphere that Habermas discusses and that still might have been somewhat intact during the Vietnam era. Further economic and political conglomeration, combined with technological and psychical shifts, rendered the classic politics of enlightenment employed by the antiwar movement more or less ineffective.

THE FUTURE OF THE PUBLIC SPHERE?

I would now like to tie together some of the strains of thought that run through this chapter. I began by discussing Habermas's analysis of the bourgeois public sphere, which I argued serves as his model for a politics of enlightenment. This, I suggested, is a double-edged sword: on the one hand, we can't really get along, either theoretically or politically, without the ideal of publicity that he holds in such high regard; on the other, these ideals were used strategically from the outset and continue to be used as such in contemporary contexts. I further discussed Habermas's own application of his version of the politics of enlightenment around two key issues that illustrate both the strengths and weaknesses of this approach. My conclusion in this context was that as we move further into the aftermath of modernity, the classical politics of enlightenment becomes less effective and more compromised. In the next section I showed further how very recent changes in the "literary public" have rendered the classical politics of enlightenment rather ineffective. I selected what I consider to be a watershed political event, where progressive opposition was systematically shunted away from the mainstream, as a case study. As has been the case, to greater or lesser degrees, throughout the history of the bourgeois public sphere, who was able to "speak" was largely determined by positional status, economic power, and media access.

Habermas's analysis of the rise and fall of the early modern public sphere showed quite nicely what happens when the revolutionary class becomes the hegemonic class; the sphere of publicity that they have created becomes an arena that they dominate. As I have attempted to show, this was precisely the case with the Gulf War. My position has been that this is part of the logic of the early modern ideal of publicness: a logic that uses the rhetoric of publicness to constitute, even determine, actual public opinion. Yet this does not seem to be a totally coherent logic. There are gaps—such as those that Habermas's himself has exploited and those that occurred during the Vietnam War—that shed light on the possibility for uncontrollable or unmediatable publics to emerge. I will now suggest some ways that these gaps can be expanded in the aftermath of the Gulf War, and, more generally, in the aftermath of modernity.

The Gulf War was fought with the threat of "another Vietnam" influencing military strategy in very important ways. In this particular situation, the centers of power clearly had the upper hand. The system seemed to learn a great deal more from Vietnam than did the opposition. Even this formulation seems symptomatic of the problem. In the '60s, it was considerably easier to define the system and to constitute opposition. In the '90s, the system is both more diffuse and more consolidated: diffuse in the sense that it has branched out, into the world, in ways that are difficult to track quickly; consolidated in the sense that internal pressure has been all but annulled. Given these systematic changes, it is not at all surprising that today's version of '60s-style opposition was ineffective; it was neither very diffuse nor very consolidated. As such, this suggests that the system/opposition dichotomy is inappropriate to contemporary progressive politics. It assumes that both poles are operating in the same public sphere. This seems to be the assumption of theorists such as Habermas as well. As his later debates suggest, however, this assumption breaks down under the pressure of the distorted world that it finds itself in. If this is the case, then opposition must, in one sense, stay out of the official public domain. This would require that a politics of enlightenment be formulated that would extend outward into the margins of society. Now the question is, can this be accomplished through reformist measures, or is something more radical needed?

The reformist, Habermasian, approach would require a government truly representative of all the people, not just the constituencies of money and power, that would then maintain the public sphere. However, there is a chicken-and-egg problem here: to reform the government we need access to the public sphere. Hence, the need for a more radical approach, one that takes advantage of the gaps in the existing public sphere, aiming to reinvigorate the possibility of expanding it. Such an approach would employ a strategy of disruption in order to create enlightenment possibilities in the aftermath of modernity. It must be guided by the same ideals that direct the reformist approach but with a different understanding of the communicative possibilities afforded by the lifeworld and with a more flexible approach to normative structures. To theorize this would be to theorize a politics of enlightenment suited to the aftermath of modernity. In the final chapter of this work, I will attempt to initiate such a theory, focusing on a version of discourse ethics that supports a radically egalitarian theory of communicative action.

CHAPTER 5

Ethical Discourse and Radical Egalitarianism: Toward a Textualization of the Lifeworld

During the past twenty years a number of important rifts have developed within Continental philosophy that can be loosely situated within the general debate between modernism and postmodernism. I have spent a good deal of time in this book discussing these rifts. My claim throughout has been that there is potential for more fruitful intersections between thinkers such as Derrida and Habermas than has taken place. In this final chapter I will attempt to demonstrate this within the thematic boundaries of the politics of enlightenment. I will begin with a discussion of the ethical theories of Habermas and Emmanuel Levinas. The purpose in doing so is to develop the ethical content that is necessary for a politics of enlightenment. Habermas clearly sees the need for this, but his discourse ethics are overly influenced by the modernist tradition. I will use Levinas's theory of alterity to flesh out some of the implications of discourse ethics that are suited to the aftermath of modernity. From these I will turn to lifeworld theory, which serves as the basis for a politics of enlightenment. I will argue that Derrida's notion of textuality is useful for developing the more radical implications of Habermas's lifeworld theory. Finally, I will conclude with a general discussion of the relationship between politics and ethics in the aftermath of modernity.

COMMUNICATIVE ETHICS IN THE FACE OF ALTERITY

Habermas has expounded at great length on the relationship between discourse and the establishment of ethical norms. It is his contention that the inherent telos of ethical discourse is to establish norms of action that attain universal status. The deep ground of this theory is located in what I would describe as a linguistified or textualized theory of the lifeworld: a theory that in my estimation does not complement the formalistic aspirations of his communicative ethics. It does, however, establish a framework within which the question of alterity can be problematized.

Levinas, on the other hand, develops a relational view of ethical conduct that is located in the ineradicable difference between "I" and "another." The ethical relation is one in which the other is passively granted his/her alterity. The language of this relationship is presystematic, prerational, and operates solely on the basis of response-ability. I am in an ethical relation when I respond to the other qua his/her alterity.

These are radically different ethical notions. The former starts with the assumption that alterity can be subsumed in forums of discourse—producing consensus-based ethical standards. The latter denies that subsumption of this sort can be characterized as ethical in any sense. While in general I am more sympathetic to Habermas's agenda, the prospect of factoring radical alterity into a communicative theory of ethics is intriguing. I will attempt here to use Levinas and Habermas in conjunction with one another in order to begin formulating some of the tenets of a postconventional discourse ethics. My aim is to thematize this project in terms of the relationship between alterity and authority, and legitimacy and authority. The goal will be to sketch consensual legitimacy and incommensurability into an ethical network that is radically postconventional. Or, in the terms I have been developing, a notion of discourse ethics that is suited to the aftermath of modernity.

The place of ethics and the place of language in Habermas's social theory can be situated in terms of the two key essays discussed in chapter 3: "On Systematically Distorted Communication" and "Towards a Theory of Communicative Competence." I will briefly review these essays in order to provide a context for the ensuing discussion. Habermas's objective is to show how irregular communicative patterns can develop into dangerous norms of conduct. The problem lurking in the background of these essays (one dealt with more explicitly by Adorno and Horkheimer) is that of manipulative propaganda. Habermas's aim is to show how language can be abusively employed in discourse such that unethical standards of action follow.

The key development in "On Systematically Distorted Communication," is the connection that is drawn between modes of discourse, the language of discourse, and norms of action (which are in fact ethical norms). It is Habmermas' objective to demonstrate that the language of discourse is not only commensurate with, but naturally suited for, establishing ethical norms. Further, insofar as the mode of discourse is determined to be the source of communication distortions that translate into normative distortions, it is necessary to develop a theory of discourse that enables language to operate in accordance with its "design."[1] As we saw in chapter 3, Habermas begins this work in "Towards a Theory of Communicative Competence," where he draws together key elements of generative linguistics (Chomsky) and speech-act theory (Austin). In doing so he is able to develop a theory that incorporates both the contingency of particular speech situations and the universality of structural grammatics. Hence we have the theory of universal pragmatics. The theory of communicative competence, and as such, the theory of ethical normativity, must be premised on a theory of universal pragmatics. This will reveal that linguistic utterances are rooted in intersubjective a priori semantic structures that are, in a sense, linguistically determined. As such, the foundation of communicative ethics is the hypothetical ideal speech situation.

Habermas realizes that the ideal speech situation—a forum of discourse that provides for pure intersubjectivity—cannot be established. Nevertheless, the analysis of communicative competence does indicate the presence of ideal structures in the rational deployment of speech acts. The model of ideal speech establishes a standard against which asymmetries that distort communication can be measured. With this addition to the theory of systematically distorted communication, Habermas provides a tool for rehabilitating communicative abnormalities.[2]

The formal work in the essays that I have discussed is put to normative work in *Legitimation Crisis* and *The Theory of Communicative Action*. Habermas's aim is to develop a theory of action in terms of the semantic structures of language and an ideal speech situation. If universal validity is built into the structures of language, and can be realized in certain discursive situations, then normative claims concerned with truth, freedom, and justice can be universalized. Habermas takes it upon himself to argue for this in volume 1 of *The Theory of Communicative Action*. His primary concern is to formulate a theory of action synchronization that hinges on clear, unrestrained communication. This requires the development of a schema for distinguishing between strategic and communicative action. Rather than depending on an analysis of psychological states, this schema relies on knowledge of the structural foundations of "reaching understanding."[3] Reaching understanding involves a rational process of argumentation that culminates in consensus among interlocutors. Habermas stresses that this process must be free of coercion; understanding has to be arrived at through free and open discussion. For him this is "the inherent telos of human speech."[4] In order for action coordination to be communicatively orchestrated two conditions have to be met: first, there must be a speech act uttered by a speaker; and, second, that speech act must be received and affirmed by a hearer. This roots the speech act in a relationship between rational agents who assume the truth of the propositional content of the utterance, the authenticity of the speakers' intentions, and an obligation on the part of the receiver to respond with the appropriate action. Insofar as semantic content is a function of the *process* of understanding—the utterances meaning is partially determined in the discursive arena—the speech act is now formulated in such a way that it can coordinate domination-free action. In chapter 3 I pursued this by investigating precisely what Habermas means by a validity claim and what criteria determine whether that claim should be accepted or rejected. In the present context, however, it suffices to note that the overarching concern is with categorizing various types of social action such that whether or not those actions are legitimate can be determined.[5]

It is on this theoretical platform that Habermas develops the more specific tenets of discourse ethics.[6] This project bears certain resemblances to Kantian ethics and social contract theory in that ethical determinations are internally formulated and subject to validation by a group of participants who will be affected by those determinations. It breaks with both of these traditions, however, in that the moral subject is not presupposed; she or he is always conceived relative to a linguistic community. Seyla Benhabib sums this up as follows: "Instead of asking what an individual moral agent could or would will, without self-contradiction, to be a universal norm, one asks: What norms or institutions would the members of an ideal or real communication community agree to as representing their common interests after engaging in a special kind of argumentation or conversation?"[7] The participant in ethical discourse is embedded within the communicative framework provided by a common language. As such, the subject is both shaped by the common denominators established by a shared language and affirmed as an individual located in the networks of reciprocity that develop within ethical communities.[8] Habermas situates this in terms of the relationship between justice (autonomy) and solidarity. He contends that in order for the principles of autonomous morality to obtain, they must be undergirded with a cohesive sense of communal solidarity. Under such conditions the purposes of justice (moral autonomy) are to preserve inviolable respect for socialized individuals and to protect the structures of intersubjectivity that provide the foundation for solidarity." Justice concerns the equal freedom of unique and self-determining individuals, while solidarity concerns the welfare of consociates who are intimately linked in an intersubjectively shared form of life—and thus also to the maintenance of the integrity of this form of life itself" (JS, 47). Benhabib calls this "the principle of egalitarian reciprocity" that necessarily attends "the principle of universal moral respect."[9] Discourse ethics presents a solution to the problem of preserving autonomy under conditions of communal solidarity by claiming that language is the source of both. As Habermas summarizes: "Thus, the procedure of discursive will formation takes account of the inner connection of the two aspects: the autonomy of unique individuals and their prior embeddedness in intersubjectively shared forms of life" (JS, 49).

While this discussion is a bit too compressed, it should provide the basis for a preliminary investigation into the relationship between Habermas's work and Levinas's reflections on the ethical relationship. The most obvious point of contact is the centrality of language for each; although as will soon be apparent, Habermas and Levinas have radically different views concerning language. Another point of contact is contact itself. Both Habermas and Levinas insist that the substance of ethics is to be found in a certain form of relationality, of contact with another. Further, both are at great pains to characterize this interaction as one that is by necessity free of domination. Finally, both place a great deal of weight upon conditions of response and responsibility. I will return to these common, although minimally so as stated, denominators in short order. At this point, however, it is necessary to move into some of Levinas's work in order to further establish basis for comparison.

Levinas and Language

My discussion of Levinas will attempt to do one of the things that Levinas seems to resist. That is, I will try to map his work onto the framework provided by Habermas. While this might not be entirely fair to Levinas, I think that it is a philosophically valuable project. If, as seems to be the case, Levinas's work is concerned with problems of domination, industrialization, and the use of systematization to coerce "beings," then it should be useful to read his work in the light of others with similar concerns.[10] I will begin by discussing Levinas's notion of the face-to-face relation. From there I will consider the connection between this relationship and ethics. Finally, I will situate this in terms of Levinas's view of language and the ethics of proximity.

Levinas states the following about the face-to-face relationship: "The face is present in its refusal to be contained. In this sense it cannot be comprehended, that is, encompassed. It is neither seen nor touched—for in visual or tactile sensation the identity of the I envelopes the alterity of the object, which becomes precisely a content."[11] This points toward the radical alterity in terms of which Levinas wants to think the ethical relationship. Insofar as the face cannot be "contained," "comprehended," or "encompassed," a conceptual relationship thematized in terms of a relational framework, is impossible. To frame alterity is at once to deny it. As such, circumscription, even within a community structured via networks of difference, denies the "absolute difference" that Levinas wants to bring into play (TI, 194–95).

On what grounds, then, can this be called a relationship at all? Levinas's curious response is that the relationship is linguistic. In fact, one might even say that radical alterity "establishes" a speech situation (although here situation must be purged of any conceptual connotations and be thought only in terms of proximity). "Speech proceeds from absolute difference." Language is the relational medium that enables contact with the other. But it is not language in the sense of common ground, means for communicating, or point of intervention. To intervene or establish common territory would be to conceptualize alterity, which is tantamount to enacting its violation. Language, for Levinas, is not a source of unity, but rather the impossibility of unification. "Language accomplishes a relation between terms that breaks up the unity of a genus." It is this interlocutionary relationship, prior to thematic unity, that annotates the ethical. "The formal structure of language thereby announces that ethical *inviolability* of the Other and without any odor of the 'numinous,' his 'holiness.'" In other words, the ethical relationship is one that is utterly independent of any active force. As such, ethics is situated in terms of domination-free speech (TI, 194–98).

This of course bears certain resemblances to Habermas's ideal speech situation. Further, I think that Levinas would want to say that, in some sense, this is an idealization.[12] Nevertheless, on the specific content of the ideal the two part company. For Habermas the ideal is domination-free intersubjectivity. For Levinas, the "inter" of intersubjectivity is already a violation. Interlocution in Levinas's "ideal speech situation" is always concerned with interrupting that in subjectivity which permits the "inter"—the bringing together of I and Other under a single conceptual rubric.[13] When "I" faces "Other," I is called into question. This questioning, Levinas maintains, is the original ethical gesture. The call of the Other is not an attack on subjectivity but rather a mandate to which I must respond. "The 'resistance' of the other does not do violence to me, does not act negatively; it has a positive structure: Ethical." Given this, the question that Levinas must address concerns the status of the ethical structure (TI, 196–97).

The face-to-face encounter involves two surfaces coming into contact with one another. This coming into contact establishes a relationship—one without depth or content. As such, it has only form; and this form is ethical. For Levinas, the form of the face-to-face relationship is ethical in the sense that it represents a resistance to power. "The face resists possession, resists my power." This, however, is not resistance that requires action in opposition to that which seeks to dominate: an annulment of power through the exercise of power. Rather, it is a resistance that defies the category of power. For the other to resist my power by exercising her/his power would be to accept the terms of a power relationship. This in turn involves an inevitable usurpation or subordination; conceptual unification—either total or through compromise—always falls from a power relationship. The other calls to me, requests my response, in a space that is outside of any totality or ontological fabrication. Here my power is inoperative; I just "am," in the proximity of the other (TI, 197–99).

For Levinas the ethical form of the face-to-face relationship serves to neutralize power. This in turn establishes a sphere of discourse. "But thus the epiphany of infinity is expression and discourse." Here again, some similarities with Habermas's ideal speech situation emerge. For both, the domain of ethical discourse lies within a formal sphere that is free of power relations. But the status of both formal and power is quite different. For Habermas, the formal aspect of the ideal speech situation is a construct that uses the resources that are available in natural language. For Levinas, ideal discourse precedes natural language. It is not concerned with the content of speech acts as it is necessarily prior to the possibility of speech acts. As such, his appeal is to a peculiar sort of transcendence: not to a transcendental philosophical a priori, but rather to a transcendence that is intricately intertwined with immanence. "The absolutely other, whose alterity is overcome in the philosophy of immanence on the allegedly common plane of history, maintains his transcendence in the midst of history. . . . Transcendence designates a relation with reality infinitely distant from my own reality, yet without this distance destroying this relation and without this relation destroying this distance, as would happen with relations within the same; this relation does not become an implantation in the other and a confusion with him, does not affect the very identity of the same, its ipseity, does not silence the apology, does not become apostasy and exstasy" (TI, 40–42). There are actually some very interesting resonances here between Levinas's view of transcendence and what Habermas has at times referred to as the quasi-transcendental character of ordinary language. With respect to the operational features of discourse, however, the similarities drop out. This situates the difference between the two concerning power as well. For Habermas, power involves the use of unreasonable tactics for gaining an advantage in negotiation. For Levinas, relations of reason and negotiation are relations of power, and the vocabulary of such discourses is inherently tainted with structures of domination (conceptualization). As such, the formal character of the ideal speech situation and the face-to-face relation represent two poles of formality: form prior to the possibility of content and form that rarefies content (TI, 200–1).[14]

Given this polarity, and what has already been noted about the role of language in Habermas's formal discursive arena, what sort of language operates within Levinas's formal structure? Levinas states the following: "This bond between expression and responsibility, this ethical condition or essence of language prior to all disclosure of being and its cold splendor, permits us to extract language from subjection to a preeminent thought, where it would have but the servile function of translating that preexistent thought on the outside or of universalizing its interior moments" (TI, 200–1). This states negatively the role of language in the face to face relationship. It is not, as for Habermas, a medium through which content is expressed, a way to fill in the space created by an empty formality; nor is it matter that can be formed into universal norms. Rather, as Levinas states positively in "Language and Proximity," the language of the face-to-face relationship, the language of ethical discourse, is anarchical; it is proximity without cognition. "This relation of proximity, this contact unconvertible into noetico-noematic structure, in which every transmission of messages, whatever be those messages, is already established, is the original language, a language without words or propositions, pure communication."[15] This is the language of ethical discourse—the presystematic array of material signifiers that originate in the "human face and skin."

These last remarks seem completely outside of the framework provided by Habermas's universal pragmatic schema. In fact, they call into question the possibility of situating ethical discourse in terms of any type of schema.[16] Yet I think that an interesting connection can be drawn. Habermas situates his schematic theory of communication and discourse in terms of a historical theory of language that is associated with the development of lifeworld structures. This, in a sense, frames the ideal features of language that ground communicative ethics in terms of a material substructure. Habermas notes that within this substructure there is a considerable amount of shifting and disruption that results in semantic ambiguity. At the same time, however, there is a considerable amount of continuity and evolutionary refinement. The universal pragmatic analysis attempts to demonstrate how these structures of continuity and refinement can be drawn upon in formal spheres of ethical decision-making.

What Habermas seems to ignore is that the language needed to construct a universal pragmatic schema is always already laced with the disruptive movement that operates within lifeworld spheres. This is where Levinas's notion of alterity becomes extremely interesting. If the disruptive movement that Habermas detects in lifeworld structures, from which the language of ethical discourse must be drawn, is traceable to the radical alterity of the face-to-face relation, then a constructive theory of ethical discourse will always be susceptible to the disruptive features of its medium of exchange. Or, in other words, the *material*, marked by alterity, will always break up the unity of the *ideal*. This claim depends upon the sense in which, for both Habermas and Levinas, transcendence and immanence are historically related.

I would like to advance this claim, although with certain reservations. I support Levinas's view that the materiality of the face-to-face relationship has ethical significance. And, with Levinas, I would claim that the importance lies in the way that alterity—*as a structural feature of language*—annuls conceptual hegemony. Contra Levinas, however, I would argue that this does not begin to exhaust the possible manifestations of ethical discourse. In fact, I think that there is much to be said for the procedural-schematic model of discourse that Habermas has developed in great detail. What is most interesting, and for the purposes of a postconventional critical theory of ethical discourse most useful, about Levinas's "analysis" is the way that it, in a sense, gets behind discourse, identifying a problem area that a theory such as Habermas's has difficulty contending with. Nevertheless, Levinas doesn't develop this analysis in a manner that is particularly useful to critical theory. In much the same way that Habermas develops an ethical theory that attempts to eliminate the problem of radical alterity, Levinas gestures away from concrete situations in which alterity can actually play a role in the disruption of structural domination. For both, the role of power and ideality in ethical discourse is characterized in an extremely limited way. I will attempt now to define these established limits and consider the ethical space that lies between them.

Real and Ideal Speech

Earlier I alluded to poles of formality that distinguish between the modes of ideal discourse that are central to Habermas's and Levinas's respective views on the ethical. As is the case with any polar opposition, there is an interesting terrain lying between these two extremities. I would characterize this terrain as a field of power. Both Habermas and Levinas attempt to exclude power from the domain of ideal speech; but in my estimation, neither is sufficiently attentive to the complexities of power relations. In general, for Habermas, power is anything that falls outside of rationality. This is not entirely true as he recognizes that in institutional contexts rational forms of power have to be used for the sake of expedient operations. But this type of rationality is fundamentally strategic—rather than communicative—and as such does not pertain to the domain of ethical decision-making. For Levinas, power is anything that attempts to circumscribe alterity. I would like to advance the position that power should be used as a heuristic term: that there are various forms of power, some of which are ethically useful and others that are ethically neutral or destructive. Further, excluding power from arenas of ethical discourse necessitates the strategic deployment of a specific mode of power. The mode of power deployed by both Habermas and Levinas, albeit in quite different ways, is authority. In what follows I will attempt to establish this by drawing upon Habermas's and Levinas's respective analyses of power, and turning them against one another in order to identify the way in which each, unintentionally but significantly, engages in an act of authoritarian exclusion.

As I noted above, Habermas's theory of communicative normativity ultimately takes recourse in his theory of the lifeworld.[17] He describes the lifeworld as the historically developed condition that allows for various forms of communication. It transcends particular discursive situations yet provides the linguistic patterns that enable communicative exchange. Likewise, it is composed of shifting structures that are in a constant process of transformation that is rooted in the historical relationship between a pool of discursive resources and specific contexts of discourse. Hence, the lifeworld serves as a preconceptual, prethematic mesh of communicative possibilities, a reserve that can be drawn upon in a manner tailored to specific discursive situations. "The background of a communicative utterance is thus formed by situation definition that, as measured against the actual need for mutual understanding, have to overlap to a sufficient extent" (TCA, 2:121). As such, the communicative reserve is always overdetermined; it exceeds the specific determinate situation in which ethical norms are established.

It is this overdeterminedness that Habermas needs to contend with if he is to successfully defend the claim that in ideal forums of discourse, universal norms can be established. In other words, it is necessary to provide an analysis of the conditions that generate surplus and to demonstrate how, within rational discourse, what is excessive in language can be filtered out. Habermas seems unconcerned with the first problem and as such does not provide a satisfactory response to the second. His attempt at a solution involves an appeal to stable structures in language that are easily transferred from the linguistic pool to specific discursive situations. "From a perspective turned toward the situation, the lifeworld is a reservoir of taken-for-granteds, of unshaken convictions that participants in communication draw upon in cooperative processes of interpretation. Single elements, specific taken-for-granteds, are, however, mobilized in the form of consensual and yet problematizable knowledge only when they become relevant to a situation" (TCA, 2:124). The question that Habermas ignores, the difficult question, concerns the linguistic material that lies behind the taken-for-granteds that become reified in historical languages. Is there disruptive movement within language that always stands in opposition to the unshaken? I will develop this in greater detail in the section that follows. What is important to emphasize in the present context are the problems that Habermas has in accounting for the relationship between the "transcendental" (loosely speaking) character of language and the immanent situations in which language is employed in moral decision-making. If, as his analysis suggests, the transcendental is somewhat indeterminate, then one would suspect that indeterminacies would show up in ethical determinations. My suggestion is that this has a bearing on the normative status of such determinations.

This is where I would argue that Levinas's concern with the anarchical disruptiveness of the language of alterity upsets Habermas's determinate situations of discourse. The materiality of the face-to-face relation—unthematizable, preconceptual differentiation—overdetermines the ethical relation in such a way that unity, consensus, can only be an aberration. As such, disturbances will be etched into the normative accord produced under the conceptual rubric of ideal speech. In order to neutralize the effects of this etching, tactics of exclusion have to be deployed. In Habermas's case this involves an appeal to the authority of coercion-free argument. But here, Levinas would claim, a power strategy is enacted. By introducing content into the discursive relationship between I and the Other, and by formulating that content in such a way that it can be shared, the alterity that originally situated the relationship is excluded. By appealing to the authority of "we," the other to whom I am responsible becomes mine.

Stating the Levinasian objection quite explicitly: Habermas's normative accord involves a political subsumption of alterity into rational agreement. It is the absolute authority of reason that is of concern. Rational consensus seems to close off, conceptually, the possibility of dissent, resistance, alterity. In Habermas's own terms, the determinate conditions of a discursive situation eliminate the possibility of radical difference. Further, the intrinsic connection between rational agreement and legitimacy strategically roots legitimacy within a power structure: that of authority. In order to preserve the pure domination-free aura of ideal speech, Habermas has to exclude the play of alterity that is situated within the language of discourse. This is achieved by appealing to the unmitigated authority of reason. As such, his attempt to exclude power from communicative ethics is itself premised on a form of power.[18]

While this anti-authoritarian strain in Levinas's conception of the ethical is a very useful critical tool, it only applies to one end of the pole of formality. Further, it rests on another type of authority that strikes me as being even more problematic than that upon which Habermas relies. My critique of Habermas's rational discourse ethic is not directed so much at rational discourse per se but rather at the authoritative application of the concept of universality (the power move that lends dominion to consensus) with which it is attended. In fact rational discourse, conceived in a certain way, seems to be one situation in which alterity can have its say. For Levinas, however, there is no place for having a say. Rather, there is only obligation to the other—regardless of what the other demands. Insofar as the other cannot be known, cannot be negotiated with, cannot be spoken to in the language of concepts and consent, I can only respond passively. In a word, the other always already has authority. Levinas seems to justify this position by claiming that there is something about otherness that is absolutely unspeakable; to speak back, or engage in discussion, is to annul alterity. As Lyotard puts it: "The irony of the commentator goes as far as persecution; the less I understand you, he or she says to the Levinasian (or divine) text, the more I will obey you by that fact; for, if I want to understand you (in your turn) as a request, then I should not understand you as sense."[19]

The authority at work in Levinas's text is more absolute than that operating in Habermas's. In the same manner, although by implication more problematically, that the rational subject, within the mediating context of intersubjective discourse, is hegemonic for Habermas, it is the aboriginal subject, the subject of the anarche, that establishes hegemony for Levinas. The I that cannot articulate itself determines, through passive self-negation, a structure of relational alterity. And since the other can't be known in any sense (and particularly not as another subject) I can only respond. It is this ineffability that is authoritative in Levinas's ethics of proximity. In order to maintain the ineffable status of the other, the possibility of a mediated subject—constituted in a network of forces that might be compared to Habermas's lifeworld—has to be excluded. It is this gesture, which I would characterize as a power strategy, that is necessary if the powerless authority of the ineffable other is to be preserved.

In between these two poles of authority, both of which stand in opposition to power but which are formed through the deployment of power, is a terrain that I stated previously could be viewed as a field of power. The power in this field is generated through the exclusionary strategies that instantiated the powerless authority that reigns at either pole. Each of these poles, I would contend, contains certain elements of both conventional and postconventional[20] notions of the ethical. The conventional in each is represented in terms of the authority structures that I have identified; for Habermas this involves an appeal to a mediated Kantian subjective rationality, while for Levinas it involves a gesture toward the absolute transcendence of an otherwise than being. The postconventional is represented in each as the space in which alterity can be freely expressed. While free expression takes on a considerably different meaning for Habermas and Levinas, this difference constitutes a field of power that is the terrain of postconventional discourse. I will now advance some tentative comments concerning the characteristics of this ethical space, before turning to analysis of its conditions of possibility.

The Postconventional Condition

The postconventional condition, and the role of universal norms, is in a sense the primary concern of Habermas's systematic social theory. With the term *postconventional*, Habermas refers to the modern epoch in general and the ongoing project of enlightenment in particular. With the rise of rationality and science, and the decline of traditional religion, an entirely new problematic emerged concerning the foundation of ethical norms. No longer could an appeal be made to the authority of a metaphysical being that possesses the power of life and death. Either morality had to be grounded in something universal that was other than God, or the very concept of morality would have to be radically altered.

The most important ethical theory that developed in coincidence with the postconventional problematic was Kant's. Kant opted to ground morality in a nondivine universality: human reason. This is the project taken up by Habermas. Quite aware of the radical critiques of rationality that have developed in the wake of the Enlightenment, Habermas's objective is to develop a theory of rationality that avoids the pitfalls noted by Nietzsche, Heidegger, and the like. Hence, he developed the communicative-intersubjective rationality that I discussed above. In this final subsection I would like to consider whether Habermas's communicative ethics are as postconventional as he claims. This will once again involve the problem of authority, legitimacy and alterity.

The convention that dominates Habermas's post-conventional ethics is that of modernity. Modernity for Habermas is not simply an historical epoch; it is also a conceptual schema. As I noted in chapter 3, the element of this schema that appeals to Habermas is its universality. Modern ideals of scientific truth, political solidarity, and individual autonomy all aspire to universality. But is this aspiration postconventional or a reformulation of more conventional approaches to these questions? My position is that the latter is, to a certain extent, the case.

The trace or surplus that carries over from the premodern to the modern in Habermas's discourse ethic is reflected in his interest in providing a philosophically cogent defense of ethical closure or totality. This in itself seems neutral enough; there are certainly good reasons for pursuing the possibilities available for a universal ethic. But when this project becomes excessively bound up with the political economy of modernity, and the way its ethical codifications shape various spheres of life, it brings with it problematic elements of the conventional. This would include the "ethics" of profit, production, and aggregated power that I discussed in chapter 3. The point is that while modern ethics, and modernity in general, move initially in the direction of postconventionality, the logic of conventionality resurfaces and draws the sequence back into a metaphysics of authority that, as I have been arguing, is rooted in the capitalist mode of production.[21] For this reason the terrain of postconventional ethics must accommodate the movement of alterity: the disruptive resistance that defies the tendency to lapse back into conventionality. At the same time, however, it would be a mistake to valorize alterity at the utter expense of rationality and conceptual thought. The role of alterity in postconventional ethics is procedural. It checks, so to speak, the authoritarian tendencies that operate at the formal pole of rationality. Construed as such, the terrain of postconventional ethics is a field of power in which the poles of authority contest one another for hegemony. In this process of struggle, competing forces hammer out ethical determinations that reconstitute the field, alter the circuitry of power, and fall themselves into the economy of reason and alterity. As such, the universal authority of reason and the anarchical authority of alterity operate upon one another in an indeterminate field that produces tentative ethical determinations.

An example of the operations that take place within this field would have to take into consideration the various social movements that have responded to specific concerns related to what some have called the postmodern condition. Groups composed of feminists, African Americans, gays and lesbians, and other marginalized sectors of this political economy have thematized their alterity (which is of course outside the main stream spheres of rationality) in terms of rational strategies of action. In deference to both Habermas and Levinas, however, their struggles have been conducted from localities on the postconventional terrain that allow them to exercise power. When one positional strategy is exhausted, another is thematized and deployed. Ethical norms are tentatively formed in a field of political contestation, and are in turn reformed as the terrain of that field assumes a different contour. Hence, the aftermath of modernity demands an ethical discourse that works both within and around the problematic of universality; a politics of relationality that has the fortitude to face up to alterity.

TEXTUALIZING THE LIFEWORLD

As is indicated by the closing remark in the previous section, my conception of a politics of enlightenment is rooted in the convergence between universalistic normative ethics—in the tradition of Kant—and a notion of politics that is appropriate to the concrete conditions that face late-twentieth and even early-twenty-first century actors with progressive agendas. While it is certainly beyond the scope of this work, and quite possibly beyond the scope of social philosophy, to lay out specific strategies that can be taken up by said actors, it is unquestionably within the domain of a critical social theory to outline the conditions of possibility that enable such strategies to take shape. I will be dealing with this problem on a rather abstract level. In doing so, however, I hope to situate further discussions that can become more concrete: those dealing with the nature of public debate and societal transformation. My assumption is that Habermas is correct to approach these questions with language and communication as his starting point.

As I indicated in chapter 1, this concluding section will utilize the work of Jacques Derrida. Critical theorists up to this point have not been particularly sympathetic to Derrida's work; one might even say they have been generally quite hostile. This has always seemed to me an attitude that runs counter to the spirit of critical theory. First-generation critical theorists appropriated Nietzsche, Freud, and a whole gamut of other controversial thinkers, in such a way that their most important insights were incorporated into radical analyses of the contemporary condition. Derrida, while not a social philosopher per se, seems a likely candidate to be appropriated in similar fashion. Before turning to the primary issue of this section, I would like to briefly respond to several critical theorists who take a somewhat dismissive view of Derrida.[22]

Habermas himself has been at the forefront of these attacks. At the core of his concern with Derrida is the omnipresent Heidegger controversy. Derrida, being under the influence of Heidegger, is viewed with considerable suspicion. This suspicion seems to be prompted by early Frankfurt School attacks on Heidegger. Both Adorno and Herbert Marcuse put a great deal of energy into more or less successful efforts to link Heidegger's philosophical work with his participation in the National Socialist movement.[23] As I discussed in chapter 4, Habermas has followed up on these critiques and extended them to Derrida, whom he considers to be an unreconstructed Heideggerian: "Derrida is correct in claiming for himself the role of an authentic disciple" (PDM, 161). Habermas's main concern with Derrida in particular and those that are located under the banner of postmodernism in general, is the way in which their antifoundational tactics and critiques of humanism disavow the possibility for political projects with emancipatory aspirations. "In his opinion, the worst of these implications is their rejection of freedom, individuality, communal solidarity, and democratic self-determination. For him, these are the very values underwriting opposition to totalitarianism."[24]

Habermas's critique is, in many respects, an important one. His concern is to show how a flippantly postmodern approach to questions of truth, emancipation, and rights is irresponsible and dangerous. As I noted in chapter 4, his general strategy is to locate key thinkers that he identifies with postmodernism in a generalized discourse that is about the business of undermining Enlightenment rationality. Derrida, according to Habermas, is representative of this trend. While these concerns are very important, it is not clear that Derrida fits unambiguously within this discourse.[25] In fact, he finds it necessary to give a caricatured account of Derrida in order to make his point. While the point is of considerable value, the representation of Derrida is misdirected and has contributed to an unduly negative perception of his work in critical social theory circles.

Habermas has not been the only, nor for that matter the first, critical theorist to attack the political implications of Derrida's work. Nancy Fraser, for example, in an article published first in 1984,[26] offers a report on the "Ends of Man" conference held in Paris in 1981, which attempts to undermine the social-theoretic value of Derrida's work, as well as the research of those that operate within the framework of his central concerns.[27] She establishes the tone of her analysis with this series of rhetorical questions:

> Does deconstruction have any political implications? Does it have any political significance beyond the byzantine and incestuous struggles it has provoked in American lit crit departments? Is it possible—and desirable—to articulate a deconstructive politics? Why, despite the revolutionary rhetoric of his writings circa 1968 and despite the widespread assumption that he is "of the left," has Derrida so consistently, deliberately and dexterously avoided the topic of politics? Why, for example, has he danced so nimbly around the tenacious efforts of interviewers to establish where he stands vis-à-vis Marxism? Why has he continued "to defer indefinitely" the encounter of deconstruction with "the text of Marx" that he has on occasion promised? (Fraser 1989, 69)[28]

Fraser suggests that two predictable "gestures" emerge out of this set of problematics: the Marxist gesture, which is represented by Gayatri Spivak, and the Hegelian gesture, which is represented by Jacob Rogozinski. The former is radical, revolutionary, and anti-establishment; the latter is conservative, individualistic, and suspicious of fundamental ruptures of any sort. Derrida himself, characteristically according to Fraser,[29] couldn't accept either of these positions and as such "deferred" taking any position at all.

Fraser proceeds by tracing this lack of positioning, as she might call it, through the rise and fall of the Center for Philosophical Research on the Political.[30] She focuses her analysis on the way that Heidegger and Arendt came to play an increasingly important role in the work of the center's members and how this led to an apolitical neoliberalism that ultimately undermined the centers aims and aspirations. The following remark summarizes her critique: "It is telling that . . . they do not debate their opponents on the latter's own—political—terms. Rather, they refuse the very genre of political debate and in this way, too, maintain the ethos of deconstruction. For there is one sort of difference that deconstruction cannot tolerate: namely, difference as dispute, as good old-fashioned political fight" (Fraser 1989, 81–82). A leap in logic is made by Fraser in this poignant but questionable assertion. Her point that certain quasi-Derridean intellectuals (Nancy and Lacoue-Labarthe) are unwilling to go to bat for their political leanings does not warrant the claim that deconstruction is antidiscursive or that a Derridean orientation is nonargumentative (one of Habermas's main complaints). As is the case with Habermas,[31] Fraser uses polemic and rhetorical gestures to undermine what she considers to be a critical approach that is dangerous because of its retreat into polemic and rhetorical gestures. As such, she employs the very strategy that she seeks to discredit, utilizing what she considers to be suspect tactics. In the words of Habermas, this results in a performative contradiction.

Another American critical theorist, Thomas McCarthy, has also played an important role in discussions concerning the political implications of Derrida's work. This began with a debate between Derrida and McCarthy in which the latter clearly represented the absent Habermas.[32] Later this was developed into a more detailed analysis in an article titled: "The Politics of the Ineffable: Derrida's Deconstructionism."[33] McCarthy takes great pains to quote frequently from remarks Derrida has made in interviews as well as from his various writings. In doing so he hopes to protect himself from the claim that he is misunderstanding Derrida.[34] McCarthy reprimands Derrida for not having a systematic analysis of social institutions, law, or rights. Likewise, he points out that when Derrida does comment on political issues he appeals to the very concepts that his "deconstructionism" leads him to undermine. Finally, McCarthy makes every effort to identify Derrida with Heidegger (as do Habermas and Fraser). These points lead him to the following conclusion:

> I have found nothing in Derrida's writings to persuade me that his quasi-apocalyptic, near prophetic mode of discourse about politics should displace the more prosaic modes available or constructible in our tradition. Even if his heart is in the right place, and even if his "anarchy" is meant to be "responsible," we know from experience that the devaluation of these modes opens a space, or rather creates a vacuum

> that can be filled in quite different ways, for instance by Heidegger's call for submission to some indeterminate authority. (McCarthy 1991, 118)

Putting aside the questionable attempt to make a Nazi out of Derrida, McCarthy's arguments hinge on two assumptions:

1. That in order have pertinence to political and social theory, one's work must be that of doing systematic social theory. While clearly systematic social theory, such as the type that Habermas does, is very important and highly commendable, it doesn't follow that this is the only way in which ethical and political questions can be broached.
2. That Derrida's critique of Western rationality is totalistic; Derrida can't legitimately undermine, or even question, certain aspects of reason without demolishing reason altogether. It seems that even a cursory reading of Derrida's work would notice that this is not the case; yet when Derrida indicates as much quite straightforwardly, McCarthy accuses him of contradicting himself.

In addition to these two fundamental problems, the same point that I made with Fraser applies to McCarthy. At the very moment that he lauds rational discourse, he relies on rhetorical operators, such as appeals to Heidegger and the loaded claims about totalistic (read totalitarian) critique. As is the case with Habermas and Fraser, these comments are far less the product of serious criticism than the mark of those who either have an axe to grind or a cross to bear.

Communication and Difference

While Habermas has a highly developed theory of communication, and has shown carefully, if not utterly convincingly, that there are important ethical implications to be drawn from his theory, it is not at all clear that the concept of language to which he continually appeals is fleshed out in a theoretically satisfactory manner. Jonathan Culler makes this point in *Framing the Sign* (FS), where he develops a succinct analysis of Habermas's "norms of language." Culler states that Habermas constructs, rather than derives, the normative features that he claims are rooted in the structures of language. It is his contention that Habermas begins with norms that serve his project and proceeds to systematically bracket off exceptions, labelling them parasitic deviances. The most notable of these, Culler suggests, is literature, which by Habermas's own standards is communicative, yet does not aspire to mutual understanding. By excluding modes of language usage that escape his normative framework, Habermas presupposes and applies norms in the course of his analysis that are supposed to be derivatives of the analysis. While Habermas chooses "norms that we all would admire," his method of legitimating them is exclusive and ultimately circular.[35]

Culler argues that at the heart of Habermas's account is a universalistic ideology, not an analysis of language. "Discussion of these matters does not belong in an account of presupposed norms, as Habermas conceives it, but perhaps to say this is to indicate that what he is analyzing is not language so much as ideologically restricted notions of understanding, communication, rationality, or more generously, a philosophical conception of communication that goes with the value choice he wishes to make normative" (FS, 199). Habermas, in a sense, naturalizes a specific mode of discourse and assigns the norms that are fundamental to this discursive form universal status.

Culler is quite correct in his assertion that Habermas's norms are implausibly derived from natural language and that mutual understanding is not a constant presupposition of participants in communication situations. At the same time, however, he provides little defense of his own view of understanding, which is premised on the "frequently counterfactual assumption of the possibility that the reader can see and grasp what the speaker failed to see and even what the author failed to see" (FS, 193). Culler makes a sweeping reversal of Habermas's privileged category (symmetry) and assigns universal status to his own choice. "Communication, one might say, is structurally asymmetrical, and symmetry is an accident and a myth of moralists, not a norm" (FS, 193). Culler's bracketing and marginalizing of features of language that are at odds with his theory bears striking resemblances to Habermas's. This reflects a tendency on the part of theorists steeped in deconstruction to ignore the communicative possibilities that are afforded by language. As was the case with Habermas, Culler sidesteps issues that pose serious threats to the universality of his central thesis.

This view of communication, as structurally fixed (whether symmetrical or asymmetrical), denies the force of the theory of language that Culler is tacitly defending: that the structures of language are always shifting and that this movement disrupts the structures of various modes of discourse.[36] It is not incompatible with this view to hold that symmetry is just as possible as asymmetry when language structures and discursive contexts adhere, although it does problematize the possibility of arranging universal patterns of mutual understanding in these contexts.

In contrast to Culler, Derrida, no champion of the inherent transparency of language, notes that under certain conditions a normatively moderated symmetrical discourse is quite realizable. In an afterword to *Limited Inc.* (LI) Derrida states the following: "And within interpretive contexts (that is, within relations of force that are always differential—

for example, sociopolitical institutions—but even beyond these determinations) that are relatively stable, sometimes apparently unshakable, it would be possible to invoke rules of competence, criteria of discussion and of consensus, good faith, lucidity, rigor, criticism, and pedagogy."[37] While this confirms my point that symmetrical discourse under certain normative standards is not precluded by a deconstructive theory of language, it is nevertheless a far cry from Habermas's teleological universalism. In fact, it is premised on the following: "In the analysis of so-called normal cases, one neither can nor ought, in all theoretical rigor, to exclude the possibility of transgression. Not even provisionally or out of methodological considerations. It would be a poor method, since the possibility of transgression tells us immediately and indispensably about the structure of law in general" (LI, 133). This point applies to both Habermas and Culler. Once the contextually desirable case is normatively naturalized, incipient and ensuing transgression is denied—leaving only obscure, irrelevant deviances in the margins.

While Habermas argues convincingly that under certain conditions symmetrical communication is possible, Culler argues with equal persuasiveness that the rules governing these conditions don't translate into universal norms. Culler, however, falls back on a normal/deviant distinction that is every bit as problematic as Habermas's. I have introduced Derrida to indicate why mutual understanding in symmetrical discourse is neither a "myth of moralists," nor "intuitive knowledge of participants themselves." As I noted above, Habermas elsewhere develops the framework for a theory of language that is more sensitive to these problems. At the base of this framework is his theory of the lifeworld. As it stands, this theory both includes and denies the deconstructive impulse that I think can serve his social theory. In the following subsection I will argue that a Derridean "textualizing" of Habermas's lifeworld provides a more acceptable basis for a theory of communicative action.

Language and Lifeworld

The first step in this portion of my discussion is to argue for a linguistic interpretation of the lifeworld. As I mentioned earlier, Habermas's semantic theory is rooted in three participant-world relations. These three "worlds"—the subjective, objective, and intersubjective—intersect and intermingle to constitute the lifeworld. Habermas seems to have recognized that the criticisms of the sort discussed above would be directed at his abstract analysis of communicative competence. In particular, he is sensitive to Culler's point that an adequate theory of language is missing. In response, Habermas develops a theory of the lifeworld that attempts to meet this deficiency. Insofar as the lifeworld is constituted by the intersecting components of speech acts, it, like language, is foundational for communication.[38]

Habermas establishes the connection between language and the lifeworld as follows:

> It is not my intention to carry further our formal-pragmatic examination of speech acts and of communicative action; rather, I want to build upon these concepts so far as they have already been analyzed, and take up the question of how the lifeworld—as the horizon within which communicative actions are "always already" moving—is in turn limited and changed by the structural transformation of society as a whole. (TCA, 2:119)

Characterized as such, the lifeworld is the historically established precondition for any form of language usage; it is the trans-situational compilation of syntactic, semantic, and grammatic structures that enable communication. Likewise it is an ever shifting, ever moving, dynamic of transformations that reflect the historical relationship between the "always already" and the immediate.

By taking this position, Habermas invalidates the type of universality that he wishes to attribute to redeemed validity claims. Insofar as validity claims are ultimately language dependent, and linguistic configurations are framed by shifting horizons of meaning, the only grounds for claiming universality would be to establish that the residual meaning that sustains horizon or boundary shifts has universal content. This is tantamount to saying that linguistic mechanisms that produce semantic fluidity are the only universal features of language. Clearly Habermas does not want to accept this. It nevertheless seems to follow from his theory of language. In order to make this case I will focus on the shifting horizons of the lifeworld and trans-situational differences that inevitably factor into specific lifeworld structures that ground contingent speech situations.

It is first necessary to specify with as much precision as possible what I mean by "language." At a very primary level language is that which enables communication of various sorts and modes. For this to take place language must have certain consistent features but at the same time must be malleable enough to accommodate changing communicative demands. These demands are constituted by the material, political, legal, cultural, and moral reproduction of the conditions that preserve and transform communities of language users. As is evidenced by history, both in the broadest sense and in numerous contemporary instances, there is tremendous tension between preservation and transformation. The fundamental medium by which and within which these tensions are played out is language; it gives rise to and limits the range of solvent activities. Likewise, these activities, which take the form of the above-mentioned modes of reproduction, feed back into language—disrupting and transforming its structural makeup. One can assume that since these tensions do not lead to final resolution, that history doesn't really ever end; tension itself is a constitutive feature of language. As such, I will define language as a dynamic network of constellations and transgressions that reflect sociohistorical conflicts, partial resolutions, further conflicts, and so forth.

With this in mind, the connection between language and Habermas's lifeworld can be neatly drawn. The reproductive matrix that I identified above as being both dependent upon and constitutive for language reproduction, encompasses the actor/world relations that Habermas claims are dependent upon and constitutive for the lifeworld. As a mesh of overlapping communicative possibilities, this matrix serves as a source pool that can be drawn upon in particular situations. "The background of a communicative utterance is thus formed by situation definition that, as measured against the actual need for mutual understanding, have to overlap to a sufficient extent" (TCA, 2:121). Situations geared toward mutual understanding cannot be sharply delineated; there is always a certain amount of shifting that accompanies situation definition, depending on the complexity of the theme that is explicated. "A situation is a segment of lifeworld contexts of relevance that is thrown into relief by themes and articulated through goals and plans of action; these contexts are concentrically ordered and become increasingly anonymous and diffused as the spatiotemporal and social distance grows" (TCA, 2:122–23). This seems like a correct description, although the metaphor of concentric circles could be replaced with a more appropriate one such as intersecting threads. Habermas proceeds to describe the degree to which lifeworld horizons shift relative to the thematic complexity of the particular situation and how as the linguistic demands placed on lifeworld resources intensify, the effect of shifting, both immediate and embedded, is felt. This reflects the constellational-transgressional dynamic that I attributed to language. In order to accept such an implication, however, Habermas would have to abandon his truth-productive semantic theory: meaning would be subject to degrees of indeterminacy that run along a spectrum ranging from something close to semantic transparency to a fairly radical polysemia.

In an attempt to avoid the repercussions that this would have on his normative theory, Habermas suggests that lifeworld (language) appropriation be carefully tailored to the specific communication situation:

> From a perspective turned toward the situation, the lifeworld as a reservoir of taken-for-granteds, of unshaken convictions that partici-

> pants in communication draw upon in cooperative processes of interpretation. Single elements, specific taken-for-granteds, are, however, mobilized in the form of consensual and yet problematizable knowledge only when they become relevant to a situation. (TCA, 2:124)

As such, the "problem" of semantic indeterminacy is overruled by a political decision: that of defining the situation. This move fails to take into consideration the flexible-reflexive character of language, a significant feature of Habermas's own semantic theory. While political moves of this nature are appropriate in some situations, perpetually forcing determinacy on fluid semantic structures will build up tension in the linguistic networks of the lifeworld. Insofar a these networks serve as the source pool from which the resources for further political decisions are drawn, built-up tension or neutralized transgression will resurface with greater intensity. This, in brief, is the problem with a conventional appropriation of the politics of enlightenment. Traditional understandings of key enlightenment categories lead to their ossification rather than dynamic reproduction. I will return to this with respect to the concept—democracy—that covers heuristically Habermas's categories of truth, freedom, and justice.

Habermas insists that this tension is not a problem. Appealing to his view that the natural end of language usage is mutual understanding, he states the following:

> So long as the participants maintain their performative attitudes the language actually in use remains at their backs. Speakers cannot take up an extramundane positioning relation to it. The same is true of culture—of those patterns of interpretation transmitted in language. From a semantic point of view, language does have a peculiar affinity to linguistically articulated worldviews. Natural languages conserve the contents of tradition, which persist only in symbolic form, for the most part in linguistic embodiment. For the semantic capacity of a language has to be adequate to the complexity of the stored-up cultural contents, the patterns of interpretation, variations and expressions. (TCA, 2:125)

Every situation either comes preinterpreted or with an unproblematic negotiable interpretation readily available. Insofar as language is essentially geared toward mutual understanding, it is this stable medium that undergirds processes of negotiation and interpretation. Language always provides common ground: "Communicative actions can no more take up an extramundane position in relation to their lifeworld than they can in relation to language as the medium of processes of reaching understanding through which their lifeworld maintains itself. In drawing upon a cultural tradition they continue it" (TCA, 2:125). In other words, the movement of language is always coherent with respect to its determinate end: transparent communication.

Language-lifeworld development is continuous and unproblematic in that it adheres to a teleological principle—that of rational speech. In order to sidestep the implications of his own lifeworld theory, Habermas has to take refuge in the most problematic aspect of his semantic theory: the natural primacy of mutual understanding. As I pointed out via Culler, this view is highly dubious. Hence, a number of questions can be raised concerning Habermas's linguistified lifeworld. What are the adaptive mechanisms that facilitate horizon movement? Is there within language a provision for the transgression of established boundaries? How can semantic evolution and linguistic paradigm shifts be explained? Habermas's response to all of these questions would involve an appeal to a continuous intersubjective development that has refined language to the point that all changes can occur smoothly and unproblematically. While this concurs with his theory of communication, I think that it is at odds with the theory of language that is embedded in his conception of the lifeworld, not to mention his analysis of late capitalism's systematic destruction of social communication. Further, I think that altering this conception of the lifeworld by fleshing out the implications of the implicit theory of language will markedly improve the theory of communicative action as a theory of a politics of enlightenment. In order to establish this, I will now turn to Derrida for some suggestions as to how Habermas's lifeworld could be "textualized."

Derrida and the Lifeworld

Derrida's view of language draws upon Saussure's observation that language is fundamentally composed of arbitrarily established differences. These differences, for example between signifier and signified, create spaces or gaps within the fabric of language: areas that shift and move, rendering meaning and truths ultimately undecidable. Derrida characterizes this as a textual or intertextual phenomenon. Texts, or textual "situations," provide evidence of this as they reflect the intertextual networks that operate under, above, around, and within the apparent boundaries that suggest distinctions between text and context. This intermingling of text and context brings into textual situations the spatial gaps in language that generate play or indeterminacy. As such, any concrete, definite manifestation of language is rife with its own deformation.[39]

As was the case with Habermas's lifeworld, Derrida's "text" is a loosely woven, historically structured matrix of overlapping linguistic components. Likewise, the text and the lifeworld are both fluid: shifting in compositional form with respect to factors that contribute to their fabrication. Further, both remain in the background—a quasi-transcendental foundation, although not solid ground—serving as the reserve from which textual instances or defined communicative situations are drawn.[40] They diverge sharply, however, with respect to the relationship between the reserve and the situation or instance. Habermas, as I noted above, contends that the shifting within the reserve does not affect properly defined situations. Derrida, on the contrary, claims that the "différance"—"'active' moving discord of different forces and of differences of forces"—of the intertextual reserve factors into every textual situation, leaving traces that seed the structure's disassembly.[41] Hence, the excluded or marginalized other, that which has to be politically neutralized in a defined or textual situation, is never quite flushed out, as the text and its situation are inseparable.[42]

Critics of Derrida have suggested that this theory of textuality-language reduces all of reality to the status of a big, self-animating book—denying real conflict, historical changes, and concrete social-political relations.[43] Derrida refutes this by indicating that the catch phrase of deconstruction, "there is nothing outside the text," means simply that "there is nothing outside context" and that this "*concept* of the text . . . does not exclude the world, reality, history" (LI, 136–37).

Derrida summarizes as follows:

> Once again (and this probably makes a thousand times I have had to repeat this, but when will it finally be heard, and why this resistance?): as I understand it . . . the text is not the book, it is not confined in a volume itself confined to the library. It does not suspend reference—to history, of the world, reality, that they always appear in an experience, hence in a movement of interpretation which contextualizes them according to a network of differences and hence of referral to the other, is surely to recall that alterity (difference) is irreducible. Différance is a reference and vice versa. (LI, 137)

As such, the text, like the lifeworld, is always in the backdrop of the subject matter that is central to critical theory. It is within this text (language), albeit in a "highly unstable and dangerous" fashion, "that responsibilities jell, political responsibilities in particular" (LI, 136–37).

Given that the material of the text and the lifeworld is essentially the same, the importance of the difference between Habermas's and Derrida's respective views on the relationship between the general and the specific comes into focus. Here I think that Derrida has a decided advantage. Habermas argues that the situations defined in specific instances of communicative action are the natural product of a language designed with this purpose in mind. As such, under the right definite conditions, language fulfills itself in universal validity claims. Derrida, on the other hand, claims that "there is always something political 'in the very project of attempting to fix the contexts of utterances'" (LI, 136). Such political actions attempt to bracket off spheres of meaning or truth production, marginalizing the intertextual movement that threatens them with disruption. It is not Derrida's point that attempting to contextualize spheres of discourse is wrong; he in fact notes that doing so is necessary if there is to be political action (my term, not Derrida's). Rather, his contention is that the borders that define these contexts are never impervious to intertextual movement or differentiation. "Hence, no context is saturable any more. No one inflection enjoys any absolute privilege, no meaning can be fixed or decided upon. No border is guaranteed, inside or out."[44] It is clear that Derrida does not want to deny the possibility of political decision-making; his point is that these decisions are never final due to contextual instability. What marks the difference between Derrida and Habermas in terms of the questions that I am pursuing revolves around the difference between thinking in terms of modernity and thinking in terms of the aftermath of modernity. For Habermas, the contextual boundaries of a politics of enlightenment are fixed insofar as they are exclusively modern. In terms of the type of politics of enlightenment that I am concerned with, Derrida is more appropriate as his theory doesn't limit the meaning of the term *enlightenment*, nor does it limit the type of values that are its spin-off, to a fixed historical epoch. As such, this textualized version of the lifeworld is more in line with a politics of enlightenment in the aftermath of modernity.

In order for Habermas to maintain the view that in communicative action, redeemed validity claims achieve universal status—in the modern sense of the word—his thesis on the "telos of speech" or the natural propensity for communication to be transparent would have to be grounded in his theory of language. But as I have attempted to demonstrate, his theory of language or lifeworld acknowledges the same tensions and movements as does Derrida's theory of intertextuality. It seems implausible to move from a general condition of instability to specific instances of universal stability. As such, Derrida's conception of ultimately unstable textual situations is the more viable theoretical derivative.

In my estimation, Habermas carefully avoids the implications of his linguistified lifeworld in order to preserve the contextual stability provided by the normative structures of modernity. Instability, in this situation, translates into tragic loss. This position has a long history in both political theory and practice; and on the surface it seems correct. In other words, it makes sense to stick with values that seem unambiguously worth retaining. Yet, as I have argued, the values of modernity are not as unambiguous as Habermas suggests. Sticking with them in an unmodified fashion could quite plausibly lead to problems that far outreach the already near-crisis conditions that Habermas has shown permeate modern societies. The sorts of pressures that build up in communities that are undermined by the cynical appropriation of modern values (and I am not implying in any way that Habermas's appropriation is a cynical one) are more likely to come chaotically unglued than are those that recognize their ultimately undecidable (read infinitely redefinable) status. A sanguine example of this are the riots that broke out as a result of the cynical appeal to justice in the Rodney King case in May 1992.[45] The pressure that builds up when such cynical notions of justice, or truth, or freedom, are reactionarily perpetuated will disrupt the borders of the political context in violent fashion. This, in fact, seems to be the most appropriate response under such conditions: conditions under which discursive asymmetries are so vast that radically different modes of communication become necessary. In other words, intertextual differentiation, in the form of the politically marginalized, will respond forcefully to domination in situations defined by manipulated values portrayed as achieved absolutes.

For both Derrida and Habermas, language qua language is that which transcends any particular linguistic establishment. Similarly, they both recognize that language, whether as text or lifeworld, is constantly shifting, bending and contracting the horizons that establish its limits. Where they diverge pertains to the degree that movement within the transcendental impacts the concrete. Habermas believes that this movement can and should be politically neutralized, while for Derrida the politics of speaking or writing internalize the play of differences native to language. I have argued that Habermas's view that the meaning of truth, freedom and justice can be determined within the horizon of modernity is both theoretically untenable and politically undesirable. My suggestion is that a textualized theory of the lifeworld, complete with the extensional properties of intertextuality, would provide the basis for a more vibrant theory of communicative action.

POLITICS, ETHICS, AND THE AFTERMATH OF MODERNITY

In order for this to begin taking form, it is necessary to flesh out what can be meant by the term *theory* as well as the modifier *vibrant*. A critical theory, by definition one might say, can never be detached from contexts of political action. That is not to say that anything like an identity relationship between theory and practice is sought; but, rather, that theory must be sensitive to the possibilities and limits presented by situations that define political movement. The modifier *vibrant* serves as an indicator that seeks to identify the most radical possibilities that are availed by such situations. In my estimation this indicator points in the direction of radical egalitarianism rather than disciplined formal democracy.

It can be argued that Habermas has been driven throughout his career by the tensions that exist between radical egalitarianism and formal democracy. From *The Structural Transformation of the Public Sphere* to *Legitimation Crisis* and beyond that in *The Theory of Communicative Action* and his more recent work on questions concerning law and ethics, Habermas has struggled with what can simply be characterized as a form/content distinction. Another way to put this is that there is tension between Habermas the radical and Habermas the liberal. That tension is captured in the following remark: "The challenges of the twenty-first century will be of an order and magnitude that demand answers from Western societies which cannot be arrived at, nor put into practice, without radical-democratic universalization of interests through institutions for the formation of public opinion and political will."[46] On the one hand, radical democracy is deemed necessary if the revolutionary potential that has been brought about by the breakdown of bureaucratic communism in Eastern Europe is to be fulfilled; on the other, the radicality of this democratic thrust has to be checked by an institutional framework. One might surmise that this is simply an acknowledgment of the need (a need I would neither deny nor bemoan) for institutionalized decision-making procedures in any large political body. As will be argued below, however, I think there is more at stake than just that.

Egalitarianism and the Aftermath of Modernity

In order to determine what is at stake, it is necessary to consider democracy as a fundamental modern political value. One of the key developments that marks the shift from premodern to modern forms of political life is the linkage established between legitimation and democratization. In a very unusual sense this imperative was first formulated, on a theoretical level, in Hobbes's proclamation that all rights must be sacrificed to the sovereign. This move, and here again in a very unusual manner, paves the way for models of political legitimation that are not attached to an explicitly metaphysical conception of sovereignty. Habermas would identify this as a movement in a "postconventional" direction. In short, political authority is legitimate only insofar as it can be traced in some way to a point of public consent. One can of course find better (although I often wonder how much better) theoretical models for this in Rousseau,

Kant, and Hegel. The point in any case is that it became necessary in early modern political theory, as well as in the constitutional democracies that emerged in Europe and America, to sustain some type of claim to being democratic.

Whether anything like substantive democracy, or what I prefer to call political egalitarianism, has ever existed in modern societies is another question. If the modern conception of democracy is salvageable in any form, it is necessary to demonstrate that at some point it either operated effectively, or at least seemed to contain egalitarian possibilities. Habermas, who is currently the most renowned defender of modernity, while at the same time a rigorous critic of the view that in late modern societies the possibilities for democracy have been leveled, is keenly aware of this need. In some of his more recent work he has attempted to defend modernity on the grounds that the universal normative ideals—truth, freedom, and justice—that distinguish modernity as a postconventional epoch, reflect a substantive shift that can be viewed as fundamentally egalitarian. This analysis, in my estimation, has as its reference point Habermas's empirical work on the operatives of the early modern public sphere. As I discussed in chapter 4, whether this defense works is contingent upon the separability of those normative ideals, and that public sphere, from the economic and political imperatives that colonize the lifeworld, eliminating the possibility for substantive democracy. I have argued in both chapters 3 and 4 that this separation cannot be sustained.

As such, the tension that I noted above, that between radical egalitarianism and formal democracy, expresses itself as a dilemma: the dilemma of modernity.[47] Insofar as we are dealing with an historical period that can be legitimately characterized as forcing us to confront democracy (often in spite of itself), while at the same time systematically preventing the realization of democracy in the thick sense of the term, a contradiction emerges. This internal contradiction is likewise reflected in Habermas's formulation of communicative action, severely limiting its political significance. For these reasons I have suggested that communicative action would take on a new vibrancy if given a Derridean, *post*-modern, twist.

I would like to draw this analysis together by discussing the conditions for solidarity, the possibility for discourse, and the framework provided by political struggle. With respect to each of these important elements of any critical social theory, I think that Habermas is correct to focus on the lifeworld. But here again, the tensions in his work—which I would now like to formulate as the tension between political movement and interpretive work that is shaped by modernity versus that which is shaped by the aftermath of modernity—presents difficulties. As

I have argued, Habermas is leery of the more radical implications of his linguistic turn with respect to lifeworld theory. While he implicitly acknowledges the heterogenous character of the lifeworld's linguistic substrata, he denies that this will have a significant effect on the discursive arrangements that are lifeworld derivatives. In other words, he wants to derive relative homogeneity with respect to speech situations from a language medium that is differential and in a constant state of transformation. That enables him to view the discourse situation as prior to, and constitutive of, political solidarity: "Owing to the fact that communication oriented to reaching understanding has a validity basis, a speaker can persuade a hearer to accept a speech-act offer by guaranteeing that he will redeem a criticizable validity claim. In doing so, he creates a binding/bonding effect between speaker and hearer that makes the continuation of their interaction possible."[48] If the argument that I have presented concerning the textual character of the lifeworld is accepted, this priority is necessarily placed in question.

For Habermas, the only kind of struggle that factors into solidarity formation is that found in argumentative discourse. This, once again, hinges upon a relatively homogenous view of discursive situations. But if one takes seriously Habermas's recognition of the heterogenous character of language, as well as the fractured state of public discourse that results from systematic colonization of the lifeworld, it would seem that a prior form of struggle is necessary if solidarity is to be achieved. In other words, when conditions are such that shared meaning cannot be accounted for either linguistically or in terms of existing social unity, the establishment of discursive situations would necessarily involve struggling within and against those conditions. Hence, solidarity, established in the context of oppositional struggle, must precede situations in which reciprocal discourse is possible.

The direction in which I would like to push this analysis is toward thinking about the possibilities for radical egalitarianism in the aftermath of modernity rather than accepting the limits of modern democracy. My claim is that the lifeworld, even in its heterogeneity, can be thematized in relation to specific political objectives that disclose a certain set of possibilities. As even Habermas has acknowledged, it is this world-disclosing feature of the lifeworld that provides alternatives to established forms of life. In this manner the lifeworld provides a matrix within which struggles can emerge that attempt to overcome the impoverishment of modes of disclosure that are systematically restrained by imperatives that are external to those situated in positions of subordination. Through such struggles, which are initially aimed at negating existing forms of hegemony, solidarity can develop in such a way that new egalitarian possibilities emerge.

My suggestion is that the lifeworld in the aftermath of modernity is textured in such a way that articulations of possible new configurations are delimited by the framework within which opposition is conducted. The instantiation of these possibilities needs to resonate with the concerns of those engaged in opposition. Through this, discursive configurations will emerge that must be measured against their capacity to empower those that intervene into established discursive regimes. The term *configuration* is useful in that it acknowledges the need for solidarity without assuming that the conditions within which it can be established are fundamentally intact. The objective must be to develop, out of an existing lifeworld matrix, discursive situations in which radical democracy can operate. As such, the criterion of empowerment, checked by the need to resonate with the objectives of oppositional politics, situates the possibility for egalitarian community. In the final analysis I think this is only possible if we give up on the modern ideal (which in some ways Habermas embraces) that there can be a final analysis or an end of history. Hence, the radical egalitarianism, which can be shaped out of the textualized understanding of the lifeworld that I have been putting forth, would be construed in terms of a politics of enlightenment geared toward the aftermath of modernity.

Having laid out, in the most basic of terms, the political dimensions of this theory, it is necessary now to return to the discussion of ethics that served as its point of departure. I began this book with a discussion of the relationship between Kantian ethics and a theory of enlightenment. I have attempted to keep the spirit of this discussion in the forefront of the analyses that have followed. My position, as articulated in the first section of this chapter, is that Habermas's discourse ethic is the version of Kantian ethics most relevant to the project that I have elaborated. By way of the modified version that I have put forth, I have argued that there are important social and political implications of this ethic. I don't, however, want to subordinate ethics to politics. This has proven in numerous instances to be detrimental to the aims and aspirations of political movements that have laudable goals but lose sight of those ends in the process of the means that I referred to as political struggle. In other words, the question that remains pertains to the ethical backdrop that must be firmly in place if the politics of enlightenment is not to deteriorate into an unenlightened form of solidarity. While I am not prepared to spell this out at length, I will conclude with some remarks that will serve as points for further discussion.

First, I will restate what I mean by the aftermath of modernity. This formulation, as I noted in chapter 2, is an attempt to move beyond postmodernists such as Lyotard and Jean Baudrillard—those whom I would call the cynical postmodernists. According to their characterizations, the emancipatory content of the Enlightenment has been thoroughly depleted. This leaves us in a vacuum of sorts, insofar as the great thinkers of emancipation—Kant, Hegel, Marx, and so forth—were all products of this tradition. While accepting that we are in a vacuum of sorts, I want to resist the conclusion that cynical postmodernists draw from this: that the best we can hope for politically is an aestheticized liberalism that celebrates incompatibility, meaninglessness, and, in a sense, confused enslavement to the mediations of postindustrial capitalism. From this perspective, the vacuum of postmodernity is not a temporaly specific stage that is open to an array of possibilities; it is an atemporal state of ontologically determined despair. I don't want to belittle the observations that have contributed to this conclusion—only the conclusion itself. It stalls at the point of giving consideration to what it might take to bring an end to the end of history. As such, my terminological break with postmodernism is first and foremost a break with cynicism.

My characterization of the aftermath of modernity begins with, and stays with, the conditions of anomie and helplessness that lead to communicative breakdown at the societal level. Such a breakdown eliminates the possibilities for radical egalitarianism. In summary of points that I have developed throughout this work, there are a number of imperatives that operate vis-à-vis the late-modern lifeworld that indicate that things can't be other than what they are. Habermas himself is at times vulnerable to this sort of conclusion. What this amounts to is the recognition that the human condition suffers from an "energy crisis," and as a result of being de-energized, it is difficult to conceive of alternate fuels. I attribute this to a communicative breakdown in that due to the massiveness of societal problems (as analyzed by Habermas and others) our resources for commitment, achieving solidarity, and resisting violent fragmentation have been all but depleted. As I noted in chapter 4, Bill Martin describes this as the flattening of consciousness that results in the impasse of postmodernity. But he also looks at the possible conditions of moving beyond that impasse—an aftermath of postmodernity or a resumption of history. While I want to stick with the spirit of this vision, I wish to depart from the terminological letter. Rather than trying to breathe new life into what I consider to be a devalued term—postmodernity—I prefer, rather, to attempt to broaden its terminological and descriptive horizons with the hope of stretching our capacity to think in terms of future possibilities.

If communicative breakdown is, as I have suggested, at the heart of the problem, then fostering solidarity needs to be at the heart of the solution. My suggestion for pursuing this involves thinking of ethically based discourse as a resource for recovering those elements of the lifeworld that have been distorted by postmodern malaise. I would argue for this being an ethics on the grounds that a politics of recovery could not be readily distinguished from cynical postmodernism. I would argue for this being a recovery on the grounds that (1) the communicative breakdown is something that political consciousness needs quite literally to recover from, and (2) that insofar as we are in the aftermath of modernity—in a vacuum, but one with far-reaching horizons—our best bet is to reclaim values and traditions that have been devalued and disintegrated due to the colonization of the lifeworld and the imperatives of the steering media.

Reclaiming involves revaluing, and possibly even renaming. In order to recover the various devalued ideals and forms of life that will help us move in the direction of radical egalitarianism we must reconfigure, reconceptualize, and reevaluate the key enlightenment ideals that serve as our most important resources. As I have argued against Habermas, however, this cannot be achieved by defending a set of values that are more or less in place. It also requires more than substituting terms such as radical egalitarianism for democracy. It is necessary to go beyond putting a new handle on a battered old cup; the cup must also be filled with new meaning that displaces its previous semantic content. In the case of ethically grounded solidarity, it would require that invaluable enlightenment ideals be reinscribed into the textures of a reinflated lifeworld. Of these, the most important, and probably most devalued, is democracy. My suggestion is that we consider radical egalitarianism as an alternative to the ideals of formally democratic societies. How this would differ from democracy would depend on its institutional base and forms of consciousness that it allowed and nurtured. In other words, for such a model to be formulated it would by necessity take into account the radical differences that would have to come into contact in order for solidarity to congeal. For this reason, a communicative ethic that is sensitive to the question of alterity can contribute to the recovery of communicative possibilities necessary for the achievement of radical egalitarianism.

The danger of operating politically within the vacuum characteristic of the aftermath of modernity should be quite clear. When meaning has been seriously deformed, any positive articulation runs the risk of being strategically assimilated. I take this to be one of Habermas's foremost concerns and uphold his hesitancy to break with values that are indispensable to the emancipatory thrust of critical theory. Yet, if reforming these values is what it takes to move beyond the disaffection that is endemic in the societies that Habermas concerns himself with, then the risks that this entails must be explored. I would be the first to admit that there is no ethical principle that can protect against this completely. But rather than acquiescing to the conservative streak in Habermas, I urge for the exploration of a revalued notion of enlightenment that has the potential to generate possibilities in the aftermath of modernity. The most concrete way to pursue this is initiated by my attempt to rethink democracy under the rubric of radical egalitarianism. If we are to survive the impasse of postmodernity, we need to develop such a mode that is rooted in ethically based solidarity and sensitive to radical difference. This, I believe, requires a politics of enlightenment in the aftermath of modernity.

NOTES

1. DIALECTIC OF DIFFERENCE

1. Arendt 1982.

2. George A. Trey, "Rethinking the Public Sphere: Arendt's Shift from the Polis to the Politics of Judgment," presented at the 1991 meeting of the Society for Social and Political Philosophy.

3. See Ingram 1988.

4. As Kenneth Baynes (1992, 12) indicates, the politics of enlightenment, which draws out the political implications of Kant's moral philosophy, is not unequivocally supported by Kant's texts. "This claim concerning the unity of Kant's practical philosophy may seem suspect to those already familiar with his political theory. After all, Kant not only drew a sharp distinction between the realm of legality and the realm of morality, he also claimed that progress in the former does not insure any improvement in the latter." In order to sustain the reading that I am forwarding, it is necessary to highlight the "dialectical" side of Kant.

5. Kant 1983, 41–48.

6. Baynes notes that Kant draws an important distinction between validity and genesis. Validity is an ahistorical criteria, whereas genesis views the political moment in terms of past development and future possibilities. For Kant, the apparent development of a free and open public sphere plays an important role in social-political genesis. I'm particularly interested in the range of possibilities that this opens up. Exploring these seem to overcome Kant's remarks about the political viability of a race of devils.

7. Kant 1983, 29–40.

8. Kant 1983, 107–43.

9. I say that Kant is being conservative in that he makes concessions to the current power structure at the expense of exploring more fruitful ideals. This clearly runs contrary to his own definition of enlightenment, resorting to a cynicism that fails to take the possibility for enlightenment seriously.

10. See for example Herbert Marcuse, "Philosophy and Critical Theory," in David Ingram and Julia Simon-Ingram, eds., 1992. Marcuse writes the following: "Kant had, of course, written essays on universal history with cosmopolitan intent, and on perpetual peace. But his transcendental philosophy aroused the belief that the realization of reason through factual transformation was unnecessary, since individuals could become rational and free within the established order" (7). If Marcuse's point is simply that Kant saw enlightenment to be attainable within the confines of the bourgeois order, that seems right. My

analysis has attempted to set up Kant's views in terms of their critical potential for getting beyond that paradigm.

11. Baynes 1992, 12.

12. Horkheimer and Adorno 1972.

13. See Dubiel 1985, 69–81. Dubiel recognizes three phases in the theoretical development of the Frankfurt circle. The phase with which I am concerned he labels "the critique of instrumental reason." This is distinguished from the previous phases—the first of which focuses on formulating Marxist materialism in light of early-twentieth-century economic conditions and the second, which develops an interdisciplinary approach to social studies—by distancing itself from question of political economy and developing a quasi-structuralist critique of Western rationality. The particular historical events that most concerned Horkheimer and Adorno were the rise of fascism, Stalinism, and the vulnerability to authoritarianism that they detected in the Allied countries.

14. Seyla Benhabib (1986, 168) notes that this project results in a paradox. "The critique of Enlightenment becomes as totalizing as the false totality it seeks to criticize." Habermas, in *The Philosophical Discourse of Modernity*, echoes this criticism. I tend to think that this problem has been overemphasized. Horkheimer and Adorno don't explicitly renounce the enlightenment tradition; rather they analyze its failure to live up to its own normative standards. For a valuable defense of their position, see Larry Ray 1989, 69–110.

15. Horkheimer and Adorno point to pre-Socratic cosmologies, as well as Platonic and Aristotelian metaphysics, as examples of this (DE, 6).

16. In contemporary semiotic theory this point would be characterized in terms of the discrepancy between signifier and signified. Insofar as the two never meet, there is no sign. Hence, there are merely chains of signification that can have either a hierarchical or relational organization. Horkheimer and Adorno's point seems to be that the inability to produce symbolic unity necessarily results in hierarchical, dominative structure. I would challenge this view by arguing for a more communitarian form of disunity. This would involve appealing to a historically fluid lifeworld as the social basis of discourse.

17. Horkheimer and Adorno are here playing on the Comtean stages of human understanding. We first understand things religiously or theologically, this develops into metaphysical or philosophical understanding; then finally, once our mode of understanding has sufficiently matured, we come to view things scientifically. Horkheimer and Adorno are attempting to refute the claim of progress that Comte wants to make. See selections from Comte in Ronald Nash, ed., 1969, 8–10.

18. As Adorno puts it: "Universal history must be construed and denied. After the catastrophes that have happened, and in view of the catastrophes to come, it would be cynical to say that a plan for a better world is manifested in history and unites it. Not to be denied for that reason, however, is the unity that cements the discontinuous, chaotically splintered moments and phases of history—the unity of the control of nature, progressing to rule over, and finally to that over men's inner nature. No universal history leads from savagery to humanitarianism, but there is one leading from the slingshot to the megaton bomb" (Adorno 1973a, 320).

19. Much of Adorno's and Horkheimer's work prefigures and surpasses Jean Baudrillard's writings on the political economy of the sign.

20. This ambiguity is pointed out in most of the critical literature. Helmut Dubiel sums the situation up as follows: "This judgment—which might be classified in terms of sociology of knowledge—about the conditions for the circle's own work is radicalized in the 1940s to the point of nullifying itself self-referentially" (Dubiel 1985, 82).

21. The independent authorship of the excursuses is not acknowledged by Horkheimer and Adorno. See Seyla Benhabib 1986, 20.

22. I am not claiming that there is a historical connection that substantiates the relationships that I am attempting to establish. The fact that there is a historical connection between Habermas and Horkheimer and Adorno is not pertinent to the argument that I am presenting. My claim is simply that *Dialectic of Enlightenment* is a seminal work concerning the question of enlightenment and rationality given the circumstances of the twentieth century, and that Foucault and Habermas address these issues from different perspectives—both of which can be derived from Horkheimer and Adorno's analysis.

23. Instrumental rationality is the use of reason in a strictly purposive fashion. The fundamental consequence of this is that the "praxis" of reason homes in on its end without considering the repercussion of its process. For a detailed discussion of this, see Benhabib 1986, 149–63, and Dubiel 1985, 88–99.

24. Adorno writes the following: "Man's domination over himself which grounds his selfhood, is almost always the destruction of the subject in whose service it is undertaken; for the substance which is dominated, suppressed, and dissolved by virtue of self-preservation is none other than that very life as functions of which the achievements of self-preservation find their sole definition and determination: it is, in fact, what is to be preserved. The irrationalism of totalitarian capitalism, whose way of satisfying needs has an objectified form determined by domination which makes the satisfaction of needs impossible and tends toward the extermination of mankind, has its prototype in the hero who emerges from sacrifice by sacrificing himself" (DE, 54–55).

25. David Ingram (1986, 314) points this out in "Foucault and the Frankfurt School: A Discourse on Nietzsche, Power and Knowledge." Having discussed the theoretical similarities between the position taken by Adorno and Horkheimer in *Dialectic of Enlightenment* and the themes that dominate Foucault's work, and with reference to the paradox that I have alluded to, Ingram states the following: "Asserting the prerogative of reason against itself or imputing a rational authority to one's own declamations that are without absolute foundation appear to be contradictions that Foucault has sought to avoid."

26. Foucault's first important work, *Madness and Civilization*, initiates a series of reflections on the consequences of the rationalization of people's everyday lives. These ideas evolved and were refined throughout his career and are represented in nearly all of his writings.

27. While for the purposes of this discussion an actual historical connection between Foucault and Adorno is not necessary, Foucault does view his work to be conducted in the spirit of critique that is characteristic of the Frankfurt School. In light of the Kantian questioning of the nature of enlightenment, which Fou-

cault understands to be a questioning of the present, he states the following about his methodological heritage: "One can opt for a critical philosophy of truth in general, or one can opt for a critical thought which has the form of an ontology of ourselves, an ontology of the present; it is this latter form of philosophy which, from Hegel to the Frankfurt School by way of Nietzsche and Max Weber, has founded a form of reflection within which I have tried to work" (1986, 96).

28. Foucault points out that there are some affinities between his approach to social theory and the objectives of the Enlightenment. For example, both insist that it is necessary to push forward with and both share the objective of increasing human freedom. Foucault disagrees rather sharply, however, on questions of science, progress, and rationality.

29. Here I think that Horkheimer would have done well to read Kant a bit more sympathetically. While there clearly is a sort of fetish to compartmentalize in the second Critique, and even more so in the first, to limit an analysis of these rich texts to that dimension is to do so at the expense of appropriating the powerful moral content in a politically radical manner.

30. Habermas 1982, 29–43.

31. Habermas 1987b, 362 (*The Philosophical Discourse of Modernity*, hereafter PDM).

32. Derrida 1982, 109–36.

33. It should be quite clear how precisely this links up with Habermas's overriding goal in developing a theory of communicative action.

34. See Trey 1989.

2. MODERNITY, LATE MODERNITY, POSTMODERNITY

1. 1986, 226.

2. Ibid., 227.

3. As I mentioned in chapter 1, the analysis of postwar twentieth-century society in *Dialectic of Enlightenment* is sobering to the point of leading one to quietism. The following samples form their most consequential subsequent works do little to dispel this deep pessimism: "The revolt of natural man—in the sense of the backward strata of the population—against the growth of rationality has actually furthered the formalization of reason, and has served to fetter rather than free nature. In this light, we might describe fascism as a satanic synthesis of reason and nature—the very opposite of that reconciliation of the two poles that philosophy has always dreamed of" (Horkheimer 1974, 122–23). "After the catastrophes that have happened, and in view of the catastrophes to come, it would be cynical to say that a plan for a better world is manifested in history and unites it. Not to be denied for that reason, however, is the unity that cements the discontinuous, chaotically splintered moments and phases of history—the unity of the control of nature, progressing to rule over men, and finally to that over men's inner nature. No universal history leads from savagery to humanitarianism, but there is one leading from the slingshot to the megaton bomb" (Adorno 1973a, 320). Given the significance of Horkheimer's and Adorno's influence upon Habermas it is remarkable that he places so much

stock in the rationality that his mentors so roundly criticized. Habermas would argue that both failed to recognize the reflexivity that developed in discourse during the modern epoch. As such, in systems where discursive communication is not systematically distorted (such as Nazi Germany—critical theory's paradigm case), norms of action can always be called into question in such a manner that reasons must be provided to support validity claims. I will take up Habermas' position later in this chapter. For his critique of Horkheimer and Adorno, see chapter 1. Also see chapter 5 of *The Philosophical Discourse of Modernity* and chapter 4 of *The Theory of Communicative Action.*

4. Habermas points out in "Psychic Thermidor and the Rebirth of Rebellious Subjectivity" that negative thinking, such as that of Horkheimer and Adorno, doesn't have to result in lamenting the horrors of the present. The third key member of the Frankfurt School provides an alternative: "No doubt, Herbert Marcuse claimed negation to be the very essence of thinking—as did Adorno and Horkheimer; but the driving force of criticism, of contradiction and contest carried him well beyond the limits of an accusation of unnecessary mischief. Marcuse moved further ahead. He did not hesitate to advocate, in an affirmative mood, the fulfillment of human needs, of the need for undeserved happiness, of the need for beauty, of the need for peace, calm, and privacy. Although, certainly, Marcuse was not an affirmative thinker, he nevertheless was the most affirmative among those that praised negativity. With him negative thinking retained the dialectical trust in determinate negation, in the disclosure of possible alternatives" (Bernstein 1985, 67). Marcuse has often been criticized for being hopelessly utopian. Habermas, nevertheless, applauds this up to a point. His primary disagreement with Marcuse pertains to the focal point of emancipatory rationality. For Marcuse, reason is embedded in human instinct (this view ties Marcuse to the same philosophy of nature that stifled Horkheimer and Adorno) whereas for Habermas it is to be found in communicative structures. See Habermas's and Marcuse's discussion of their respective views in "Theory and Politics: A Discussion with Herbert Marcuse, Jürgen Habermas, Heinz Lubasz and Telman Spengler," in *Telos* 38 (1978–79):124–53.

5. 1986, 227.

6. This thesis is developed in a number of Marx's writings (many in collaboration with Engels). See for example *Manifesto of the Communist Party, The Marx-Engels Reader*, pp. 469–500. While Marx substantiates his theory with considerably more data in later works, such as the mammoth *Capital*, the general idea is conveyed effectively and enthusiastically in this pamphlet.

7. See David McLellan 1973, 280–84. Here McLellan provides an account of Marx's indebtedness to the bourgeois tradition of political economy (Smith and Ricardo in particular). It seems quite clear that Marx never dreamed that the state would save capitalism through political intervention. This would run contrary to the enlightenment view (Smith's invisible hand) that things left to themselves always balance out. While Marx of course was highly critical of this theory, he didn't suspect that the political magnates operating the bourgeoisie superstructure would also recognize its limits.

8. Habermas considers Marx's fundamental error to be his failure to recognize the resilience of capitalism: "Capitalism's capacity to adapt is very great:

it is an incredibly flexible order, which still possesses significant cultural and motivational reserves. It is surprising how it has been able to combine different forms of social integration" (Dews, ed., 1986, 64).

9. See in particular Marx's *Theory of Surplus Value.*

10. Dews 1986, 65.

11. Habermas uses these criteria for evaluating all societies. His analysis, which develops a "social-scientific concept of crisis" examines three increments of social evolution: primitive, traditional and liberal-capitalist (see chart in LC, p. 24). This exhibits Habermas's view that societies all evolve along similar lines that result in their either becoming Western-like or stagnating prior to that point. Benhabib is quite critical of this view. Developmental sequences cannot be determined with respect to social orders in the same way that they can in human individuals as there exists no determinate end to societies (I would contest that there is a determinate end for individuals also). As such, no confirmable model by which existing societies can be measured for regressive or deviant developments is available. On the other hand, the future is always unknown and unknowable; there is no available data about futures that allows the theorist to do more than anticipate and project what will be. "To put the objection I am raising to Habermas in a nutshell: if the problem with early critical theory seemed to be that their conception of utopian reason was so esoteric as not to allow embodiment in the present, the difficulty with Habermas' concept is that it seems like such a natural outcome of the present that it is difficult to see what would constitute an emancipatory break with the present if communicative rationality were fulfilled" (Benhabib 1986, 276–77). This is a crucial point. My central argument against Habermas will take this up in subsequent chapters.

12. I am of course referring here to Adam Smith's famous invisible hand metaphor. See Smith 1937, 423.

13. This occurs in several ways, the most obvious of which is to "buy off the proletariat." Wages are much higher but the worker is still at the mercy of the industrial complex. Another way is through the shifts in class. Marx's model holds that classes are defined purely in terms of socioeconomic status and that this is reducible to the distinction between owner and worker. In advanced capitalism different distinguishing characteristics become more determinate. For example, the rise of "pink-collar workers," women in low-paying service jobs, indicates that gender plays an important role in exploitation in advanced capitalism. See Ben Agger, "The Dialectic of Deindustrialization: An Essay on Advanced Capitalism," in Forester 1985, 9, 10, 16–19.

14. In addition to *Legitimation Crisis* I am drawing upon Habermas's essay "What Does Crisis Mean Today? Legitimation Problems in Late Capitalism" (LPC).

15. When asked why advanced capitalist countries have not yet experienced legitimation crises, Habermas's response is simply that we tend toward crisis; it cannot be determined at what point irremedial economic dysfunctions will emerge as actual crises. He does, however, identify the following phenomena as strong indicators that crisis is immanent: failure to vote by a large percentage of the population, disintegration of the two-party system, success of a third-party platform, and the emergence of a socioeconomic class

that experiences a great deal of discomfort. See Dews 1986, 66.

16. See Habermas's discussion in "Conservatism and Capitalist Crisis," in Dews 1986, 67–68. Here he states in unequivocal terms that democratic forms of life are part of the human telos (or one might say human nature). This seems to cohere with the claim that intersubjective communication is the telos of language. Neither of these assertions can be verified empirically or argued for convincingly. Habermas's enlightenment aspirations clearly shape his interpretation of human nature and the ends of language. This also represents a reaction to the "stalemated" critical theory that emerges after *Dialectic of Enlightenment.* As I will argue later, a shift away from the goals of *the* Enlightenment does not necessarily lead to pessimistic quietism. While I agree that participatory forms of government is the route to go, I see no reason to think that social evolution will lead to this. As such, normative theory needs to consider strategies that promote more revolutionary modes of action.

17. See Habermas's introduction to *Theory and Practice*, "Some Difficulties in the Attempt to Link Theory and Praxis." The section subtitled "Objectivity of Knowledge and Interest" is particularly relevant to the argument that I am developing. It fails to meet my objections for reasons that will become clear shortly.

18. See Habermas's discussion of the Heidelberg Research Project in Systems Analysis in *Towards a Rational Society*, pp. 70–73, for an example of this.

19. Ben Agger, in "A Critical Theory of Discourse," an article that contests the practicability of Habermas's theory of discourse, indicates the importance of the powerless setting the agenda for dialogue. While Agger regresses in the direction of orthodox Marxism at times, and settles for the philosophically questionable theories of Herbert Marcuse, this is a crucial point that Habermas fails to accommodate. By insisting on a movement toward discursive symmetry by way of therapeutically transforming those who are not presently competent, he ignores the fact that within the boundaries of many populist movements symmetry already exists, and that this is a source of power. I would argue that the power embodied in these corporate units should be exercised against the established sectors of power. This of course pits power against power—something that rationalists like Habermas would loathe. My argument will be that this is necessary if the gap between the empowered and the subordinated in late modern society is to be dissolved.

20. For a critical discussion of this see Anthony Giddens's "Reason without Revolution? Habermas' Theorie des kommunikativen Handelns," in Bernstein 1985, 95–121. See in particular pp. 112–21.

21. For Habermas's view of social evolution, see *Legitimation Crisis*, pp. 20–23. His view is that all societies evolve along similar lines in a manner that is characterized by increasing rationality and increasing freedom. For a critique of this, see Benhabib 1986, 270–77.

22. See "The Entwinement of Myth and Enlightenment," *The Theory of Communicative Action*, and *The Philosophical Discourse of Modernity.*

23. See Schutz and Luckmann 1973.

24. Habermas draws a parallel between social evolution and ontogenesis in humans. Following Lawrence Kohlberg, he contends that in the same way that

children develop such that they achieve increasing ability to resolve conflicts, societies evolve so that they are more capable of resolution. This of course would be the case if consensual communication were visibly the main medium of dispute and resolve (see *Communication and the Evolution of Society*, pp. 69–94, and TCA, 2:172–79). The analogy Habermas draws is quite obviously questionable. "Is the structural isomorphism between the two developmental schemas strong enough to justify the way of proceeding? The homology is strongest, Habermas observes, in the case of cognitive development, weaker in the case of moral development. In both cases one can observe roughly parallel paths of decentration. Nevertheless, there are places where the analogy breaks down. The pattern of individual development cannot mirror that of social evolution, since even the most primitive societies have institutionalized (at the adult level) relatively advanced interactive competencies involving reciprocity and generalized expectations. Again, the sorts of crises confronting the individual personality differ from those encountered by the social system and hence call for different developmental solutions" (Ingram 1987, 133).

25. Klaus Hartmann (1985) states that Habermas fails to recognize that the steering media of the capitalist economy are in fact linguistic (p. 152). Habermas does not commit this error, as a careful reading clearly reveals. When Habermas uses the term "delinguistification," he does not mean to imply that activities such as negotiation and "dealing," which are central to the capitalist mode of exchange, are engaged in simply by flashing great rolls of money. Rather, his point is that the linguistic aspect is secondary and does not utilize the "understanding reaching" capacity that is inherent in language.

26. Here Habermas follows Marx in pointing out that bourgeois law and bourgeois democracy do not reflect the enlightened ideals that they are supposed to objectively preserve. As long as there is class differentiation based on access to steering media (money and power), there will be discrimination in these spheres.

27. Specifically the faith in rationality, science, and technology. Late modern phenomena such as the Holocaust, nuclear war, the arms race, and environmental crises suggest that these Enlightenment ideals produce the exact opposite of what was intended.

28. Bill Martin expresses this concern in terms of the loss of the possibility for community: "Humanity is on the verge of forever losing the sense of community, even as this sense seems to have been recreated in thousands of diffuse ways. Though the word, 'community,' is a commonplace of public discourse it is a mere trace of its former self" (1992, 1). Martin goes on to argue that the loss of the meaning of the word *community* is virtually equivalent to the loss of the meaning of what it is to be human, a possibility that he associates with "the impasse of postmodernity." I see strong resonances between Martin's concern with the loss of meaning and Habermas's concern with the colonization of the lifeworld that issues in the new obscurity. Both focus on the question of the regeneration of human-being through semantic analyses that lay out the possibilities for renewal. See the third chapter of Martin's *Matrix and Line* for an important critique of Habermas's semantic theory.

29. This is a key point in the argument that I am developing in that here Habermas explicitly recognizes that importance of Foucault's analysis of ratio-

nalized processes of "normalization": "It is this reifying and subjectivating power that Foucault has traced into even the thinnest capillary branchings of everyday communication. The distortions within such a regulated, analyzed, controlled, and watched-over lifeworld are certainly more subtle than the obvious forms of material exploitation, and impoverishment; but these conflicts, shifted into the domains of the psychological and the bodily, internalized, are no less destructive for all that" (TNO, 9). This points precisely to the gap that I am trying to thematize—that between modernity and postmodernity—within which a different notion of the politics of enlightenment needs to take shape.

30. Also see Habermas's discussion of new social movements in TCA, 2:391–96.

31. For an interesting discussion of this, see the introduction to Hannah Arendt, *The Life of the Mind.*

32. I am intentionally couching this discussion in a vocabulary that highlights the internal incoherence that Habermas finds with postmodernism. While one wearies of hearing him harp on about performative contradictions, there are points at which he is just right about this.

33. I feel as though this is a charitable reading of Lyotard's remark. Less charitably I would say that it's a bit silly to think that the impossible can be violent. The very fact that it is possible brings about the threat of violence. Habermas is also guilty of this sort of double talk. His concern with violence is a more legitimate one but nonetheless problematic. Any viable theory of emancipation must be able to recognize that violence is *always* within the realm of *possibility.*

34. It is a point of interest that a theory that is so deeply committed to reciprocity has painfully little to say about listening. We get an elaborate characterization of the way that speech acts operate but there is an assumption that the reception of speech acts is unproblematic. The question of listening, which is a hot topic in popular psychology, of all places, is flagrantly ignored in what I consider to be the most sophisticated theory of communication available. This strikes me as an important issue for critical theorists to address.

35. Both these points are addressed by Habermas to a certain extent in *The Philosophical Discourse of Modernity*, where he refigures the subject so as to accommodate poststructuralist critiques of the modern version of subjectivity, and also recharacterizes the narrative of emancipation. These responses might not satisfy Lyotard, and don't entirely satisfy me, but they do show how to get beyond the dichotomy between the totally fragmented subject that Lyotard propounds and the idea of subject as absolute totality that follows from one reading of Kant. Axel Honneth's discussion of this at the 1992 meeting of the Society for Phenomenological and Existential Philosophy is instructive on this point.

36. It is significant that Lyotard attempts to identify his normative postmodernism with maturity. This is of course the way that Kant defines enlightenment. In his view enlightenment meant waking up to our own capacity for freedom. For Lyotard, maturity is precisely the opposite of this. Lyotard explicitly writes off this side of Kant's work in *Just Gaming* as being totalizing. "But nonetheless it goes without saying for Kant—and it is very clear in the article on "Enlightenment," and in "The Cosmopolitan Idea," or in the "Project of Perpetual Peace"—that humanity must form a whole" (JG, 86). For this reason it is

Kant's third Critique that plays the most important role in Lyotard's "postmodern" Kantianism (Ingram 1988).

37. See Ludwig Wittgenstein, *Philosophical Investigations*.

38. Lyotard's model is really more economic than linguistic and the game is much more like monopoly than chess. His views reflect that side of modern life that Habermas associates with system imperatives. Rather than show the normative depravity of this, however, Lyotard attempts to describe it in a manner that celebrates the constant strife and contestation that prevents the realization of a social or political totality.

39. This sounds like a typically superficial growth-economy claim. For a careful critique of the normative failure of growth economics theory, see David Schweickart, *Against Capitalism*, chapter 4.

40. Jameson 1990, 5.

41. Originally published in 1984, this essay is reprinted in its entirety in *Postmodernism, or, The Cultural Logic of Late Capitalism* (CLC).

42. For a useful summary of Jameson's Marxist approach to postmodernism, see Callinicos 1990, 128–32.

43. Norris 1990, 7.

44. As I indicated in chapter 1, I believe this sort of analysis distorts the potential that lies in a Kantian political philosophy.

45. See the introduction to CLC.

3. MODERN NORMATIVITY

1. References to fascist propaganda are made throughout *Dialectic of Enlightenment*. A more focused analysis can be found in Adorno's "Freudian Theory and the Pattern of Fascist Propaganda" (1982). The objective of this critique is to demonstrate that language can function as a dangerous weapon; when properly deployed it literally circumscribes vast numbers of people, penetrating their minds with fascist ideology. Horkheimer and Adorno, in their general discussion of language in DE, seem to want to pin the development of this phenomenon on, in Horkheimer's case, polluted Enlightenment rationality, or in Adorno's case, virtually every manifestation of rationality from Homer on. While they don't present their case as such, it is quite clear that they use the language of fascism as an interpretive guide. Adorno in particular has a propensity to smell conspiracy in every nook and cranny of history.

2. Thomas McCarthy 1978, 273.

3. See Dallmayr 1984, 123–25.

4. Habermas cites three basic criteria for discerning incomprehensibility in communicative practices: (1) rule deviation—either syntactic or semantic; (2) context disorientation—use of linguistic gestures that are inappropriate to a given situation; (3) lack of congruency—a disintegration in the coherence between linguistic symbols, action, and nonverbal gestures (SDC, 206–7).

5. Two meaning constitutives supplement the semantic structure of the propositional content of performative utterances: interactional indicators and situational determinants.

6. As I mentioned above, Habermas's acute awareness of the potential for communicative practice to lapse into dominating modes seems to be shaped by fascism. As such, grasping the social-structural contexts that allow language to be abused in the way that it was in fascist propaganda is crucial. This is why Habermas insists on taking the pragmatic dimension of communication so seriously.

7. For a useful summary of this, see McCarthy's discussion in *The Critical Theory of Jürgen Habermas*, pp. 273–76, or John Thompson's essay, "Universal Pragmatics," in *Habermas: Critical Debates*, edited by Thompson and David Held.

8. Habermas goes into considerable detail about the relationship between the mode and objective domain of analysis. He provides a summary of this discussion in a chart on p. 33 of UP.

9. Habermas identifies three basic types of action, all of which fall under the general rubric of social action: Symbolic action utilizes expressive modes that are incapable of conveying propositional content (instrumental music or dance). Strategic action is action that is oriented exclusively to the success of the speaker (generally manipulative or domineering, but not necessarily so). Communicative action is action that strives for mutual understanding (as modeled by the ideal speech situation). At this point Habermas directs his analysis toward communicative action.

10. Habermas makes the point that nonsocial or "instrumental action" can play a role in social action. "Instrumental actions can be connected with and subordinated to social interactions of a different type—for example, as the 'task elements' of social roles" (TCA 1, 285).

11. This is an extremely important move for Habermas. He does not want to work from the philosophical foundation of subjectivity or abstract consciousness.

12. Habermas defends this in terms of the universal pragmatic (or formal pragmatic as he calls it here) semantic analysis. Insofar as there is little new development in this context I will not discuss it any further.

13. For a detailed account of the development of Habermas's latest version of the theory of communicative action, see Ingram 1987, chapter 3.

14. Jameson makes several direct references to Habermas in this discussion. "They think (along with the Habermassians today, perhaps) that the revolutionary ideals of the bourgeois society—freedom and equality—are properties of real societies." His point, as is mine, seems to be that even those on the more radical side of liberalism will always balk at the idea of fundamentally transforming society. Habermas has deemed it unrealistic to think that such change is possible. This, Jameson would accord, is a simple case of ideological deception.

15. Since the question that I am addressing focuses on twentieth-century capitalism I will concentrate on the problems of that period. Both Foucault and Habermas (and more importantly Marx) recognize that the forms of domination which have developed in the twentieth century have historical antecedents. Recent phenomena, however, take on a distinctly different character that can be linked to the way that capitalism has developed.

16. I borrow the term "cure" from Bill Martin. See his "The Enlightenment Talking Cure: Habermas, Legitimation Crisis and the Recent Political Landscape." This is in fact a crucial point as Habermas has consistently used medical terminology (distortion, crisis, pathology) to describe flaws in the modern system. This protects the much talked about, but rarely exemplified, modern sense of normativity.

17. I am using Habermas's language here for the sake of expediency. I do not accept either the category of system or lifeworld per se. I am particularly suspicious of Habermas's notion of the lifeworld. His characterization of the lifeworld lends itself to the interpretation that it is a pure, but lost origin of modernity and as such his theory is suggestive of return to an untainted past. If my position is valid the entire idea of the isolated lifeworld is put into question. If all the practices that are supposedly grounded in the modern lifeworld are hypothetical, then what is left of the foundation?

18. An obvious example of this would be the explicit slave labor of the seventeenth through nineteenth centuries in the United States, what for all practical purposes was slave labor in both Europe and the United States as industry developed, the "apartheid"-like setups that exist in most large urban areas in the United States, and the type of "enslavement" referred to earlier in this section that is less explicit—the type that Habermas acknowledges Foucault as revealing.

19. I want to be clear that I am not renouncing productivity per se (as does Bataille in some instances and as Foucault has been accused of doing). I am opposing in this context the types of production that are needed to maintain consumerism: production that is grounded in the normative concept of profit rather than justice.

20. For an excellent discussion of this, framed in considerable historical detail, see Roberto Mangabeira Unger, 1976, chapters 2 and 3.

21. This, of course, is essentially the argument made by Horkheimer and Adorno (1972) as well as Herbert Marcuse (1964). Habermas's response to these works questioned the conventional Marxist notion of ideology to which they appealed. While the concept of false consciousness is certainly problematic, the critique that these authors produce seems to stand without a deep committment to the specifics of Marxian ideology critique. For Habermas's response, see Habermas 1970a, chapter 6.

22. For a detailed discussion of this problem, see Stanley Aronowitz 1988, chapter 1. See also in Aronowitz an account of the dialogue between first and second generation critical theorists concerning modern science (chaps. 4 and 5).

4. THE POLITICS OF ENLIGHTENMENT

1. Calhoun 1992, 2.

2. For a useful discussion of this, see part I of Helmut Dubiel, *Theory and Politics.*

3. I would suggest that this essay looks to a theory of the aftermath of modernity—a theory that can only develop through a radical appropriation of

modern thinkers such as Kant, Hegel, Marx, Nietzsche, and Freud. The simple fact that critical theory is so eclectic is in and of itself a sign that it attempts to move beyond modernism.

4. For a general discussion of this, see Held 1980, 29–39. Susan Buck-Morss also makes this point, although hers is directed more at Adorno. She goes so far as to claim that Adorno never was invested in the proletariat. "Whereas Jay [Martin] has written of the Frankfurt Institute in general and Horkheimer in particular that they reluctantly gave up belief in the revolutionary power of the proletariat only after Hitler's consolidation of power and still not fully until the outbreak of World War II, it is impossible to document such a gradual disillusionment in the case of Adorno. This does not necessarily prove that Adorno never placed his hope in the proletariat. What it does indicate is that he refused to incorporate this class within the foundation of his theory, to allow theory's validity to be in any way dependent upon the existence of a collective revolutionary subject or the possibility of its direct application to political praxis" (Buck-Morss 1977 24–25). Kathleen League, in "Adorno: No Sell Out," takes strong exception with those who claim that Adorno is a cynical quietist. Her response to this position, which is rooted in a careful analysis of *Aesthetic Theory*, is that the emancipation of oppressed peoples has always been at the heart of Adorno's work and comes to fruition in his theory of art. My own position is somewhere between these poles. The question for me is whether there is emancipatory potential in the later works of first-generation critical theorists. While I want to answer that question affirmatively I think it is necessary to establish linkages between there work and that of the more explicitly emancipation-oriented Habermas.

5. For an interesting discussion of this, see Fredric Jameson, *Late Marxism: Adorno, or the Persistence of the Dialectic*, pp. 1–12, and 15–24. Adorno dealt with this problem most directly in *Negative Dialectics*.

6. If *The Structural Transformation of the Public Sphere* is an example of such an effort—which I think it is—it is not one that met with the approval of the first-generation Frankfurt School higher-ups. Habermas submitted this work to Horkheimer and Adorno as his Habilitationschrift. They rejected it on the grounds that it was not critical enough of the enlightenment tradition of democracy and too radically attached to the idea of egalitarianism. For a discussion of this, see Calhoun 1992, 4.

7. See Nancy Fraser, "What's Critical about Critical Theory," in Fraser 1989, 113–43; and Ryan 1989, 27–45. Also see Martin 1992, chapter 3.

8. An entire volume of *Social Text* was devoted to this topic. Also, a conference was held at the University of North Carolina at Chapel Hill that resulted in a volume entitled *Habermas and the Public Sphere*. Both offer a broad range of perspectives on Habermas's early work on the public sphere. The latter includes an article by Habermas titled "Further Reflections on the Public Sphere," as well as a transcribed discussion between the conference participants and Habermas.

9. See in particular Geof Eley, "Nations, Publics and Political Culture: Placing Habermas in the Nineteenth Century"; Mary Ryan, "Gender and Public Access: Women's Politics in Nineteenth-Century America"; and Nancy

Fraser, "Rethinking the Public Sphere: A Contribution to the Critique of Actually Existing Democracy," all in Calhoun 1992.

10. In Habermas's recent reflections on the public sphere he is more sensitive to the exclusionary character of the ideal type of the bourgeois public sphere. He notes that the "exclusion of the culturally and politically mobilized lower strata entails a pluralization of the public sphere in the very process of the emergence. Next to, and interlocked with, the hegemonic public sphere, a plebeian one assumes shape" ("Further Reflections on the Public Sphere" [FRPS], 426). This, he contends, has altered his understanding of the normative theory that he extracts from the bourgeois public sphere, moving him toward communication theory as the foundation for modern normativity (FRPS, 442). This sort of foundation has the benefit of being deeper, but it loses some of its critical potential in that it becomes, to a certain extent, dehistoricized. Then the question of how modern it is in fact becomes more important. My own view is that the theory of communicative action is ahistorical and that modernity become simply a conceptual, rather than historical, construct in Habermas's theory.

11. *Social Text* 1991, 25/26:56–80.

12. Joan Landes, *Women and the Public Sphere in the Age of the French Revolution* (Ithaca, N.Y.: Cornell University Press, 1988).

13. In Calhoun 1992.

14. This is essentially the argument that I was presenting concerning modern normativity in chapter 3.

15. The title of this section is clearly borrowed from Holub's book.

16. Most readers will recall such attempts by several American revisionist historians in the early 1980s. The revisionists in Germany are nowhere near the fanatical positions forwarded by this group.

17. Habermas repeatedly refers to the revisionists as "modern" historians. My guess would be that such remarks are tongue in cheek and that what he really wants to convey is a deviation from modern standards. This would further advance my view that the Historikerstreit is as much a debate about postmodernism as is the postmodernism debate itself.

18. In Habermas 1989a.

19. It is important to note that the debate to which I, and other authors are referring, is not really a debate at all. It has tended to be rather onesided—with Habermas writing extended polemics against the so-called postmodernists, and with them making brief and merely occasional responses. Authors such as Holub, Kellner, and Best extend Habermas's comments on Derrida, Foucault, etc. to Lyotard—the only self-proclaimed postmodernist that Habermas even mentions—but in fact it is with Lyotard that there has been the least engagement.

20. Habermas's first intervention into the Historikerstreit took place at the Romereburg colloquium. His comments here made explicit his efforts to link revisionism to Heideggerianism. See *The New Conservatism*, pp. 207–11.

21. See "Closing Remarks," in *The New Conservatism*, pp. 241–48.

22. Bill Martin, *Matrix and Line* (1992).

23. See Bagdikian, 1989 and 1990.

24. Bagdikian 1990, ix.

25. Kellner 1990, 34.

26. The *New York Times* had a number of articles dealing with pool reporting in the first three weeks of January 1991, none of them complete and none of them publishing the actual regulations. Once the war began, there was a small notice in each edition of the paper, buried in the middle pages of the war coverage, titled "Censors Screen Pooled Reports." However, in stating that the "system" was "worked out beforehand," the notice leads readers to believe that (1) the media participated in drawing up the guidelines (which is false); (2) that a paper as respected as the *Times* does not object to the arrangement (which may well be true); and (3) that, therefore, the arrangement is not problematic.

27. Sydney Schanberg, "A Muzzle for the Press," collected in M. Sifry and C. Cerf, eds., *The Gulf War Reader*, p. 369.

28. Schanberg 1991, 373.

5. ETHICAL DISCOURSE AND RADICAL EGALITARIANISM

1. It should be noted that Habermas's naturalistic or teleological view of the purpose of discourse has always been reserved and has arguably been rejected (by Habermas). I think that it is important to note that he has, at times, used this sort of language as it does suggest ways in which other terminology is being used in other contexts. I'm not claiming here that Habermas is a language metaphysician, or that I think there is something dreadful about this even if he is. My point is simply that the Aristotelian notion of design occasionally surfaces in his rhetoric, and to a certain extent in his theory.

2. For a good summary of "On Systematically Distorted Communication" and "Towards a Theory of Communicative Competence," see Fred Dallmayr 1984, 123–25.

3. This is an extremely important move as he does not want to root his theory in subjectivity. In spite of this his theory of intersubjectivity seems to rely on an unproblematic, almost Kantian, view of the subject. As such, he still has an idealized subject as the basic unit in his theory of communicative action.

4. Jürgen Habermas 1984, 284–88 (hereafter TCA 1). Certain types of strategic action are of course necessary. Mutual understanding is not needed before I feed my fish in the morning. It is when strategic reasoning factors into normative discourse that problems arise. Here again, considering the use of propaganda by various political regimes is instructive. In such cases language is used coercively to bring about a certain desired end. It is such political mythology that Habermas seeks to avoid. It would seem that for Habermas, any mythos within the political or moral logos is illegitimate.

5. For a detailed discussion of the relationship between the theory of communicative action and Habermas's theory of communicative competency, see Ingram 1987, 32–42.

6. Habermas lays out the historical background for and basic tenets of discourse ethics in "Diskursethik, Notizen zu einen Begrundungsprogram," *Moralbewusstein und kommunikatives Handeln* (Frankfurt: Suhrkamp, 1983).

7. Benhabib 1989, 1.

8. Habermas 1989, 46–51 ("Justice and Solidarity," hereafter JS).

9. Nancy Fraser (1986, 425–29) criticizes Benhabib's earlier attempt to square discourse ethics with Carol Gilligan's ethic of care. It is her position that this results in autonomy's being privileged over solidarity. Her call is for an ethical discourse that is more attentive to existing "sociocultural means of interpretation." From this she develops a more intersubjective concept of autonomy. I think that this problem exists in both Benhabib's and Habermas's most recent formulations. Habermas in particular attempts to deal with this problem but seems reluctant to go far enough. My suspicion is that the modes of alterity that would have to be contended with in a radically embedded discourse ethic are what hold him back.

10. One hint that this is what Levinas is really concerned with is the stunning dedication that sets off *Otherwise Than Being*: "To the memory of those who were closest among the six million assassinated by the National Socialists and of the millions on millions of all confessions and all nations, victims of the same hatred of the other man, the same anti-semitism." Also see "Ideology and Idealism," Difficult Freedom," and "Ethics and Politics" in *The Levinas Reader*, ed. Sean Hand (Oxford: Basil Blackwell, 1989).

11. Levinas 1969 (*Totality and Infinity*, hereafter TI).

12. See Levinas's discussion in "Ideology and Idealism" in *The Levinas Reader*.

13. My reference here is Maurice Blanchot's "Interruptions," *The Sin of the Book*, ed. Edmond Jabes. Here Blanchot identifies four types of communication. The first three, as he puts it, "tend toward unity." The fourth, however, involves "no unifying effort." In this mode of communication there is no attempt to establish common ground. "Now, what is at stake is the strangeness between us, and not only that obscure part which escapes our mutual knowledge and is nothing but the obscurity of being within the 'I'—a strangeness which is still relative (an 'I' is always close to another 'I,' even in difference, competition, desire, and need). What is at stake now and has to be accounted for is all that separates me from the other, that is to say, the other insofar as I am infinitely separate from him: separation, cleft, gap which leaves him infinitely outside me, but also claims to found my relation with him on this very interruption which is an interruption of being—of otherness through which he is, I must repeat, for me neither I, nor another existence, nor a modality of universal existence, nor a superexistence (god or non-god), but the unknown in its infinite distance" (48). This seems to nicely summarize Levinas's ethical relationship.

14. This polarity will be important in my discussion of authority, legitimacy, and alterity in the following section.

15. Levinas 1987, 119.

16. Levinas was already developing a discourse on the impossibility of critical discourses on discourse in the 1950s. See particularly "The Ego and Totality," in *Collected Philosophical Papers*.

17. It is well beyond the limits of this discussion to go into the details of Habermas's theory of the lifeworld. I think that it can be established that this theory is not completely compatible with the schematic theory that it supports. The lifeworld has a textured, multidimensional quality that the universal prag-

matic analysis seems to try to iron smooth. For Habermas's discussion of the lifeworld, see 1987a, 119–53 (hereafter TCA 2), and 1987b, 294–327.

18. The political element in Habermas's communicative ethics is what would strike Levinas as being most problematic. Political decisions always, for him, involve exclusionary unity (see in particular "Ethics and Politics"). This is a point upon which I disagree adamantly with Levinas. The political sphere, I would argue, under certain conditions, is where alterity can be most effectively expressed.

19. Lyotard 1986, 116.

20. The term *postconventional* is one Habermas borrows from Kohlberg. He uses it to define foundational devices that do not appeal to some form of metaphysical authority. I will use the term in a somewhat similar fashion, but will alter it slightly.

21. Benhabib (1989) criticizes the view that the telos of ethical discourse should be consensus: "If I am correct that our goal is the process of such dialogue, conversation, and mutual understanding, and not consensus, discourse theory can represent the moral point of view without having to invoke the fiction of the homo economicus or homo politicus" (22–23). Her call is for "ongoing moral conversation" (12–13).

22. For a comprehensive study of the importance of Derrida for social theory, see Martin 1992. This is an extremely thoughtful and creative text that demonstrates the role that Derrida's work can play in a radical critical theory of society.

23. See Adorno 1973b and Marcuse 1968.

24. Ingram 1990, 204.

25. See Norris 1990, chapter 3.

26. Reprinted in Fraser 1989.

27. While I don't want to accept the implication that Derrida's work can only be put to spurious use in social theory, I do agree with Fraser that the participants at this conference have generally produced what I consider to be useless "interventions" into "the political." So up to that point I agree with Fraser. It strikes me as a bit reductive, however, to take the position that this is the only route that one can take in using Derrida within the framework of a social theory.

28. As most readers know, Derrida has since this remark written significant works on politics and Marxism. I would argue that this work is an extension of the work that Fraser refers to here. See Derrida, 1992 and 1994.

29. Here again, I agree with Fraser for the most part. The fact, however, that Derrida hasn't always been the most astute translator of his work into political terms doesn't render its political implications insignificant.

30. An organization that was formed as a result of the "Ends of Man" conference.

31. See Trey 1989.

32. This took place at the Eastern Division meeting of the American Philosophical Association in 1989.

33. In McCarthy 1991.

34. This is a typical charge made by Derrideans against people who disagree with Derrida. The upshot is that if you are not a zealous follower of Der-

rida, it must be because you are incapable of understanding his work. Such charges usually do nothing more than encourage a less than serious reading of Derrida's books and articles.

35. Culler 1988, chapter 11.

36. "And what is true of a word is true of language in general: the structure of a language, its systems of norms and regularities, is a product of events, the product of prior speech acts. However, when we take this argument seriously and begin to look at the events which are said to determine the structures, we find that every event is itself already determined and made possible by prior structures. The possibility of meaning something by an utterance is already inscribed in the structure of language. The structures themselves are always products, but however far back we try to push, even when we try to imagine the 'birth' of language and describe an originary event that might have produced the first structure, we discover that we must assume prior organization, and prior differentiation" (Culler 1982, 95–96).

37. Derrida 1988, 146.

38. Culler plays little attention to the role played by the lifeworld in the theory of communicative action.

39. Derrida develops this theory in a number of his writings. For a useful discussion of text and textual situations, see Gasche 1983.

40. Habermas notes this transcendental character of language in several places. By *transcendental* he does not mean something metaphysical; rather, language is transcendental insofar as it survives or transcends the immediate, contingent forms that it takes in discourse. It is somewhat more controversial to claim that Derrida has a transcendental theory of language. Nonetheless, I would hold that he does—in the same sense as Habermas. I am confirmed in this view by Gasche 1983. I would formulate this as a temporal, rather than spatial, type of transcendence.

41. I hesitate to use the term *différance* as it is rather silly and has been appropriated by Derrideans in some ridiculous ways. I prefer to call what Derrida labels "différance" intertextual differentiation. I think that such a term is more descriptive and less subject to ontological hyperbole.

42. See Derrida 1982, *Margins of Philosophy*, 20–25 (hereafter D).

43. McCarthy (1991) serves as a primary example of this line of critique. See also Habermas's analysis in PDM.

44. Derrida 1979, 78.

45. For a powerful discussion of these events, see Martin 1996, chapter 12.

46. Habermas 1989c, 21.

47. I borrow the phrase "the dilemma of modernity" from Lawrence E. Cahoone's book of the same title. See Cahoone 1988.

48. Habermas 1990, 59.

WORKS CITED

Adorno, Theodor. 1973a. *Negative Dialectics*. Trans. by E. B. Ashton. New York: Continuum.

———. 1973b. *The Jargon of Authenticity*. Trans. by Knut Tarnowski and Frederic Will. Evanston, Ill.: Northwestern University Press.

———. 1982. "Freudian Theory and the Pattern of Fascist Propaganda," in *The Essential Frankfurt School Reader*. Ed. by Andrew Arato and Eike Gebhardt. New York: Continuum.

Agger, Ben. 1981. "A Critical Theory of Discourse." *Humanities in Society* 4:7–30.

Arendt, Hannah. 1971. *The Life of the Mind*. New York: Harcourt Brace Jovanovich.

———. 1982. *Lectures on Kant's Political Philosophy*. Chicago: University of Chicago Press.

Aronowitz, Stanley. 1988. *Science as Power: Discourse and Ideology in Modern Society*. Minneapolis: University of Minnesota Press.

Austen, J. L. 1962. *How to Do Things with Words*. Cambridge: Harvard University Press.

Bagdikian, Ben. 1989. "The Lords of the Global Villiage." *The Nation* 248.23 (12 June 1989).

———. 1990. *The Media Monopoly*. 3rd ed. Boston: Beacon Press.

Baynes, Kenneth. 1992. *The Normative Grounds of Social Criticism: Kant, Rawls, Habermas*. Albany: SUNY Press.

Benhabib, Seyla. 1986. *Critique, Norm and Utopia: A Study of the Foundations of Critical Theory*. New York: Columbia University Press.

———. 1989. "In the Shadow of Aristotle and Hegel: Communicative Ethics and Current Controversies in Practical Philosophy." *The Philosophical Forum* 21:1–31.

Benhabib, Seyla, and Fred Dallmayr, eds. 1990. *The Communicative Ethics Controversy*. Cambridge: MIT Press.

Bernstein, Richard, ed. 1985. *Habermas and Modernity*. Cambridge: MIT Press.

Braten, Jane. 1991. *Habermas' Critical Theory of Society*. Albany: SUNY Press.

Buck-Morss, Susan. 1977. *The Origins of Negative Dialectics: Theodor W. Adorno, Walter Benjamin, and the Frankfurt Institute*. New York: Macmillan.

Cahoone, Lawrence E. 1988. *The Dilemma of Modernity: Philosophy, Culture, and Anti-Culture*. Albany: SUNY Press.

Calhoun, Craig, ed. 1992. *Habermas and the Public Sphere*. Cambridge: MIT Press, 1992.

Callinicos, Alex. 1990. *Against Postmodernism: A Marxist Critique*. London: St. Martin's Press.
Chomsky, Noam. 1968. *Aspects of the Theory of Syntax*. Cambridge: MIT Press.
Culler, Jonathan. 1982. *On Deconstruction: Theory and Criticism after Structuralism*. Ithaca, N.Y.: Cornell University Press.
———. 1988. *Framing the Sign: Criticism and Its Institutions*. Norman: University of Oklahoma Press.
Dallmayr, Fred. 1984. *Language and Politics*. Notre Dame, Ind.: University of Notre Dame Press.
Derrida, Jacques. 1978. *Writing and Difference*. Trans. by Alan Bass. Chicago: The University of Chicago Press.
———. 1979. "Living On: Border Lines," Trans. by James Hulbert, in *Deconstruction and Criticism*. Ed. by Harold Bloom. New York: Seabury Press.
———. 1981a. *Positions*. Trans. by Alan Bass. Chicago: University of Chicago Press.
———. 1981b. *Dissemination*. Trans. by Barbara Johnson. Chicago: University of Chicago Press.
———. 1982. *Margins of Philosophy*. Trans. by Alan Bass. Chicago: University of Chicago Press.
———. 1992. *The Other Heading: Reflections on Today's Europe*. Trans. by Pascale-Anne Brault and Michael B. Naas. Bloomington: Indiana University Press.
———. 1994. *Specters of Marx: The State of the Debt, the Work of Mourning, & the New International*. Trans. by Peggy Kamuf. New York: Routledge.
Dews, Peter, ed. 1986. *Habermas: Autonomy and Solidarity*. London: Verso.
———. 1987. *Logics of Disintegration: Post-Structuralist Thought and the Claims of Critical Theory*. London: Verso.
Dubiel, Helmut. 1985. *Theory and Politics: Studies in the Development of Critical Theory*. Trans. by Benjamin Gregg. Cambridge: MIT Press.
Foucault, Michel. 1984. *Foucault Reader*. Ed. by Paul Rabinow. New York: Pantheon Books.
Fraser, Nancy. 1986. "Toward a Discourse Ethic of Solidarity." *Praxis International* 8:425–29.
———. 1989. *Unruly Practices: Power, Discourse and Gender in Contemporary Social Theory*. Minneapolis: University of Minnesota Press.
———. 1991. "Rethinking the Public Sphere." *Social Text* 25/26:56–80.
Gasche, Rudolph. 1983. "Joining the Text: From Heidegger to Derrida." In *The Yale Critics*. Ed. by J. Arac, W. Godzich, and W. Martin. Minneapolis: University of Minnesota Press.
Habermas, Jürgen. 1970a. *Toward a Rational Society*. Trans. by Jeremy Shapiro. Boston: Beacon Press.
———. 1970b. "On Systematically Distorted Communication." *Inquiry* 13.3:206–18.
———. 1970c. "Towards a Theory of Communicative Competence." *Inquiry* 13.4:206–18.
———. *Legitimation Crisis*. 1975. Trans. by Thomas McCarthy. Boston: Beacon Press.

———. 1978–1979. "Theory and Politics: A Discussion with Herbert Marcuse, Jürgen Habermas, Heinz Lubasz and Telman Spengler." *Telos* 38:124–53.

———. 1979. *Communication and the Evolution of Society*. Trans. by Thomas McCarthy. Boston: Beacon Press.

———. 1981. "Modernity vs. Postmodernity." *New German Critique* 22:13–30.

———. 1982. "The Entwinement of Myth and Enlightenment: Re-reading Dialectic of Enlightenment." *New German Critique* 32:13–30.

———. 1984, 1987a. *The Theory of Communicative Action*, 2 vols. Trans. by Thomas McCarthy. Boston: Beacon Press.

———. 1985. "Remarks on the Concept of Communicative Action." In *Social Action*. Ed. by G. Seebass and R. Tuomela, 151–78. New York: Reidel.

———. 1987b. *The Philosophical Discourse of Modernity*. Trans. by Frederick Lawrence. Cambridge: MIT Press.

———. 1988. *Limited Inc*. Trans. by Weber and Mehlman. Evanston, Ill.: Northwestern University Press.

———. 1988a. "A Kind of Settling of Damages." Trans. by Jeremy Leaman. *New German Critique*. Spring/Summer, 25–39.

———. 1988b. "Concerning the Public Use of History." Trans. by Jeremy Leaman. *New German Critique*. Spring/Summer, 40–50.

———. 1989a. *The New Conservatism: Cultural Criticism and the Historians' Debate*. Trans. by Shierry Weber Nicholsen. Cambridge: MIT Press.

———. 1989b. "Justice and Solidarity." *The Philosophical Forum* 21:32–53.

———. 1989c. "What Does Socialism Mean Today? The Rectifying Revolution and the Need for New Thinking on the Left." *New Left Review* 183:3–21.

———. 1989d. *The Structural Transformation of the Public Sphere*. Trans. by Thomas Burger. Cambridge: MIT Press.

———. 1990. *Moral Consciousness and Communicative Action*. Trans. by Christian Lenhardt and Shierry Weber Nicholsen. Cambridge: MIT Press.

Hartmann, Klaus. 1985. "Human Agency between System and Lifeworld: Habermas' Latest Version of Critical Theory." *The Journal of the British Society for Phenomenology* 16:145–55.

Heidegger, Martin. 1959. *An Introduction to Metaphysics*. Trans. by Ralph Manheim. New Haven, Conn.: Yale University.

———. 1962. *Being and Time*. Trans. by John Macquarrie and Edward Robinson. New York: Harper & Row.

Held, David. 1980. *Introduction to Critical Theory: Horkheimer to Habermas*. Berkeley: University of California Press.

Holub, Robert C. 1991. *Jürgen Habermas: Critic in the Public Sphere*. New York: Routledge.

Honneth, Axel, and Hans Joas, eds. 1991. *Communicative Action*. Trans. by J. Gaines and D. L. Jones. Cambridge: MIT Press.

Honneth, Axel, and Thomas McCarthy et al., eds. 1992. *Philosophical Interventions in the Unfinished Project of Enlightenment*. Cambridge: MIT Press.

Horkheimer, Max. 1972. *Critical Theory: Selected Essays*. Trans. by Matthew J. O'Connell et al. New York: Continuum.

Horkheimer, Max, and Theodor Adorno. 1972. *Dialectic of Enlightenment*. Trans. by John Cumming. New York: Continuum.

Ingram, David. 1986. "Foucault and the Frankfurt School: A Discourse on Nietzsche, Power and Knowledge." *Praxis International* 6:311–27.

———. 1987. *Habermas and the Dialectic of Reason*. New Haven, Conn.: Yale University Press.

———. 1987–88. "Legitimacy and the Postmodern Condition: The Political Thought of Jean-François Lyotard." *Praxis International* 7:284–303.

———. 1988. "The Postmodern Kantianism of Arendt and Lyotard." *The Review of Metaphysics* 42:51–77.

———. 1990. *Critical Theory and Philosophy*. New York: Paragon House.

Ingram, David, and Julia Simon-Ingram, eds. 1992. *Critical Theory: The Essential Readings*. New York: Paragon House.

Jameson, Fredric. 1990. *Late Marxism: Adorno, or The Persistence of the Dialectic*. New York: Verso Press.

———. 1991. *Postmodernism, Or, The Cultural Logic of Late Capitalism*. New York: Verso Press.

Kant, Immanuel. 1983. *Perpetual Peace and Other Essays*. Trans. by Ted Humphrey. Indianapolis: Hackett.

Kelly, Michael, ed. 1990. *Hermeneutics and Critical Theory in Ethics and Politics*. Cambridge: MIT Press.

Kellner, Douglas. 1989. *Critical Theory, Marxism and Modernity*. Baltimore: Johns Hopkins University Press.

———. 1990. *Television and the Crisis of Democracy*. Boulder, Colo.: Westview Press.

Landes, Joan. 1988. *Women and the Public Sphere in the Age of the French Revolution*. Ithaca, N.Y.: Cornell University Press.

League, Kathleen. 1991. "Adorno: No Sell Out." Unpublished manuscript.

Levinas, Emmanuel. 1969. *Totality and Infinity*. Trans by Alphonso Lingis. Pittsburgh: Duquesne University Press.

———. 1981. *Otherwise Than Being or Beyond Essence*. Trans. by Aphonso Lingis. Boston: Martinus Nijhoff.

———. 1987. *Collected Philosophical Papers*. Trans. by Alphonso Lingis. Boston: Martinus Nijhoff.

———. 1989. *The Levinas Reader*. Ed. by Sean Hand. Oxford: Basil Blackwell.

Lyotard, Jean-François. 1984. *The Postmodern Condition: A Report on Knowledge*. Trans. by Geoff Bennington and Brian Massumi. Minneapolis: University of Minnesota Press.

———. 1985. *Just Gaming*. Trans. by Wlad Gozich. Minneapolis: University of Minnesota Press.

———. 1986. *The Differend: Phrases in Dispute*. Trans. by George Van Den Abbeele. Minneapolis: University of Minnesota Press.

Marcuse, Herbert. 1964. *One Dimensional Man: Studies in the Ideology of Advanced Industrial Society*. Boston: Beacon Press.

———. 1968. *Negations: Essays in Critical Theory*. Trans. by Jeremy Shapiro. Boston: Beacon Press.

Martin, Bill. 1988. "The Enlightenment Talking Cure: Habermas, Legitimation Crisis and the Recent Political Landscape." *Southwest Philosophical Review* 4:33–43.

———. 1992. *Matrix and Line: Derrida and the Possibilities of Postmodern Social Theory*. Albany: SUNY Press.

———. 1996. *Politics in the Impasse: Explorations in Postsecular Social Theory*. Albany: SUNY Press.

Marx, Karl. 1973. *Grundrisse*. Trans. by Martin Nicolaus. New York: Vintage Books.

———. 1978. *The Marx-Engels Reader*. New York: W.W. Norton.

McCarthy, Thomas. 1978. *The Critical Theory of Jürgen Habermas*. Cambridge: MIT Press.

———. 1991. *Ideals and Illusions: On Reconstruction and Deconstruction in Contemporary Critical Theory*. Cambridge: MIT Press.

McLellan, David. 1973. *Karl Marx: His Life and Thought*. New York: Harper & Row.

Nash, Ronald, ed. 1969. *Ideas of History*. New York: E. P. Dutton.

Norris, Christopher. 1990. *What's Wrong with Postmodernism? Critical Theory and the Ends of Philosophy*. Baltimore: Johns Hopkins University Press.

Offe, Claus. 1983. *Contradictions in the Welfare State*. Cambridge: MIT Press.

———. 1985. *Disorganized Capitalism*. Cambridge: MIT Press.

Poster, Mark. 1989. *Critical Theory and Poststructuralism: In Search of a Context*. Ithaca, N.Y.: Cornell University Press.

Rasmussen, David, ed. 1990. *Universalism and Communitarianism: Contemporary Debates in Ethics*. Cambridge: MIT Press.

Ray, Larry. 1989. "Foucault and the Decomposition of the Historical Subject." *Philosophy and Social Criticism* 13:69–110.

Ryan, Michael. 1982. *Marxism and Deconstruction: A Critical Articulation*. Baltimore: Johns Hopkins University Press.

———. 1989. *Politics and Culture: Working Hypotheses for a Post-Revolutionary Society*. Baltimore: Johns Hopkins University Press.

Schanberg, Sydney. 1991. "A Muzzle for the Press." In *The Gulf War Reader*. Ed. by Michael L. Sifry and Christopher Cerf. New York: Random House.

Schutz, Alfred, and Thomas Luckmann. 1973. *The Structures of the Lifeworld*. Trans by Richard M. Zaner and H. Tristram Engelhardt Jr. Evanston, Ill.: Northwestern University Press.

Schweickart, David. 1996. *Against Capitalism*. Boulder, Colo.: Westview Press.

Searle, John. 1969. *Speech Acts: An Essay in the Philosophy of Language*. New York: Cambridge University Press.

Smith, Adam. 1974. *The Wealth of Nations*. New York: Penguin Books.

Thompson, John, and David Held, eds. 1982. *Habermas: Critical Debates*. Cambridge: MIT Press.

Torpey, John. 1988. "Habermas and the Historians." *New German Critique*. Spring/Summer, 5–24.

Trey, George A. 1989. "The Philosophical Discourse of Modernity: Habermas' Postmodern Adventure." *Diacritics* 1989 (No. 2):67–79.

———. 1991. "Modern Normativity and the Politics of Deregulation," *Auslegung: A Journal of Philosophy* 19 (No. 2):137–48.

———. 1992. "Communicative Ethics in the Face of Alterity: Habermas, Levinas and the Problem of Postconventional Universalism." *Praxis International* 11:412–27.

———. 1993. "Rethinking the Public Sphere: Arendt's Shift from the Polis to the Politics of Judgment." Unpublished manuscript.

Trey, George A., and David I. Gandolfo. 1993. "Free Speech and Public Debate: A Discourse Theory of the Gulf War." In *The Bill of Rights: Bicentennial Reflections*. Ed. by Yeager Hudson and Creighton Peden. Lewiston: The Edwin Mellen Press.

Unger, Roberto Mangabeira. 1976. *Law in Modern Society*. New York: Free Press.

von Wright, G. H. 1971. *Explanation and Understanding*. Ithaca, N.Y.: Cornell University Press.

White, Stephen K. 1988. *The Recent Work of Jürgen Habermas: Reason, Justice and Modernity*. New York: Cambridge University Press.

Wittgenstein, Ludwig. 1958. *Philosophical Investigations*. Trans. by G.E.M. Anscombe. New York: Macmillan.

Wren, Thomas, ed. 1989. *The Moral Domain*. Cambridge: MIT Press.

INDEX